Merry
Chistmas 202___

In addition —

to the aliens, You are
never alone — Yay
Family!
Love
Mom

MW00443733

WE
ARE
NOT
ALONE

ALSO BY MARC HARTZMAN

*Chasing Ghosts: A Tour of Our Fascination
with Spirits and the Supernatural*

The Big Book of Mars: From Ancient Egypt to The Martian,
A Deep-Space Dive into Our Obsession with the Red Planet

*Found on eBay: 101 Genuinely Bizarre Items
from the World's Online Yard Sale*

*American Sideshow: An Encyclopedia of History's
Most Wondrous and Curiously Strange Performers*

*God Made Me Do It: True Stories of the Worst Advice
the Lord Has Ever Given His Followers*

*The Anti-Social Network Journal: A Place for All the
Thoughts, Ideas, and Plans You Don't Want to Share*

The Embalmed Head of Oliver Cromwell: A Memoir

WE
ARE
NOT
ALONE

The Extraordinary History
of UFOs and Aliens Invading
Our Hopes, Fears, and Fantasies

MARC HARTZMAN

QUIRK BOOKS
PHILADELPHIA

Copyright © 2023 by Marc Hartzman

All rights reserved. Except as authorized under U.S. copyright law, no part of this book may be reproduced in any form without written permission from the publisher.

Library of Congress Cataloging-in-Publication Data
Names: Hartzman, Marc, author.
Title: We are not alone : the extraordinary history of UFOs and aliens invading our hopes, fears and fantasies / Marc Hartzman.
Description: Philadelphia : Quirk Books, [2023] | Includes bibliographical references and index. | Summary: "A pop history of UFOs, aliens, and extraterrestrial encounters, including photographs and illustrations"— Provided by publisher.
Identifiers: LCCN 2023007338 (print) | LCCN 2023007339 (ebook) | ISBN 9781683693352 (hardcover) | ISBN 9781683693369 (ebook)
Subjects: LCSH: Unidentifed flying objects—Sightings and encounters. | Human-alien encounters.
Classification: LCC TL789 .H375 2023 (print) | LCC TL789 (ebook) | DDC 001.942—dc23/eng/20230310
LC record available at https://lccn.loc.gov/2023007338
LC ebook record available at https://lccn.loc.gov/2023007339

ISBN: 978-1-68369-335-2

Printed in China

Typeset in Kiro, Kopius, Maxular, and Poster Gothic

Designed by Andie Reid
Production management by John J. McGurk

Full photo credits appear on page 296.

Quirk Books
215 Church Street
Philadelphia, PA 19106
quirkbooks.com

10 9 8 7 6 5 4 3 2 1

TO THE
PEOPLE OF
EARTH
AND
WHOEVER
ELSE

~~~~~

CONTENTS

GREETINGS,
EARTHLING READERS

I t seems only fitting to start a book about unidentified flying objects
and aliens with an otherworldly story from Roswell, New Mexico.
Not the Roswell crash in 1947 (we'll discuss that tale later), but the
one I heard over lunch during my pilgrimage to the flying saucer mec-
ca on a clear November day.

I had spent the previous two days working on this book just outside
Albuquerque, New Mexico, at the home of UFO researcher and historian David Marler. His curated collection is a massive archive of UFO
documents, photographs, books, original newspapers, and every form
of audiovisual media imaginable. During our conversations he told me
the story of a man he'd tracked down in Roswell who was attacked by a
UFO in 1964. His name is Charles Davis, and he was just eight years old
when the incident occurred on a Tuesday afternoon on June 2 in the
small town of Hobbs, New Mexico. Knowing I was headed to Roswell to
continue my research, Marler texted Davis and asked if he'd be willing
to meet with me. He said yes.

The next morning, with the rising sun nearly blinding me at the outset of the three-hour trip, I drove from Albuquerque to Roswell. There was little to be seen over the last hundred miles leading into town, except for some cliché tumbleweed that occasionally rolled across the road in front of me. But once I got to Roswell, aliens greeted me everywhere I looked. The lampposts dotting the main drag were topped with alien heads. The Dunkin' Donuts sign was held up high by a twenty-foot extraterrestrial. The McDonald's was shaped like a flying saucer and surrounded by metallic alien statues and, naturally, there were plenty of shops selling whatever they could put an alien face on— including a store selling Abduction Beef Jerky.

My plan was to spend the day at the International UFO Museum and Research Center. It has an enormous collection, including more than 8,000 books and 30,000 files. I didn't quite get through them all, but after a few hours of gathering as much information as possible, I took a break and met Davis and his wife for lunch at a nearby Mexican restaurant. It was crowded and loud and, for Davis, not the ideal place to discuss the traumatic event of his youth. But he had moments when he felt comfortable enough to share a few of his memories.

"If you were to ask me today if I'm a believer or a nonbeliever, I'd tell you I don't know," he said as I cut into my enchiladas. "I just know something weird happened. It was unexplainable."

The weird thing that happened involved a black, metallic object shaped like a spinning top hovering about two stories high. Davis was playing in the back lot of DeLuxe Laundry when he spotted it across the street. It seemed fixated on the young boy, and he knew it. So he moved to the left, and it moved to the left. Then he moved to the right, and it followed.

"I remember knowing I was seeing something I shouldn't be seeing," he said. "I remember hearing a loud noise and within seconds— boom—it was on me."

The strange craft whooshed directly over Davis's head and belched out fire, giving him second-degree burns across his face and ears. His grandmother heard the commotion and rushed out of the laundromat in time to witness the strange event. She told reporters her grandson was "covered with black, his hair standing on end and burning. . . .

Drivers along Highway 285 in New Mexico are welcomed to Roswell by a UFO.

I grabbed him and tried to smother out his hair, which was on fire."

Once she'd extinguished the flames, she rushed him to a hospital. Fortunately for Davis, a burn specialist happened to be working there that day and treated him immediately. Davis told police and doctors that he was burned by "a fire that came out of the sky" and added, "I guess I should have ducked."

According to a local newspaper report about the story, police investigated dozens of theories to understand what had happened, but found no answers. A Roman candle had not been thrown at him; no burning lint blew out of the laundry; no fire belched from the boiler; and no release of steam had caused the burns. There weren't even any scorch marks on the ground. It was just something . . . unidentified. The FBI questioned Davis's family but came up empty as well. As for the object itself, Davis said it had whooshed back from whence it came and disappeared.

Aside from a little hearing difficulty in one ear, he made a full recovery. I looked as closely as possible, but no scars were evident on his face, though he told me "from a certain point up my ears were inside out. They wouldn't give me a mirror in my room, because my face was so disfigured."

Whatever had happened, Davis had put it on "a back shelf" of his mind. In fact, he had not spoken of the incident in some forty years until Marler learned of the case and tracked Davis down in 2019. I was the second person Davis had discussed it with since the late 1960s. This was clearly not something he'd ever tried to publicize, exploit, or cash in on, though early on that's what people suspected.

"You get accused of insurance fraud, or that you made it up—there were a lot of skeptics at the time," Davis said. "I will tell you this, I know something happened and I don't care what anyone says."

I thought Davis seemed genuine in his recounting of the tale, and Marler had come to the same conclusion based on his interviews with Davis. "These are the last people that you would think would concoct a UFO story," he told me of Davis and his family. "They lived in conservative Hobbs, New Mexico, in the sixties and were devout Pentacostal. He doesn't care about UFOs. . . . I can't find any legitimate reason to disbelieve the story, as crazy as it is. But there it is, nonetheless."

That last person Davis had spoken with about the case before Marler was Dr. James McDonald, in 1968. The physicist worked with the Institute of Atmospheric Physics at the University of Arizona and had been investigating the UFO phenomenon. After questioning Davis and his mother on the phone for twenty minutes, McDonald acknowledged this event was particularly unique. "It's very weird, and unlike any other case I've run into," he told Davis's mother. (I obtained a recording of the conversation from Marler's archive.) "Almost all UFO cases are fairly weird, but this one is different from anything that I have ever heard of myself."

And the story just gets weirder. Marler's research found that black top-shaped objects were spinning around the country in the weeks before and after the 1964 Hobbs incident. And almost always on Tuesdays. One week before Davis was burned, newspapers reported that residents of Morgantown, West Virginia, saw a "burst of fire" in the sky coming from an unidentified object described as "top-shaped and glowing like an overheated stove."

On June 30, a couple of weeks after Davis's encounter, a man driving through northwestern Georgia spotted a strange circular object flying by his car. "I was traveling about 65 or 70 miles per hour, but when the object approached, the car's engine began to slow down," he told a reporter. The object was about six feet high and as long as his car. The man described it as resembling "a giant top." As his car decelerated, he pulled off the road, at which point, according to a newspaper article, the object "gave off heat and burned his arm," then left a foul odor and residue on his car.

The following Tuesday a group of neighbors in Tallulah Falls, Georgia, witnessed a similar object that also smelled "terrible." Exactly a week later an article reported that a young girl in the same area claimed to have seen a "weird contraption" with a "bad smell" as she and a friend rode bicycles. That night, in anticipation of more Tuesday top sightings, residents grabbed their cameras and telescopes and set up watch parties.

What the heck was happening on Tuesdays in the middle of 1964? There is simply no good answer.

"If you and I were living in 1964 and we got a bunch of UFO researchers we want to pull the wool over on and concoct a story, you're not going to come up with a small, black, top-shaped object belching flames, you're going to fit a story that falls along the known narrative," Marler explained to me. "You're going to come up with, 'I saw this sleek thirty-foot-diameter silver disk and it moved silently and it caused vehicle interference with my car.' You're going to tell a story they're going to believe because this is the narrative that's out there. But people were describing a black top-shaped object belching smoke and flames that basically behaved not like some advanced aircraft from another world, but almost like a bad lawnmower. It makes no sense."

As you'll read in these pages, there's a lot about UFOs that doesn't make sense. Sure, UFO sightings often have perfectly natural explanations, but all too often they don't. And they're continuing to happen today. In recent years, multiple U.S. Navy pilots have reported anomalous objects flying over the oceans in ways that defy physics—and the government has even declassified and released three navy videos showing UFOs (see page 269 for more). At a public congressional hearing on May 17, 2022—the first focused on UFOs in more than fifty years—the government's Unidentified Aerial Phenomena (UAP) Task Force admitted that it had insufficient data to identify a number of physical objects witnessed in U.S. airspace.

That means that the U.S. government itself has finally admitted what many people have long believed: that UFOs are real. Whether or not these UFOs are flying saucers containing little green men is up for debate, of course, but there are—without a doubt—unidentified flying objects in our skies. The UAP Task Force is now tasked with providing annual unclassified reports to Congress, which will hopefully start to include more data. Contemporary scientists are also openly exploring the phenomenon and gathering data to understand it through organizations such as the Search for Extraterrestrial Intelligence (SETI) Institute and the Galileo Project.

Many of these witnesses and investigators—who include government officials, navy pilots, police officers, and thousands of everyday people who have seen flying objects in the shapes of saucers, triangles, and even eggs since the 1940s—are respected members of the community, not kooks telling tall tales. Their compelling testimonies have helped destigmatize the UFO conversation and led to an uptick in the number of believers. Gallup reported in August 2021 that 41 percent of Americans believe UFOs involve alien spaceships from other planets. That's nearly half the country. And even more believe that aliens exist somewhere out there in the universe: two-thirds of Americans, according to a 2021 Pew Research Center survey. Wherever flying saucers may be coming from, it's clearly not the fringe.

So, what exactly is this strange phenomenon that's captured our imaginations for decades—and throughout that time led to conspiracy theories, cultlike beliefs, science fiction brilliance (and schlock), scientific study, and suffocating taboos? Now that we finally have proof that UFOs are out there, the question remains: *what are they?* And beyond that, are UFOs proof of what we both hope and fear: that we're not alone in the universe?

This book is a collection of possibilities, filled with beliefs, stories, facts, and conjecture spanning the entirety of the human experience. Though I can't say I've personally seen a UFO, my journey in gathering all of the above has included interviews with former members of the military, journalists, researchers, and everyday people who *have*—and have no doubt that what they've seen was not of this earth. My research has also involved conversations with scientists, a trip to the National Press Club in Washington, DC, to hear about saucers appearing over nuclear facilities, visits to the homes of UFO investigators and collectors, and several days of attending presentations and hobnobbing at the Mutual UFO Network (MUFON) International Symposium—not to mention virtual conferences, deep dives into online newspaper archives and centuries' worth of books, and occasional forays into cavernous rabbit holes. Many of the stories and photographs I uncovered are being published here for the first time.

So consider this volume your voyage through the chapters of humanity and our encounters with whatever or whoever else might be zooming through our skies. As you read the evidence, the lack of evidence, the passionate testimonies, and the skeptical responses, you won't find a smoking gun explaining the UFO phenomenon. But when pondering if we're alone in the universe, you just might find yourself armed with more informed and endlessly fascinating questions.

The U.S. government itself has finally admitted what many people have long believed: that UFOs are real. Whether or not these UFOs are flying saucers containing little green men is up for debate, of course, but there are—without a doubt—unidentified flying objects in our skies.

CHAPTER 1

ATTACK OF THE FLYING SAUCERS

A Modern Phenomenon Begins

> "If the egos of Earthmen are hurt when
> we realize that we may be the country cousins of the
> Universe, what is so terrifying about that? If we are cut
> down to size maybe we can begin to grow up."
>
> —EDWARD M. CASE in "Scientist Reports Talk with Visitor
> from Venus," *Daily Press*, Newport News, October 23, 1953

Say what you will about little green men and big-headed gray aliens, but the very questioning of their existence is precisely what makes us human. It's our relentless curiosity and ability to reason that set us apart from earth's other creatures. So it's only natural that we look up at the sky and ask ourselves if we are just one of many intelligent species in the universe—or if our blue marble is the only one asking such questions.

If you happened to be a U.S. Air Force cadet in the late 1960s, you would've been taught that not only are we not alone, we've *never* been alone. One of your lessons would have even taught you that aliens might be watching us like we're nothing more than a zoo. "A zoo is fun to visit, but you don't 'contact' the lizards," as Chapter 33 of *Introductory Space Science*, written and published in 1968, said. Or maybe, as the text continued, we are "the object of intensive sociological and psychological study."

Chapter 33 of *Introductory Space Science* was heavily revised in 1970 after the air force ended its official investigations of UFOs in December 1969, but until then cadets were thoroughly warned about what might be out there as they traversed the skies. According to the textbook, otherworldly observers were most commonly described as being about three and a half feet tall with round heads (which might be helmets) and arms reaching to or below the knees, wearing silvery space suits or coveralls. "Other aliens appear to be essentially the same as Earthmen, while still others have particularly wide (wrap around) eyes and mouths with very thin lips," the textbook added. "And there is a rare group reported as about four feet tall, weight of around 35 pounds, and covered with thick hair or fur (clothing?)." These last aliens were believed to be "extremely strong."

Visits by alien—or at least intelligently controlled spacecraft—were considered hardly a recent occurrence. As the chapter's conclusion stated, "the UFO phenomenon appears to have been global in nature for almost 50,000 years." It based that estimate on carvings in granite on a mountain in China's Hunan province from 45,000 BC. These carvings show humanoid figures with elephant trunks, which the text suggests might be aliens wearing breathing apparatus. Cylindrical objects floating in the sky (the earliest known depiction of UFOs?) have similar creatures standing atop them.

Chapter 33 noted more recent—as in 6,000 BC—rock paintings on the Tassili n'Ajjer plateau of the Sahara desert that appear to show more alien visitors. In 1958, French archeologist Henri Lhote likened the strange figures with round helmet-like heads and apparent spacesuits to Martians and called the largest the "great Martian god." Other scientists suggest the frescoes simply portray humans wearing ritual masks and costumes.

Intriguing as these and other reports of ancient anomalies are, the textbook stated, "the subject of UFOs really was thrust upon the American public shortly after World War II when Kenneth Arnold on 24 June 1947 reported seeing nine 'saucer like' objects near Mount Rainier."

We'll explore more ancient alien reports in sidebars throughout this book, but first let's dive deeper into Kenneth Arnold's relatively recent experience—and the beginning of the modern flying saucer era.

A Man from Boise Launches a Flying Saucer Craze

When Kenneth Arnold took off from Chehalis, Washington, in his small utility plane, he wasn't in search of the fantastic and unknown. He was simply looking for a lost C-46 Marine transport that had gone down in the mountains. It was June 24, 1947, and he'd just finished installing firefighting equipment for his employer, Central Air Service. Rather than call it a day, he was lured in by a $5,000 reward for locating the missing plane. What he found instead forever changed his life—and the lives of millions of others convinced by his tale.

At 3:00 p.m. on that perfectly clear summer afternoon, the thirty-two-year-old pilot from Boise, Idaho, witnessed nine shiny, flat objects whizzing and weaving through the sky in a chain-like formation over Mount Rainier. He estimated their speed at a whopping 1,200 miles per hour and their elevation at about 10,000 feet. The event lasted just a few minutes, and at first Arnold wondered if the unidentified flying objects were some sort of new jet aircraft or experimental guided missiles. Or maybe even geese. Yet they were too big to be birds, they had no tails, and their speed was nearly twice what any plane could achieve at that time. Arnold didn't know what exactly he'd seen; he just knew they were peculiar.

After initially landing in Yakima, Washington, and sharing his story with other pilots, Arnold refueled and set off for an air show in Pendleton, Oregon. Upon his arrival, he discovered someone from Yakima had already phoned in his story, which quickly spread. The media awaited and swarmed him upon his landing nearly as fast as the UFOs had. When Arnold told them the objects appeared like saucers skipping on water, reporters ran with the visual and termed them "flying saucers." Neither our skies nor our vocabulary have been the same since.

Arnold settled on the idea that the saucers must've been "robotly controlled" guided missiles from the government. Few, if any, shared this opinion and the next several days were a whirlwind of unwanted attention for Arnold. Reporters and press agencies pestered him for his story. Could these "saucers" be from another planet? Intelligent life on Mars had been frequently discussed by respected scientists in the preceding decades, as we'll explore in Chapter 4, so to many, the idea

The Flying Saucer as I Saw it... by Kenneth Arnold
Per copy 50¢

Kenneth Arnold described the aerial objects as looking like disks, saucers, and even pie pans and claimed at least one of them was crescent shaped, as seen on the cover of this autographed booklet from 1950.

of their arrival may have seemed plausible.

"I didn't share the general excitement," Arnold later wrote in his 1952 privately published book, *The Coming of the Saucers*. "I can't begin to estimate the number of people, letters, telegrams and phone calls I tried to answer. After three days of this hubbub I came to the conclusion that I was the only sane one in the bunch."

That hubbub included unwanted public recognition. "Half the people I see look at me as a combination Einstein, Flash Gordon and screwball," Arnold told the United Press just days after the sighting. One of those people was a woman who spotted him in a café and, shrieking and sobbing, shouted, "There's the man who saw the men from Mars!" Arnold, however, would soon have plenty of company. In the weeks that followed, a rash of additional sightings suggested the same fleet of saucers were touring America.

A sixty-year-old railroad engineer in Illinois claimed to have seen a group of "about nine" flying disks flying in formation and "going faster than any airplane I ever saw." His sighting occurred just hours before Arnold's, though he didn't think much about seeing something so extraordinary until after hearing the report from Mount Rainier.

The following day, a Kansas City, Missouri, carpenter spotted nine saucers speeding overhead as he worked on a roof. Soon after, three aeronautical experts at a Utah airport saw the busy saucers "flying eastbound at terrific speed."

Saucers had quickly become all the rage. Within the next twelve days, sightings were reported in thirty-nine states. Some of them were easily explained, like the "whole flock" of flat objects glimmering in the sky that residents reported seeing in Lawton, Oklahoma. They turned out to be handbills dropped from an airplane.

The skies were so crowded that one Virginia airport left a bulletin board notice to pilots stating: "Two thousand feet vertical and horizontal clearance required between aircraft operating from this field and any 'flying saucers.'" Sincere or not, safety first is always a good policy.

Were these witnesses validating Arnold's claim, or had he simply opened the floodgates for others wanting to piggyback on his sudden fame? Either way, skeptics had their hands full, and explanations began pouring in within days. A preacher in Texas, for example, called Arnold directly to tell him the mysterious objects were harbingers of doomsday. One meteorologist suggested people were simply seeing a "spotlight somewhere playing on the clouds," while another believed Arnold may have had a touch of snow blindness. A retired high-school principal told reporters that he agreed with Arnold's original theory that the saucers were merely geese or white swans. Their size was an illusion, he proposed, and he explained how different the birds look when seen from above: "They have a swirling motion that gives a disk-like effect, especially when the sunlight is reflected from just the right angle."

Crazy as the entire experience was, Arnold took the situation seriously. "It's God's truth—I will swear it on a Bible," he told curious reporters. In a written statement sent to the air force just days after the event, he added:

> I look at this whole ordeal as not something funny as some people have made it out to be. To me it is mighty serious and since I evidently did observe something that at least Mr. John Doe on the street corner or Pete Andrews on the ranch has never heard about, is no reason that it does not exist. Even though I openly invited an investigation by the Army and the FBI as to the authenticity of my story or a mental or a physical examination as to my capabilities, I have received no interest from these two important protective forces of our country.

The air force eventually investigated and in its written report concluded that the nine objects were nothing more than a mirage: "Mr. Arnold's statement concerning how smooth and crystal clear the air was is an indication of very stable conditions which are associated with inversions, and increase the refraction index of the atmosphere." However, this statement did nothing to quell the UFO mania that had seized the country.

> ## "I didn't mean it to be what it was, and I was amazed at the public reaction—more so than at the sighting."
>
> —KENNETH ARNOLD, reflecting on the events of 1947 eighteen years later in the *Minneapolis Star*, August 11, 1965

Foo Fighters and the Battle of Los Angeles: The UFOs of World War II

The military had, in fact, been dealing with flying saucers years before the term was coined by Arnold and the press. In the wee hours of the morning of February 25, 1942, just a couple months after the Japanese attacked Pearl Harbor and yanked the United States into World War II, anti-aircraft guns fired upon a mysterious entity appearing along the southern California coast. Radar first detected the unidentified object at 1:44 a.m. moving slowly south from Santa Maria toward the Los Angeles area.

Air-raid alerts sounded and spotlights converged on the strange object as it took on more than 1,400 rounds of ammunition. Bursts of shrapnel dotted the sky all around it, yet the target wasn't brought down. In fact, the aircraft seemed oblivious to the attack as it kept moving south, disappearing along the coast toward Long Beach before changing course and heading north toward Santa Monica. According to a CBS radio broadcast, "The guns went into action again, hurling round after round of shells at the object. The second barrage appeared to be closer to downtown Los Angeles, since watchers could hear the concussion of the guns more clearly and the flash of bursting shells was brighter. Then the ship disappeared for the second time over the ocean."

Meanwhile, as the battle commenced, a blackout was ordered from Santa Monica to San Diego for five hours, which led to three deaths caused by accidents and another two from heart attacks.

Early reports indicated the entity might have been a blimp, which certainly matched the oval shape of the object the searchlights focused on. However, the barrage of anti-aircraft shots fired would have surely brought down such a harmless craft. Other articles suggested it was an enemy Japanese aircraft, perhaps launched from a submarine. Just thirty-two hours earlier, Japanese subs had shelled the Ellwood oil fields north of Los Angeles.

The day after the battle with the mysterious aircraft, secretary of the navy Frank Knox said the whole thing was a false alarm due to "jittery nerves" and that "there were no planes over Los Angeles last night." In a contradictory statement, Secretary of War Henry Stimson claimed the UFOs were commercial planes "operated by enemy agents" to detect air defense positions and demoralize civilians.

Leland M. Ford, a member of Congress from California, demanded that people be told the truth about the raid and be given a "proper explanation" by Knox and Stimson. Speaking from the House floor, he stated that the people of California are not "jittery or hysterical, but are beginning to believe the Army and Navy are."

As UFO researcher and historian David Marler stressed to me, "Jittery war nerves can't be photographed. And jittery war nerves can't be tracked on three separate radar systems with an inbound target that preceded this event where this object was tracked over the Pacific coming inland for 120 miles."

Knox's and Stimson's contradictory theories added to the public confusion. "They never had one cohesive explanation," Marler added. "They were always at odds with each other."

After the war, the Japanese, who gladly took credit for the oil field shelling, denied having aircraft in the area during the encounter, which came to be known as the Battle of Los Angeles.

In 1949, an explanation from the United States Coast Artillery Association claimed the anti-aircraft artillery was firing at a meteorologi-

The Battle of Los Angeles made national headlines, including this one from the *Boston Traveler* on February 25, 1942.

WALL ST. STATE ST. FINAL

Boston Traveler

New England's Largest Evening Circulation Complete Associated Press and United Press Wire Services

EST. 1825 — 117th YEAR — NO. 197 WEDNESDAY, FEB. 25, 1942.   32 PAGES   5 CENTS

War Extra!

LOS ANGELES BATTLES MYSTERY AIRCRAFT

Anti-Aircraft Guns in Heavy Barrage
Balloon-Like Object Hit, Brought Down

In the early hours of February 25, 1942, spotlights converged on an unidentified flying object off the southern California coast. Some believe it may have had otherworldly origins.

cal balloon. Like the blimp hypothesis, this seemed highly unlikely, though one witness claimed to have seen debris from a balloon that may have simply been caught in the crossfire. As Marler summed up the counterargument: "Do we really think one or two weather balloons were launched, drifted 120 miles out to the Pacific, circled back around, and came in, becoming the source of the radar target, which was then fired upon, but happened to dodge every little piece of shrapnel and every little shell that went up, to disappear and, twenty minutes later, reverse course and then come back over and get fired on a second time, only to disappear over the Pacific? I'll tell you what, that's one hell of a balloon."

In an op-ed featured in the February 28, 1942, edition of the *Los Angeles Times*, a local resident named Halbert P. Gillette suggested the object was a rare meteorological phenomenon called ball lightning, which drops out of a thundercloud and drifts away like an incandescent balloon. If this is the case, its back-and-forth journey would've been even rarer than its occurrence. Still, to Gillette it was a sounder theory than a weather balloon, since, as he noted, "no balloon has been reported" and because "it failed to collapse under intense and apparently accurate shellfire." That left him with the one question that still remains today: "What, then, was it?"

Was there a genuine spacecraft in the skies over Los Angeles that night? The involvement of hundreds of witnesses, military engagement, and radar evidence, plus the inclusion of an official press photo, make it a particularly compelling case.

"I think it's a genuine UFO," Marler has said in lectures on the event. "I don't think any of the prosaic explanations fit. It does seem to be of an unknown origin. I'm not saying it's extraterrestrial, but it's highly suspicious in nature. I think we at least need to concede it's a possibility that we were dealing with someone else's technology in '42 over Los Angeles."

As World War II raged on, more UFOs were spotted in the winter of 1944, when multiple fighter and bomber pilots in German territory reported seeing reddish glowing lights like "balls of fire" in the night sky. Lieutenant Donald Meiers told the press he'd seen them flying in vertical rows, right alongside the planes—and in one instance, as a group of fifteen lights in the distance "like a Christmas tree up in the air," flickering on and off. He called them "foo fighters," based on a nonsense word used in cartoonist Bill Holman's popular comic strip *Smokey Stover*.

Meiers was also chased by a foo fighter for twenty miles as he sped through the Rhine Valley at 360 miles per hour. "It kept right off our wing tips for a while and then zoomed up into the sky," he told the Associated Press. "When I first saw the things off my wing tips, I had the horrible thought that a German on the ground was ready to press a button and explode them."

Fortunately, Meiers didn't experience any physical attacks. Nor did any other pilots. But Allied forces did believe that Nazis had developed a new radio-controlled secret weapon and feared the worst—the Nazis certainly excelled at the worst. And if their luminous balls couldn't detonate in the air, perhaps they could interfere with radio signals and radar detection.

After the war, American intelligence officers searched for evidence of foo fighter weaponry but found none. Captured airmen from Germany and Japan claimed to have also seen the reddish balls of light. Scientists suggested they might have instead been natural phenomena such as ball lightning or St. Elmo's fire, but the maneuverability described by the pilots would seem to discount both possibilities. It was also suggested the pilots simply imagined what they saw, but witnesses were adamant they were no hallucinations. Other theorists believed the foo fighters were extraterrestrial, and that the visitors might be monitoring the world's increasingly destructive military capabilities. Alien or not, as World War II ended and the Cold War began, UFOs were a new force for the government to contend with.

The Many Incidents at Roswell

After the swarm of saucer stories took off in late June 1947, it only took about a week for one of them to crash. Perhaps even more amazing, on July 8, the United States Army Air Forces actually announced it. A "flying disk," it acknowledged, had been found on a ranch near Roswell, New Mexico, and was in the army's possession. So began what would become the biggest UFO conspiracy story in history. But before we get into alien bodies being recovered from the wreckage and concealed from the public, let's run through the precipitating events as they unfolded before the world over a two-day roller coaster ride of nationwide headlines.

Reports claimed the saucer went down sometime at the beginning of July or as early as three weeks prior. If the latter were true, the event would have occurred before the Kenneth Arnold UFO sighting, suggesting that perhaps those nine saucers were looking for a missing tenth. Regardless of the specific timing, a rancher named W. W. "Mack" Brazel eventually discovered strange debris scattered across a square mile of his land, located on the outskirts of Roswell. These mysterious bits and pieces appeared to be tin foil and wooden beams.

On Saturday, July 5, Brazel headed into town for a drink, where he heard about the flying saucer hoopla sweeping the country. Having no radio at the ranch, he'd been oblivious to the flurry of reports, not to mention the $3,000 reward that the press was offering to anyone who could produce one of these saucers. If the idea of aliens didn't pique his interest, the cash prize surely did.

The next day, Brazel gathered a bundle of foil and beams and hauled it into the Roswell sheriff's office. Their curious nature compelled the sheriff to alert the Roswell Army Air Field, which began an immediate investigation. Base commander Colonel William H. Blanchard assigned intelligence officer Major Jesse Marcel of the 509th Bombardment Group and Sheriden Cavitt of the Counter Intelligence Corps to follow Brazel back to his ranch to investigate. Marcel and Cavitt were ordered to load any strange wreckage they retrieved onto a B-29 plane and deliver their findings directly to General Roger Ramey at the Fort Worth Army Air Field. In the meantime, Blanchard issued a press release to his public information officer, Lieutenant Walter Haut, who delivered the following statement to the press:

> The many rumors regarding the flying disks became a reality yesterday when the intelligence office of the 509th (atomic) bomb group of Eighth air force, Roswell army air field, was fortunate enough to gain

> possession of a disk through the cooperation of one of the local ranch-
> ers and the sheriff's office of Chaves county.
>
> The flying object landed on a ranch near Roswell some time last
> week. Not having phone facilities, the rancher stored the disk until
> such time as he was able to contact the sheriff's office, who in turn
> notified Major Jesse A. Marcel, of the 509th bomb group intelligence
> office.
>
> Action was immediately taken and the disk was picked up at the
> rancher's home. It was inspected at the Roswell army air field and sub-
> sequently loaned by Major Marcel to higher headquarters.

That day, newspapers across America ran the remarkable statement, including headlines like the one plastered on the front page of the *Roswell Daily Record*: "RAAF Captures Flying Saucer on Ranch in Roswell Region." Sensational as that sounded, a radio announcement described the alleged twenty- to twenty-five-foot craft as unlikely to achieve intergalactic travel, noting that "nothing in the apparent construction indicated any capacity for speed and there was no evidence of a powerplant." It also claimed that the disk "appeared too flimsy to carry a man."

Flimsy or phenomenal, this major announcement startled Washington as much as anyone else—so much so that the powers that be discussed the matter with Ramey, and by July 9, newspapers had a new announcement. According to Ramey, the "flying disc" was nothing more than a high-altitude weather balloon. Suspended from this type of balloon was a six-sided star covered with a shiny material, like tinfoil, designed to be traced by radar and to reveal air currents. As the Associated Press put it, the mysterious object "was rudely stripped of its glamour."

"I don't say these devices are what people have called discs," Ramey said. "There is no such gadget (as the disc) known to the army at least this far down the line."

That was it. One day the army had captured a flying saucer, and the next day it was a balloon. Skeptics of the official explanation continue to note that the 509th Bomb Group was the elite military group that dropped the bombs on Japan just a couple years earlier and was perfectly familiar with weather balloon technology, and that a conventional weather balloon crash would hardly necessitate inspection and identification by army higher-ups.

Decades later, Roswell made a grand return to the public consciousness. It all began when a nuclear physicist and ufologist named Stanton Friedman happened upon the story while researching a separate UFO event. The witness he'd been speaking with suggested that Friedman interview the witness's mother, Lydia Sleppy, who had worked at KOAT Radio in Albuquerque at the time of the Roswell incident. According to her tale, she had received a call from the station's Roswell affiliate and was asked to type a memo on the news wire stating that a flying saucer had crashed and that the wreckage was being transported to Wright-Patterson Air Force Base in Ohio. Before she could complete the story, a bell dinged alerting her to an incoming message, which read: "Do not continue this transmission, FBI." Friedman attempted to contact people Sleppy mentioned during their interview, hoping to corroborate the story, but had little luck learning anything more. So he filed the story away.

In 1978, several years after meeting Sleppy, Roswell leapt to the forefront of Friedman's research while he was at a radio station in Baton Rouge, Louisiana, to promote an upcoming lecture on UFOs. As he waited for one of the reporters to arrive, the station manager approached him and said, "The guy you really ought to talk to is Jesse Marcel." Coincidentally, the manager and Marcel had been ham radio friends, and Friedman followed up on the lead.

After thirty-one years, Marcel broke his silence on his involvement in the Roswell incident and told Friedman there was more than what had been reported by the press. Marcel revealed that upon his arrival at Fort Worth, he brought the debris to Ramey's office and was then led to a map room and asked to point out the location of the wreckage. This, he believed, was less about information and more about a diversion, because when he returned to the office, the wreckage he'd delivered had been replaced by weather balloon debris. It was this debris, he claimed, that he'd been famously photographed with.

Marcel's son, Jesse Marcel Jr., who has spoken and written about the event often, can see the conspiracy in his father's expression. "The

The *Roswell Daily Record* edition from July 8, 1947, the day the air force claimed to have recovered a flying saucer.

Leased Wire
Associated Press

Roswell Daily Record

RECORD PHONES
Business Office 2288
News Department 2287

VOL. 47. NUMBER 99. ESTABLISHED 1888.   ROSWELL, NEW MEXICO, TUESDAY, JULY 8, 1947.   5c PER COPY.

Movies as Usual

GRAND

Levees broke and flood waters rolled into the town of Grand Tower, Ill., but while the manager of this movie theater sweeps out the water that has entered the lobby, these youngsters are standing in line for tickets for the night's performance. (AP Wirephoto)

Some of Soviet Satellites May Attend Paris Meeting

Claims Army Is Stacking Courts Martial

Indiana Senator Lays Protest Before Patterson

Washington, July 8 (AP)—Senator Jenner (R-Ind.) contended today that "the high command in the European theatre is stacking the courts against defendants in court martial."

In a letter to Secretary of War Patterson demanding a full investigation of army military trial procedure, Jenner offered what he said was documentary proof that:

1. "Prisoners are not being permitted to employ either civilian or military counsel of their own choice in the preparation and presentation of their defense."

2. "Every effort is being made to prevent attorneys who were connected with the infamous Lichfield prison case to practice in courts martial in the European theatre."

The Indiana senator made public a copy of an informal "routing slip" which he said was signed by Brig. Gen. Cornelius E. Ryan, assistant deputy military government headquarters for the military government for Germany, and written by Col. Francis H. Vanderwater. Jenner told newsmen that the routing slip substantiated his charges.

The slip, addressed to the chief of staff, USFET (presumably US forces, European theatre), was dated last Oct. 23.

It called attention to the impending arrival of Earl J. Carroll and Thomas Lester Polcy, California attorneys, to act as special defense counsel for five prisoners then awaiting trial by...

House Passes Tax Slash by Large Margin

Defeat Amendment By Demos to Remove Many from Rolls

Washington, July 8 (AP)—The house passed today the Republican-backed bill to cut income taxes by $4,000,000,000 annually for 49,000,000 taxpayers, beginning Jan. 1.

It goes to the senate where approval also is forecast.

The vote was 302 to 11, or more than the two-thirds majority needed to override a presidential veto.

The action, which may encounter another presidential veto, came after Speaker Martin (R-Mass.) personally appealed to the house to pass the bill by such a decisive vote—as to persuade the president that the people should have this delayed justice.

The measure is identical with one vetoed by President Truman June 16 as "the wrong kind of tax reduction at the wrong time"—except that the effective date is changed from July 1, 1947 to Jan. 1, 1948.

Security Council Paves Way to Talks On Arms Reductions

Lake Success, July 8 (AP)—The United Nations security council today approved an American blueprint for arms reduction discussions despite a Russian warning that the plan would bring about a collapse of arms regulation efforts.

The vote was 9 to 0, with Russian and Poland abstaining.

In view of Russia's firm stand against the U. S. plan it had been believed she might invoke the big power veto to block it.

Soviet Deputy Foreign Minister Andrei A. Gromyko gave his warning before the United Nations security council in a new effort to revive the Soviet working plan which already had been rejected by the commission for conventional armaments.

His challenge was taken up promptly by French delegate Alexandre Parodi and U. S. Representative Herschel V. Johnson, who announced their opposition to any substitute for the American plan.

Gromyko insisted that no program for arms regulation could succeed unless the plan was linked directly with an absolute prohibition of atomic weapons.

He declared that the U. S. plan...

No Details of Flying Disk Are Revealed

Roswell Hardware Man and Wife Report Disk Seen

The intelligence office of the 509th Bombardment group at Roswell Army Air Field announced at noon today that the field has come into possession of a flying saucer.

According to information released by the department, over authority of Maj. J. A. Marcel, intelligence officer, the disk was recovered on a ranch in the Roswell vicinity, after an unidentified rancher had notified Sheriff Geo. Wilcox, here, that he had found the instrument on his premises.

Major Marcel and a detail from his department went to the ranch and recovered the disk, it was stated.

After the intelligence office here had inspected the instrument it was flown to "higher headquarters."

The intelligence office stated that no details of the saucer's construction or its appearance had been revealed.

Mr. and Mrs. Dan Wilmot ap-...

Ex-King Carol Weds Mme. Lupescu

Former King Carol of Romania and Mme. Elena Lupescu relax aboard the S. S. America bound for Cuba and Mexico in May, 1941. A member of Carol's household in Rio de Janeiro said the ex-king and his companion for 23 years in reign and exile were recently married at their hotel, Copacabana Palace suite. (AP Wirephoto)

RAAF Captures Flying Saucer On Ranch in Roswell Region

Major Jesse A. Marcel at Fort Worth holding debris from the Roswell, New Mexico, UFO crash site in July 1947.

look on his face is quite telling: 'You gotta be kidding me, this is not what I saw,'" Marcel Jr. said at the 2013 Citizens Hearing on Disclosure at the National Press Club in Washington, DC. "So this is where the cover up began—in General Ramey's office."

Marcel Jr., a medical doctor, flight surgeon, and helicopter pilot, also shared his memories of his father coming home late at night with debris from the crash before delivering it to Fort Worth. Just eleven years old at the time, Marcel Jr. claimed his father woke him and his mother up to show them what he'd collected.

"My dad, knowing he'd seen something very special, wanted my mother, myself, to look at this also, because as he said, you'll never see this again," Marcel Jr. told the hearing's committee of former politicians.

He described seeing a smattering of this strange debris spread out on the kitchen floor. "Look at this," his recalled his father saying, "I think this is what you call a flying saucer or the remains thereof."

Marcel Jr. noted three types of flying saucer remains: a thick, foil-like metallic gray substance that when bent would unfold to its original form; a brittle, brownish-black plastic-like material; and fragments of what appeared to be I-beams. These I-beams, Marcel Jr. claimed, featured "a type of writing" embossed on the inner surface. "The figures were composed of curved, geometric shapes. It had no resemblance to Russian, Japanese or any other foreign language."

By the time his father returned from the base, he told Marcel Jr. and his mother the only thing he was allowed to say: "You will never talk about this. This is a non-event." The major kept silent until finally speaking to Friedman about his experience.

Walter Haut, the lieutenant who delivered the initial statement to the press, corroborated Marcel Jr.'s version of the story in a 2002 sworn affidavit that remained sealed until after his death in 2005. In it the former public information officer mentioned a few more details he decided to finally share at the age of eighty. He described seeing a metallic "egg shaped" object about twelve to fifteen feet in length and six feet high being loaded into the B-29 on the tarmac. It had no portholes, wings, or landing gear. More curious was his observation of what appeared to have been inside the crashed object:

> From a distance, I was able to see a couple of bodies under a canvas tarpaulin. Only the heads extended beyond the covering, and I was not able to make out any features. The heads did appear larger than normal and the contour of the canvas suggested the size of a 10-year-old child.

Haut further stated that he was convinced that what he witnessed "was some type of craft and its crew from outer space." Beyond seeing these alleged extraterrestrials, the lieutenant also claimed that a temporary morgue had been set up to accommodate the recovered bodies.

Roswell mortician Glenn Dennis had been on the job that day, and when others started talking, he began sharing his memories as well. On CNN's *Larry King Live* in 2003, he told King that he had received a call from the mortuary officer at the base, he said, "asking me how many infant hermetically sealed caskets we had, three and a half to four feet, in stock."

Dennis responded that he had only one but could get more by the next day. When he asked what was going on, the army air field officer responded, "That's not important." The mortuary officer then allegedly called again to ask how the embalming chemical would alter the tissues and the stomach contents and what their preparation process was like for bodies laying out in the elements for days. Ultimately, no casket order was placed.

Back in 1994, before any of these details reached the public, the air force had offered a new explanation for the Roswell incident that didn't quite align with the claims of Marcel Jr. and Dennis or with Haut's affidavit. Its report came at the urging of New Mexico congressman Steven H. Schiff and stated that the strange debris was indeed something more than a weather balloon: it was a top-secret balloon system designed to spy on the Russians, known as Project Mogul. The goal was to float the high-tech balloon through the upper atmosphere and detect evidence of nuclear-test blasts. These types of efforts helped the U.S. government discover the Russian's nuclear capabilities in 1949.

According to the report, the air force had been interested in investigating early UFO reports because it believed that the objects might have been advanced technology sent from Moscow—halfway around the world—not from another world entirely. Were the Soviets spying on U.S. military efforts? Were they attempting to showcase capabilities superior to the atomic bomb? With the Cold War underway, the air force had no choice but to take everything seriously.

So when Brazel reported the wreckage scattered across his ranch, the RAAF may have felt safer announcing it was a "flying disc" than sharing its secret about new spying technology. A crashed UFO *was* the cover story. After taking another minute, the RAAF may have realized that "weather balloon" would have been easier for the world to digest and then forget about.

As for the mysterious markings on the debris, famed astrophysicist Dr. Carl Sagan suggested their origin was more local than ufologists contend. "The radar targets carried by the balloons were partly manufactured by novelty and toy companies in New York, whose inventory of decorative icons seems to have been remembered as alien hieroglyphics many years after the fact."

Sagan's skepticism was also targeted toward what he described as "diverse recollections simmering over the years, and memories refreshed by the opportunity for a little fame and fortune." He also noted that the rash of UFO sightings in the late 1940s coincided with the military's conversion of nuclear weapon delivery from aircraft to missiles. Some sightings may have been test launches or nose cones reentering the atmosphere—all of which would have been extremely top secret, meaning even high-level military personnel may have been kept in the dark.

"Air Force officers and civilian scientists thinking back on it in later years might very well conclude that the government had engineered a UFO cover-up," Sagan wrote. "If nosecones are judged UFOs, the charge is a fair one."

On the other hand, Walter Haut, who opened Roswell's International UFO Museum and Research Center in 1991, wasn't buying the air force's new story. "It's a bunch of pap," he told the *New York Times* following the release of the 1994 report. "All they've done is given us a different kind of balloon. Then it was weather, and now it's Mogul. Basically I don't think anything has changed. Excuse my cynicism, but

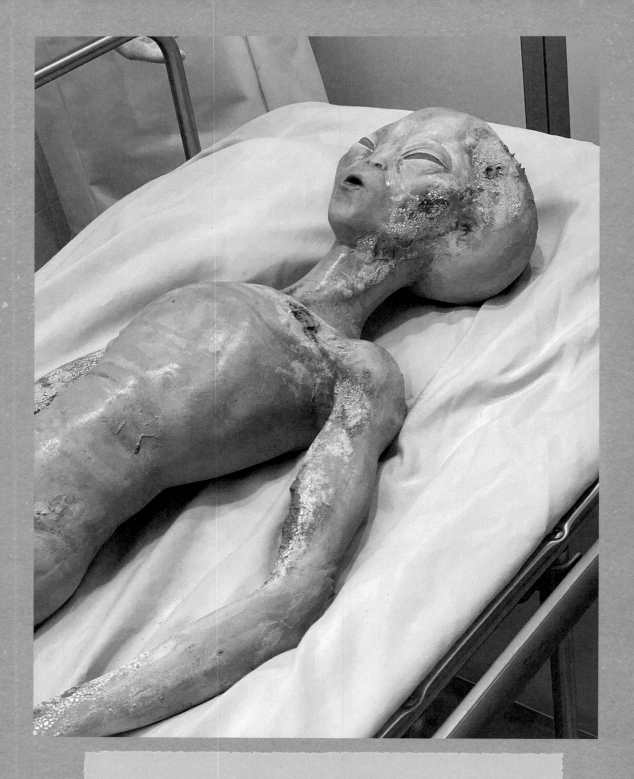

This alien model is on display at the International UFO Museum and Research Center, founded by Roswell incident witness Walter Haut, as part of its exhibit covering the lore around the 1947 event.

let's quit playing games."

But Haut was wrong. Things did change. Retired army intelligence officer Colonel Philip J. Corso added to the Roswell lore with his own recollections in 1997—just a year before his death. In a memoir titled *The Day After Roswell*, he claimed to have supervised the "seeding" of alien technology to big business in 1961. Companies like IBM, Bell Labs, and Dow-Corning began reverse-engineering the extraterrestrial technology to revolutionize the world with such modern wonders as the transistor, fiber-optic lasers, integrated circuit chips, night-vision eyewear, particle-beam weapons, and more. Aside from granting us the gift of new and improved gadgets and gizmos, the UFO also aided the development of the defense technology that helped end the Cold War.

Then there were the extraterrestrials' bodies. Haut caught a glimpse of them, but Corso got a close look at one of the bodies in Fort Riley, Kansas, while it was allegedly being transferred to Wright-Patterson. Prying open the lid of a small shipping crate, he shined his flashlight inside and nearly got sick from what he saw. His initial thought was that what he was looking at, submerged in a light blue liquid, was a dead child. "But this was no child," he wrote of the gray-skinned figure. "It was a four-foot human-shaped figure with arms, bizarre-looking four-fingered hands—I didn't see a thumb—thin legs and feet, and an oversized incandescent lightbulb-shaped head."

The Roswell incident was ballooning—and not in an atmospheric spying way. So the air force did some more digging and put together a document entitled *The Roswell Report: Case Closed* in 1997. Although the title sounded like something straight off of the History Channel, the new report left the case anything but closed. At least in the minds of ufologists. The document claimed that bodies that had been found were merely dummies that had likely broken apart upon impact, which might explain why witnesses described them as about four feet tall. However, the report also states that anthropomorphic dummies weren't used until 1953, and that "dummies of these types were most likely the 'aliens' associated with the 'Roswell Incident.'" Yet the incident took place in 1947. This created a six-year gap in the air force's story. That gap opened the Roswell rabbit hole even wider.

When Colonel John Hayes faced the media about the report, his only response to that discrepancy was that witnesses had compressed time in their memories. Dummies were used in Roswell throughout the 1950s, and military vehicles would race to retrieve them and use body bags. According to Hayes, these incidents were what people remembered. He also clarified—and stressed—that Project Mogul was unmanned and used no dummies, deepening the confusion and anger of ufologists and believers.

Oddly enough, the *Case Closed* report also highlights a 1993 account from local resident James Ragsdale, who allegedly witnessed the actual crash and saw portions of the debris in 1947. "I'm sure that [there] was bodies . . . either bodies or dummies," he stated. "They was using dummies in those damned things." Did Ragsdale mix up his dates, too?

The air force report concluded that "the witnesses or the UFO proponents who liberally interpreted their statements were either 1) confused, or 2) attempting to perpetrate a hoax."

Not surprisingly, those "confused" people came to different conclusions. As a staff member at the International UFO Museum and Research Center in Roswell quipped following Hayes's press conference, "Someone said they think the story of the dummies was put out by dummies. I think it's another cover-up."

To this day, many people agree. For Karen Jaramillo, the museum's current executive director, the number of witnesses and their character makes it difficult to believe the government's story. "I don't see how so many people lied," she told me as we discussed the case in the research library. "Why would they lie? They didn't get nothing out of it by telling their story. None of them became rich or anything from letting us know what happened. One old man came in, and when he started reading he started crying and crying. The emotions we see from the people, you know, there's just no way they're lying."

But what if the cover-up was covering up something besides aliens and Cold War spy technology? What if there's an entirely different explanation that accounts for witnesses who believed they saw small gray bodies recovered and whisked away after the crash in the desert?

When I reached out to Dr. Pascal Lee—a planetary scientist at the SETI Institute and chairman of the Mars Institute, whom I met while writing *The Big Book of Mars* in 2019—to get his thoughts on the UFO

"The psychology is simple: People believe what they want to believe. In New Mexico, flying-saucerism has become a minor industry. There are whole museums dedicated to the presentation of outrageous fictions."

—ALBERT C. TRAKOWSKI, retired air force officer who ran Project Mogul, in an interview with the *New York Times* on September 18, 1994

"Rule #1 for debunkers is, 'Don't bother me with facts, my mind is already made up.'"

—STANTON FRIEDMAN, nuclear physicist and ufologist, citing a quote frequently used in his lectures phenomenon and the possibility of extraterrestrial life, he offered a much different theory on Roswell (along with many other fascinating thoughts that we'll get to later). He has no specific data to back it up; it's pure speculation. Yet it's an idea with a fully plausible (fully terrestrial) explanation: Lee believes that any recovered bodies may have belonged to monkeys.

The United States space program sent numerous primates into space to study the physiological effects that it would have on them in order to understand the possible effects on humans. Astrochimps Ham and Enos were famously launched into space in 1961. They were even trained to pull levers in response to certain signals and received banana pellets as a reward. But before them, there was Albert, a nine-pound anesthetized rhesus monkey who, on the morning of June 18, 1948, was stuffed inside a pressurized capsule in the nose of a V-2 rocket and shot into the upper limits of earth's atmosphere. Indications from the test suggest Albert may have suffocated in the cramped capsule before it even launched. The project experienced various operational failures, including the parachute system. So even if Albert had survived the flight, the impact upon his return would've done him in. This occurred, as you might have guessed, in New Mexico.

Did Albert have predecessors being tested for the military's high-altitude spying program? If so, it's probable the air force would have shaved the monkeys in order to put electrodes all over their bodies as part of their body behavior testing. "Now if you shave a chimpanzee the skin is yellowish-gray," Lee noted. "And a shaven chimpanzee looks very alien. It's got a big head, long limbs. So, quite simply, what I think happened in Roswell is a balloon came down with three chimpanzees on board."

The monkeys may have been in pressure suits, like the ones Ham and Enos wore. Mylar might have accounted for the strange foil that was found. At the time, Mylar was a new material that would have appeared mysterious to those not involved in the radar-tracking of stratospheric balloons, which was almost everyone.

Lee believes the tests may have gone beyond the physiological. In this era before automation and robotics, monkeys may have also been undergoing training to take pictures as the high-altitude balloons soared over Soviet targets. Perhaps, he speculates, the goal of that training was—similar to Ham and Enos—to have the astrochimp learn to pull a lever to take a photo, with a banana as a reward.

"You try to get intelligence on a site, you try to get as close as possible, launch the balloon, track it, when it's in the right place, you send a signal to feed the banana and the monkey will pull the lever and take the picture," Lee proposed. "At least what I'm suggesting is completely plausible and consistent with the trends of the time, the reality of the space program, the reality of our flight tests, the reality of our use of primates and what they look like."

But why, I asked, would the air force keep such a story under wraps?

"I suspect in large part because they don't want to open the can of worms about experimenting on animals in those days, which must have been horrific," Lee said. "Subjecting apes to low pressure till they blow up, essentially. Subjecting them to high altitude radiation. It must have been a pretty gory program of testing on primates to open the way for humans to go into space."

From monkeys and dummies to top-secret tech and actual aliens, if nothing else the Roswell incident has been a boon for business and tourism in town, not to mention television, Hollywood, and pop culture. Sci-fi fans can binge the *Roswell* teen drama television series and Steven Spielberg's *Taken* miniseries, watch *Futurama*'s take in the third season episode "Roswell That Ends Well," or read Bongo Comics' *Roswell: Little Green Man*. And like the theories on what really happened, there is no shortage of documentaries to further stir imagination.

The UFO That Shot Down an F-51 Fighter. Or Didn't.

Flying saucers continued to fill the skies in the months after Roswell, but while none of them crashed, one appeared to cause a crash. In January 1948, Captain Thomas F. Mantell of the Kentucky Air National Guard died in a wreck after allegedly chasing a UFO in his fighter plane. The twenty-five-year-old decorated World War II fighter pilot was one of three officers investigating a report of a circular glowing object in the sky above Madisonville, Kentucky.

After about thirty minutes of pursuit, Captain Mantell radioed in a transmission to the control tower: "It's directly ahead of me and moving at about half my speed. I'm closing in now to take a good look. The thing looks metallic and is tremendous in size."

Minutes later Mantell made contact once more. "It's still above me, making my speed or better. I'm going up to twenty thousand feet. If I'm no closer, I'll abandon chase."

That was the last anyone heard from him. Searchers found the scattered ruins of his downed plane less than an hour later.

An air force intelligence officer initially claimed that rather than a spacecraft, the pilot had been chasing a daytime view of Venus, which happened to be near its peak brilliance that day. As with the event in Roswell, the explanation was soon revised: Mantell had seen a new type of high-altitude research balloon. This particular type of balloon, however, belonged to the navy's secret Project Skyhook and was first launched in September 1947. It had a diameter measuring about 100 feet, reached a height of 100,000 feet, and, if caught in a jetstream wind, could travel at more than 200 miles per hour. When seen from a distance its spheroid shape would look more like a disk. So to those unaware of the covert balloons, they fit the classic UFO description. According to the air force's *Roswell Report*, "The large balloon, which matched eyewitnesses' descriptions at the time, was released the previous day, and its ground track placed it precisely in the area where the unidentified object was sighted the next day."

Air Technical Intelligence Center (ATIC) officials suggested that by reaching an altitude of more than 22,000 feet, Mantell blacked out from a lack of oxygen during his pursuit and never regained consciousness. The theory was bolstered by the fact that his plane's canopy lock was still in place after the crash, indicating that Mantell had not attempted to abandon the aircraft. "The UFO was in no way directly responsible for this accident," ATIC claimed. "However, it is probable that the excitement caused by the object was responsible for this experienced pilot conducting a high altitude flight without the necessary oxygen equipment."

Others weren't so quick to accept the theory, given the pilot's expertise and experience. A search of the sky after Mantell's crash found no sign of the object. A balloon, it seemed, should've remained in view. "I think he either collided with it, or more likely they knocked him out of the air," one of the other pilots said. "They'd think he was trying to bring them down, barging in like that."

In the days that followed, headlines such as AIRMAN KILLED IN CHASE OF "FLYING SAUCER" led people who were already caught up in saucermania to believe that these mysterious objects might also be a serious threat. But rather than train pilots to evade or engage with alien aggressors, the air force stuck with ATIC's terrestrial theory and recommended briefing pilots more effectively on the effects of oxygen deprivation at high altitudes.

Still, fifteen months later the air force changed its tune yet again and announced that the "mysterious object which the flyer chased to his death" remained unidentified.

The Colorful Pages of Project Blue Book

The rash of sightings in the late 1940s kept the air force busy chasing saucers for answers. On September 23, 1947, Lieutenant General Nathan F. Twining of the Air Materiel Command issued an official opinion on the matter in a memo to Washington's commanding general of the Army Air Forces, General Carl Spaatz. Based on report data and studies by his command, Twining concluded "the phenomenon is something real and not visionary or fictitious."

This was a powerful statement. He acknowledged, however, that the strange objects could be part of a high security domestic project not known to him or his command, or that they could belong to a foreign nation with propulsion technology beyond the United States' capabilities. Twining also noted there was a lack of physical evidence which would "undeniably prove" the existence of these flying objects.

He recommended the Army Air Forces "issue a directive assigning a priority, security classification and Code name for a detailed study of this matter." ATIC investigators had already been documenting cases under the moniker Project Saucer, but they renamed it Project Sign in January 1948.

Shortly after, the air force brought in Ohio State University astronomer Dr. J. Allen Hynek to serve as a technical consultant. The goateed, pipe-smoking scientist was tasked with resolving the overwhelming number of flying saucer cases thrust upon the air force by the public, as well as with assuring people that despite the mysterious sightings, earth was not being swarmed by alien invaders. If Americans doubted the air force, perhaps the calming presence of a professor would offer greater trust.

"I was to see how many of the reports up to that time could be explained rationally and astronomically as meteors, twinkling stars, and bright planets," Hynek wrote in his 1977 book, *The Hynek UFO Report*. "Obviously, few of the many daylight discs could be so explained. No astronomical object appears as a metallic flying disc violently cavorting through the daytime sky. But there were many others that could and did have astronomical explanations."

Meteors or fireballs (unusually bright meteors) and comets were frequent culprits, as was the planet Venus. Hynek claimed the latter was the target of "many rounds of ammunition" in both world wars with "each side thinking this bright planet was a device of the enemy."

Other cases proved much more challenging. In August 1947, for example, a group of citizens and members of the police department in Twin Falls, Idaho, reported a light blue object with a reddish glow whisking over trees and racing through the Snake River Canyon at an estimated 1,000 miles per hour. The air force evaluation of the sighting, known as Case 75 in Project Saucer, stated: "There is clearly nothing astronomical in this incident. Apparently it must be classed with the other bona fide disk sightings." Yet, based on the sky-blue color and a farmer's description of the object passing over trees, which "spun around on top as if they were in a vacuum," Project Saucer offered a potential natural explanation: "Could this, then, have been a rapidly traveling atmospheric eddy?"

Project Sign lasted just a year before adopting a new name: Project Grudge. But in that short time a top-secret "Estimate of the Situation" was allegedly written by ATIC investigators and submitted to higher-ups at the air force—and rejected. According to Captain Edward J. Ruppelt, who eventually lead Grudge's next iteration, Project Blue Book, "The

Dr. J. Allen Hynek with his trademark pipe. The air force consulted the astronomer throughout its Project Blue Book UFO investigations, from the late 1940s to December 1969.

situation was the UFOs; the estimate was that they were interplanetary!"

Project Grudge aimed to change that estimate. The name, as Hynek noted, had an "extremely negative" sound to it and operated under the premise "that UFOs simply *could not be*." As such, it concluded by August 1949 that all UFO sightings could be explained one of four ways:

1. As a misinterpretation of various conventional objects
2. As a mild form of mass hysteria and war nerves
3. As the observations of individuals who fabricate such reports to perpetrate a hoax or to seek publicity
4. As the observations of psychopathological persons

"I, too, thought at the time that UFOs were just a lot of nonsense," Hynek recalled. "I enjoyed the role of debunker even though I had to admit that some of the original 237 cases I studied were real puzzlers."

The air force, apparently unconcerned with the "puzzlers," officially terminated the program by December 1949. The release of retired U.S. Marine Corps major Donald Keyhoe's article in *True* magazine that same month, "The Flying Saucers Are Real," probably didn't help the government's cause. Keyhoe firmly believed UFOs were interplanetary and wasn't shy about speaking up or publicly contradicting the air force's claims—despite working closely with its investigations. In his article, he concluded that aliens have been visiting earth for 175 years and observations had "increased markedly" over the previous two. The article grabbed the attention of the national press.

"Within twenty-four hours the Pentagon was deluged with telegrams, letters, and long-distance calls," Keyhoe wrote in his 1950 book of the same name. "Apparently fearing a panic, the Air Force hastily stated that flying-saucer reports—even those made by its own pilots and high-ranking officers—were mistakes or were caused by hysteria."

Grudge was officially over, but it trudged on till the end of 1951 since the phenomenon it studied certainly was not. In need of further investigation, the program morphed into Project Blue Book. The new name was inspired by the booklets used in college tests because, as Ruppelt described it, "Both the tests and the project had an abundance of

2

PROJECT 10073 RECORD CARD

1. DATE	2. LOCATION	12. CONCLUSIONS
October 1947	Dodgeville, Wisc	☐ Was Balloon ☐ Probably Balloon ☐ Possibly Balloon
3. DATE-TIME GROUP	4. TYPE OF OBSERVATION	☐ Was Aircraft ☐ Probably Aircraft ☐ Possibly Aircraft
Local 2300 GMT	☒ Ground-Visual ☐ Ground-Radar ☐ Air-Visual ☐ Air-Intercept Radar	☐ Was Astronomical ☐ Probably Astronomical ☐ Possibly Astronomical
5. PHOTOS ☐ Yes ☒ No	6. SOURCE Civilian	
7. LENGTH OF OBSERVATION	8. NUMBER OF OBJECTS	9. COURSE	☐ Other____ ☐ Insufficient Data for Evaluation ☒ Unknown
one hour	One	NW to S	

10. BRIEF SUMMARY OF SIGHTING	11. COMMENTS
No description, except that a "saucer" was to the NW, moving slowly to the south. All at once in a sudden burst of speed it circled from right to left in a huge circle and moved toward the south at the same time. No sound, smell, or trail. Very high rate of speed in making the circles.	Unidentified.

ATIC FORM 329 (REV 26 SEP 52)

PROJECT 10073 RECORD CARD

1. DATE	2. LOCATION	12. CONCLUSIONS
25 Apr 58	3800 N 5430 W In Atlantic Ocean	☐ Was Balloon ☐ Probably Balloon ☐ Possibly Balloon
3. DATE-TIME GROUP	4. TYPE OF OBSERVATION	☐ Was Aircraft ☐ Probably Aircraft ☐ Possibly Aircraft
Local GMT 25/1330Z	☒ Ground-Visual ☐ Ground-Radar ☒ Shipboard ☐ Air-Intercept Radar	☐ Was Astronomical ☐ Probably Astronomical ☐ Possibly Astronomical
5. PHOTOS ☐ Yes ☒ No	6. SOURCE Civilian	
7. LENGTH OF OBSERVATION	8. NUMBER OF OBJECTS	9. COURSE	☐ Other____ ☒ Insufficient Data for Evaluation ☐ Unknown
not given	one	SW	

10. BRIEF SUMMARY OF SIGHTING	11. COMMENTS
Cigar shaped obj bluish color, very high and headed north, Did not appear to be a/c or falling star.	Insufficient info for evaluation.

ATIC FORM 329 (REV 26 SEP 52)

PROJECT 10073 RECORD CARD

1. DATE	2. LOCATION	12. CONCLUSIONS
11 Apr 58	60 mi W of Argentia, Nwflnd.	☐ Was Balloon ☐ Probably Balloon ☐ Possibly Balloon
3. DATE-TIME GROUP	4. TYPE OF OBSERVATION	☐ Was Aircraft ☐ Probably Aircraft ☐ Possibly Aircraft
Local GMT 11/0615Z	☐ Ground-Visual ☐ Ground-Radar ☒ Air-Visual ☐ Air-Intercept Radar	☒ Was Astronomical Meteor ☐ Probably Astronomical ☐ Possibly Astronomical
5. PHOTOS ☐ Yes ☒ No	6. SOURCE Military	
7. LENGTH OF OBSERVATION	8. NUMBER OF OBJECTS	9. COURSE	☐ Other____ ☐ Insufficient Data for Evaluation ☐ Unknown
15-20 sec	one	— — —	

10. BRIEF SUMMARY OF SIGHTING	11. COMMENTS
Cockpit illuminated by brilliant obj believed to be decay of Sputnik 2 by witnesses on flight over Newfoundland. Obj observed for 15-20 secs. Intensity of welding torch. A/c at 8,000 ft. Obj disappated in shower of red sparks. No return on Radar.	Sputnik II did not decay until 14 apr. Obj has dracteristics of bolide observation of long duration. Case evaluated as a meteor sighting.

ATIC FORM 329 (REV 26 SEP 52)

Project Blue Book's record cards accompanied case files for each investigation.

equally confusing questions." The air force retained Hynek as a lead investigator until Blue Book was closed in December 1969. Hard evidence remained elusive since the scientist's small team of investigators (reportedly just four) could only study, as he later wrote, "UFO *reports*, not UFOs."

Throughout his years of interviews and investigations, Hynek admitted that he'd gradually gone from skeptic to "a scientist who felt he was on the track of an interesting phenomenon." How could he not be intrigued after investigating 12,618 documented UFO sightings spanning the three programs—including 701 that remained "unidentified"?

Headquartered at Ohio's Wright-Patterson Air Force Base, Hynek's team tackled the cases armed with little more than curiosity and a healthy knowledge of astronomical, aeronautical, and weather phenomena. Let's explore just a few of Project Blue Book's more colorful pages, starting with the chapter in which flying saucers invaded Washington, DC.[+]

Flying Saucers Invade Washington

On July 21, 1952, the Associated Press reported that the air force had "received reports of an eerie visitation by unidentified aerial objects—perhaps a new type of 'flying saucer'—over the vicinity of the nation's capital." If aliens were finally going to land on the White House lawn and announce themselves, it appeared this might be their big moment. But instead, the eight objects caught on radar around midnight traveled at a relatively slow 100 to 130 miles per hour over the DC area, occasionally moving rapidly up and down or hovering in one position, then simply sped off.

Officials at the Air Traffic Control Center at Washington National Airport observed the radar blips in disbelief. One object appeared and then zipped away so fast it seemingly accelerated from 130 miles per hour to 500 miles per hour in about four seconds. Another object took an abrupt ninety-degree turn—a movement beyond the capability of

---

+ After you finish this book, you can read all the Project Blue Book files online at the National Archives (*catalog.archives.gov*).

any airplane. These unusual maneuvers went on for several hours and rattled the controllers' nerves enough for them to alert the air force at nearby Andrews Base.

"Some had laughed off the idea of visitors from other planets," wrote Major Donald Keyhoe in his 1953 book *Flying Saucers from Outer Space*. "But now they were badly shaken. For the simultaneous radar tracks and visual sightings added up to only one answer. Up there in the night some kind of super-machines were reconnoitering the capital. From their controlled maneuvers, it was plain they were guided—if not manned—by highly intelligent beings."

Whatever the objects were, they only vanished for about a week. By the evening of July 26, radar caught them once again raiding Washington. If Keyhoe's concern about a scouting mission was correct, this second visit might be even more cause for alarm. This time the air force dispatched jet fighter planes to intercept the objects, but no contact was made. In a statement, officials said, "One of the jet pilots reported sighting four lights in front approximately ten miles and slightly above him but he reported he had no apparent closing speed. They disappeared before he could overtake them."

While the threat appeared legitimate enough to unleash fighter planes, Air Force Major General James A. Samford dismissed the entire episode as a bunch of hot air—more specifically, a weather phenomenon called temperature inversion. This occurs when a layer of warm air forms in the lower atmosphere and traps a layer of cool air beneath, which can reflect ground objects on a radar screen and make them appear as if they were in the sky. These reflections can even appear to be moving at great speeds. Such temperature inversions are common during the summer months in DC, but as Hynek pointed out in *The Hynek UFO Report*, "on many nights that summer the inversion was greater but no radar UFOs appeared."

The radar observers at the nearby National Airport also dismissed the possibility of temperature inversion. "When we see something there, there is something there," one of the radar men told the press, expressing confidence in his equipment. "It's not weather, clouds, and such, because that takes a different shape on the screen and it's either stationary or moving with the winds. It's not a hallucination because

Headlines like this one from July 29, 1952, ran in papers across the country after Washington, DC, appeared to be invaded by flying saucers.

5¢

U.S. Weather Forecast
THUNDERSTORMS
(Details on Page 2)

Daily Mirror

4c in N.Y.C.
5c Elsewhere

5¢

Vol. 29. No. 31.   NEW YORK 17, N. Y., TUESDAY, JULY 29, 1952   CO   FINAL EDITION ★★

ORDER ALL JETS CHASE SAUCERS

Air Force Alerts Fliers to 24-Hr. Duty

On May 31, 1952, the skies of Fort Worth, Texas, were filled with thousands of saucers—not from another world, but from a frozen dessert company. Vandervoort's capitalized on the UFO hoopla by having an airplane drop promotional "saucers" good for a free sundae cup.

radar isn't very imaginary. It's just something."

A lot of somethings filled the skies in 1952, totaling 366 flying saucer reports and fifty-five sightings left unidentified in July alone.[†] Ruppelt, who by then was the head of Blue Book, later noted that "the sightings beat the Democratic National Convention out of headline space" and that "they created such a furor" that he had President Truman asking for answers and the international press sniffing for details.

The Robertson Panel: Controlling the Narrative

With UFO reports spinning out of control like a malfunctioning saucer, the CIA sponsored a panel of distinguished scientists to investigate the situation and determine how to handle it. Chaired by Dr. Howard Robertson, the director of the Defense Department Weapons Evaluation Group, the SWAT team of physicists, including Hynek as an associate member, was dubbed the Robertson Panel. Among the notable members was Luis Alvarez, who would later win the 1968 Nobel Prize in Physics.[††]

For five full days, starting on January 14, 1953, the men discussed the methods used by Blue Book's investigators, explored case histories, and even studied films of seagulls in flight. The latter exercise helped them determine that a film taken the previous July of multiple UFOs in Tremonton, Utah, in fact captured imagery of ducks or other birds. This conclusion contradicted the report that came back from the photo reconnaissance laboratory at Wright-Patterson Air Force Base, which specifically said they couldn't be birds because the objects appeared to be a light source, not something reflecting light (without more data, it declined to speculate on the nature of the objects).

Ultimately, the Robertson Panel determined that the thousands of flying saucer sightings were clogging up the system and getting in

---

[†] UFO stories flooded newspapers so heavily in 1952 that Illinois's *Ottawa Daily Republican-Times* announced a ban on them by August. "We're not printing them anymore," the paper's managing editor told their 12,000 readers. "We've chosen sides. And we invite the 1,700 other daily newspapers in the nation to join in a fight against feeding pap to the newspaper reading public."

[††] Luis Alvarez's son, Walter, is credited with discovering that the extinction of the dinosaurs was caused by an asteroid.

the way of other important business. This contributed to a "danger of being led by continued false alarms to ignore real indications of hostile actions, and the cultivation of a morbid national psychology in which skillful hostile propaganda could induce hysterical behavior and harmful distrust of duly constituted authority." The panel recommended training the public to be better equipped to identify known objects and therefore reduce the number of reports, and for Blue Book to debunk as many sightings as possible to lessen the public's interest and ideally put an end to the entire situation. In a nutshell, as Hynek said years later, "The CIA was fearful not of UFOs, but of UFO *reports*."

So Project Blue Book debunked UFO claims, whenever and however it could. Its efforts, along with the outrageous claims made by people claiming to have met and been abducted by Venusians and other spacemen (we'll meet them in the next chapter), made ridicule a powerful tool against those who might dare to report a UFO sighting—and against other scientists who might have an interest in investigating the phenomenon.

"Today I would not spend one additional moment on the subject of UFOs if I didn't seriously feel that the UFO phenomenon is real and that efforts to investigate and understand it, and eventually to solve it, could have a profound effect—perhaps even be the springboard to a revolution in man's view of himself and his place in the universe."

—DR. J. ALLEN HYNEK, in *The Hynek UFO Report*, 1977

CLOSE ENCOUNTERS OF THE HYNEK KIND

Without the work of Dr. J. Allen Hynek, thousands of UFO reports over the decades may have gone without evaluation or explanation. The world might have also been deprived of one of the great science fiction films of all time: *Close Encounters of the Third Kind*.

Steven Spielberg's 1977 classic took its name from the UFO encounter classification system Hynek established in his 1972 book *The UFO Experience: A Scientific Inquiry*.

"It was purely an observational classification system, much like an astronomer might use to classify different types of stars or a zoologist different types of beetles that he came across in his explorations," Hynek said.

The first three categories cover strange lights seen in the night sky ("Nocturnal Lights"), sightings during the day ("Daytime Discs"), and unusual detections by radar ("Radar-Visual"). A separate set of categories deals with sightings observed within a few hundred feet "or at least close enough so that the witness is able to use his stereoscopic vision and discern considerable detail." Hynek defined three kinds of close encounters as follows.

The First Kind: A sighting in which there is no interaction with the UFO, but the object is close enough for the witness to be sure that it's not a conventional aircraft, and certainly not Venus.

The Second Kind: A sighting in which the UFO interacts with the environment and frequently with the witness. This can include a burnt ring on the ground beneath the spot where the UFO was seen hovering, mechanical interferences (a car ignition, for example), and burns, nausea, or temporary paralysis suffered by the witness.

The Third Kind: A sighting that involves an encounter with the occupants of the UFO.

Spielberg, who in the mid-seventies had wanted to make a movie about UFOs, was enamored with the Third Kind. And according to Hynek, there were "hundreds" of such encounters with intelligent beings reported across the globe in the previous decades.

The film centers around a fictional sighting by Indiana suburbanite Roy Neary (played by Richard Dreyfuss) and others, and a group of scientists investigating strange discoveries of long-lost vehicles and aircraft around the world. Two characters inspired by Hynek and French UFO investigator Jacques Vallée lead the team.

Spielberg hired Hynek as the film's technical advisor (he also makes a cameo appearance), which is evident in the authentic portrayals of the sightings experienced by Neary and other characters. For example, the blackout that swept across Indiana early in the film paralleled an East Coast power failure in November 1965 that left everyone in darkness. UFO researcher and physicist James McDonald appeared before a congressional committee in July 1968 and claimed flying saucers may have been responsible for it. "There are too many instances of sightings of UFOs hovering near power plants," he said, adding that there had been hundreds of sightings during the outage, including "reports in upstate New York of a glowing object at the instant the lights went out." The blackout was believed to have originated in the upstate New York area.

In another scene, the passing flying saucer affects Roy's truck by killing its engine and dimming its lights. A similar incident took place late at night on November 2, 1957, near Levelland, Texas. At least nine witnesses described the UFO as egg or oval shaped, about two hundred feet long, and glowing like a neon sign. Several claimed their car's headlights went out and their engines died as it approached them over the road.

"That's just the way an electromagnetic force field would operate," said Donald Keyhoe, who by then served as the director of the National Investigations Committee on Aerial Phenomena (NICAP). "This isn't the first time we've heard of such things happening."

After taking statements from numerous witnesses, Project Blue Book investigators attributed the sighting to ball lightning. This rare meteorological occurrence appears as a floating sphere that changes color from blue to orange to yellow and may disappear in seconds. Weather conditions in Levelland that night offered the ingredients necessary for ball lightning to form. As Blue Book noted, "all but one observer mentioned lightning or lightning flashes and the exis-

The title of Steven Spielberg's 1977 film *Close Encounters of the Third Kind* comes from Dr. J. Allen Hynek's UFO encounter classification system.

tence of rain or mist in the area."

In *Close Encounters*, eventually Neary and a local woman who shared the local extraterrestrial experience are drawn to Devils Tower National Monument in Wyoming, where the scientists and military meet with humanoid aliens who release long-missing abductees from their mothership.

The film was a box office success and earned eight Oscar nominations, but perhaps of greater significance, it impacted the way many people thought about the UFO subject.

"It's often pieces of fiction that help move the needle on the public discourse," said Paul Hynek,

son of J. Allen, on Lee Speigel's *Edge of Reality Radio* podcast in 2020. "I think *Close Encounters* the movie did a lot of service to the community and made a lot of people feel more comfortable talking about this highly stigmatized area."

Ufologists expanded Hynek's scale in the years following the film to include a fourth and fifth kind of close encounter. The former refers to UFO abductions, and the latter involves direct communication between extraterrestrials and humans. Both have offered fodder for many more sci-fi movies, including Spielberg's 1982 classic *E.T. the Extra-Terrestrial*, and the 2009 hypnotherapy thriller *The Fourth Kind*.

"There is compelling evidence to suggest some kind of unexplained presence on Earth. Although it's obviously an important and fascinating question as to where (when?) this presence comes from, not knowing the origin doesn't impact the strength of the evidence. My father felt that as important as it is to have an open mind as to the existence of a potential new phenomenon, it's just as important not to rush and grab the best available answer to just to tie a bow around it. The universe and its mysteries doesn't come gift-wrapped."

—PAUL HYNEK, son of J. Allen and Miriam Hynek and an entrepreneur, professor, and futurist, in a 2022 email to the author

Little Green Men Visit Kentucky:
The Kelly-Hopkinsville Incident

Regardless of the Robertson Panel's conclusions and directives, UFO reports were not going away. While the White House lawn remained untouched by extraterrestrials, by 1955 it appeared visitors had chosen a less provocative landing site: a farm in Kelly, Kentucky, just north of Hopkinsville.

At around 7:00 p.m. on August 21, 1955, Billy Ray Taylor was outside his friend Elmer Sutton's farmhouse when he witnessed a flash in the clear night sky, followed by what appeared to be a saucer swooping down toward the ground and landing in a nearby field. He ran inside to tell Elmer and the rest of the Sutton family. They didn't take him seriously until they looked outside and saw a luminescent creature approaching. It resembled a small man no taller than three feet and had a large round head, arms that nearly reached the ground, yellowish eyes, and webbed hands with claws. The matriarch of the family, Glennie Lankford, likened it to a monkey that appeared to be "made out of aluminum foil."

Suddenly, Billy Ray didn't seem so crazy anymore. He, Elmer, and Elmer's brother, J. C., grabbed shotguns and a rifle and started shooting at the alleged alien, to no avail. Elmer swore the bullets bounced off the creature "like from a concrete pavement." He claimed to have shot it twice and knocked it to the ground, only to watch it jump up and run off. But it soon returned, this time with reinforcements that began crawling up the trees and across the farmhouse roof.

Finding themselves seemingly under attack from extraterrestrials, Billy Ray and the Suttons fled to the Hopkinsville police station for help. With the authorities at their side, they returned home to either reengage in battle, or perhaps to have the aliens arrested. Unfortunately, the police found no spacemen. To the Suttons' credit, the cops also found that none of the witnesses had been drinking that night.

Sheriff's deputy George Batts told reporters, "I think it was imagination that built up from talk that got started among the people. They just got themselves worked up over nothing."

Police chief Russell Greenwell was more open-minded. Although police found no evidence of prowlers and no tracks from creatures of any kind, Greenwell acknowledged that the ground was "so hard and dry that a tractor wouldn't have left much trace on it." So the lack of footprints didn't surprise him. "Something scared those people," he told the press, stressing the level of fear that drove the Suttons into Hopkinsville. "These aren't the kind of people who normally run to the police for help. When they feel themselves threatened, what they do is reach for their guns."

Elmer stood by his word, telling reporters, "I hold up my hands to God and swear on my mother this is true." As for the lack of physical evidence, he explained that "you can't see them except in the dark, and the police used lights all over the place."

Project Blue Book did not officially investigate the case, but Major John E. Albert from Fort Campbell, about twenty miles south of Hopkinsville, drove to the scene in Kelly and found no evidence to support the story. In a statement given two years later, he suggested an escaped circus monkey may have given "the appearance of a small man." A circus train was known to be in the area just a day earlier, opening up the possibility that Albert was right, and that the monkey-like creatures were in fact monkeys that had escaped during the night.

This was Hynek's initial suspicion too, though he had not personally investigated the case and his search for nearby circuses came up empty. His Center for UFO Studies (CUFOS)—which he founded in 1973 as a way to continue his work after the closure of Project Blue Book—issued a report in 1978 that further rejected the monkey hypothesis largely because the theory asks people to believe that seven adults "persisted, for three hours, in mistaking hairy, long-tailed, noisy, vulnerable creatures for silvery, silent creatures with no tails, that were not injured by bullets fired at them at point-blank range."

As Hynek later put it, "Under a barrage of gunfire from Kentuckians, over a somewhat extended period, it is unthinkable that at least one cadaver would not have been found."

The CUFOS report also rejected the notion of hallucinations and concluded that the Suttons were telling the truth. Hynek categorized it as a Close Encounter of the Third Kind, which, in his estimation, "are *by no means infrequent.*"

This image of the creature from Kelly, Kentucky, appeared in the 1978 CUFOS report *Close Encounter at Kelly and Others of 1955*.

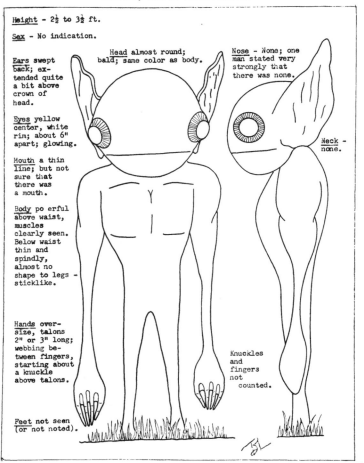

Figure 10. "Little Man" as described by Elmer Sutton, J.C. Sutton and O.P. Baker drawn by Andrew (Bud) Ledwith

Height - 2½ to 3½ ft.

Sex - No indication.

Head almost round; bald; same color as body.

Nose - None; one man stated very strongly that there was none.

Ears swept back; extended quite a bit above crown of head.

Eyes yellow center, white rim; about 6" apart; glowing.

Mouth a thin line; but not sure that there was a mouth.

Body po erful above waist, muscles clearly seen. Below waist thin and spindly, almost no shape to legs - sticklike.

Neck - none.

Hands over-size, talons 2" or 3" long; webbing between fingers, starting about a knuckle above talons.

Knuckles and fingers not counted.

Feet not seen (or not noted).

Story Of Space-Ship, 12 Little Men Probed Today

Kelly Farmhouse Scene Of Alleged Raid By Strange Crew Last Night; Reports Say Bullets Failed To Affect Visitors

Aliens landing on farmland made front-page news in the August 22, 1955, edition of the *Kentucky New Era*.

Though without definitive evidence one way or the other, the Associated Press may have put it best days after the initial event by stating, "the space ship story is still up in the air." The widespread media attention splashed the phrase "little green men" across nationwide headlines. Though the phrase had been used before, notably in Fredric Brown's 1955 book *Martians, Go Home* and earlier in a 1952 article about Venusian visitors, its frequent use in coverage of the Hopkinsville case helped cement the cliché in pop culture.[+]

<hr />

[+] Technically, Brown's little green men appeared even earlier, since his book was first published in *Astounding Science Fiction* magazine in September 1954.

DR. HYNEK LAUNCHES THE CENTER FOR UFO STUDIES

After the closing of Project Blue Book in 1969, there were still other private organizations investigating UFO reports, namely MUFON (which at the time stood for the Midwest UFO Network), the National Investigations Committee on Aerial Phenomena (NICAP), and the Aerial Phenomena Research Organization (APRO). Dr. J. Allen Hynek wanted to continue his search for answers but didn't want to duplicate the efforts of the other groups. Instead, he started the Center for UFO Studies (CUFOS) in 1973 as a scientific think tank that would build on his background as a professional astronomer, his Blue Book experience, and the contacts he'd made over the decades.

Early on, a small team of investigators explored select cases with potential scientific value. One of the first examples was a 1973 incident over Mansfield, Ohio, in which helicopter pilot Captain Lawrence Coyne witnessed a "big, gray, metallic-looking" object darting straight at him. With little time to respond, Coyne braced for impact, but no crash occurred. The strange object stopped right over the pilot and his three-man crew and seemingly took control of the helicopter, elevating it more than a thousand feet before releasing it and disappearing to the west. CUFOS investigator Jennie Zeidman's thorough examination of the case demonstrated that the anomalous object was visible to crew for at least five minutes, clearly proving it wasn't a meteor.

After Hynek's passing in 1986, his protégé Dr. Mark Rodeghier succeeded him as scientific director and to this day continues to run CUFOS. I spoke with him about what he learned from Hynek, and how it's helped the team gather information.

"[Hynek] was sometimes more like a social scientist because he liked to talk to people, and you don't find that in most hard scientists," Rodeghier said. "And that's one of the reasons that he survived and thrived all those years with Blue Book." Hynek collected data from witness reports, not from the purported objects themselves. That meant meeting with them and building a rapport to extract information as best as possible. "You had to get to know them and treat them with respect, and let them know that you were going to handle their information confidentially if that's what they wanted," Rodeghier added. "And you had to learn how to elicit information and also, once in a while, see if somebody was hoaxing or, more likely, you tried to figure out when they were going beyond their memory."

A Cartoonist Draws a UFO in Shreveport, Louisiana

On October 22, 1960, Henry Schlensker and his wife were driving north on Route 71 toward Shreveport, Louisiana, at around 5:30 p.m. when a yellowish object shaped like a teardrop caught their attention as it interrupted a perfectly blue sky. Initially, Schlensker suspected it was a weather balloon, but the twisting of its tail seemed unnatural, as did a sudden change to a "vapor trail" with a white dot at its head. This, he determined, "destroyed the balloon theory." The teardrop shape began shifting into a crescent, with the convex and concave sides switching back and forth as the sun set. Soon the thing was right overhead, as if it might be watching them.

The experience lasted just over ten minutes before the UFO diminished in size and dissolved into the darkening sky. Like so many reports, Schlensker didn't have photos to substantiate his claim. He did, however, have a cartoon. Schlensker was known for his daily comic strip, *Buz Sawyer*, and submitted a full-page watercolor cartoon detailing the event to Project Blue Book investigators.

Perhaps realizing that a UFO claim in cartoon form might exacerbate the doubt that clouded most cases from the outset, Schlensker included a letter emphasizing the fact that he was a member of the Air Force Ground Observer Corps for several years during World War II and had considerable experience in looking up.

Though his cartoon surely offered a welcome break from the usual submissions, he didn't receive a response. Nearly two years later, he wrote again to stress the importance of investigating not just his case but the UFO phenomenon at large.

"The power of what I observed dwarfs anything—even the missile at the cape, and I've seen a few take off at closer range than most," he wrote. "Whatever performed for my wife and me had power to do most anything."

Schlensker hoped that a "sincere and sane effort" to better observe, evaluate, and understand what was happening in our skies might avoid problems later and actually lead to some good. "The more people who know, the less chance for someone to pull a trigger," he added.

"Why shoot them down when maybe they want to come down?...We will eventually spend millions to compete with the UFO when we have a potential of unlimited free information with a properly instructed public."

When Project Blue Book investigators finally looked into the case, they didn't agree with Schlensker's perspective—at least not with respect to this particular case. They determined that what Schlensker and his wife had seen was "probably a condensation trail" left by an aircraft illuminated by the setting sun. Changes in the wind caused the contrail's shape to change. And Venus, ever the culprit, "probably became evident as the sun went further down and the witness associated it with the trail." The planet's visibility then disappeared due to the setting sun.

A Flying Egg Lands in Socorro, New Mexico

Of the many cases Project Blue Book categorized as "unidentified," a 1964 sighting by a police officer in Socorro, New Mexico, may be the most puzzling. Investigators were no longer dealing with rural Kentuckians or a traveling cartoonist. Lonnie Zamora was a cop with a solid reputation.

On the afternoon of April 24, Officer Zamora was chasing a speeding car on the outskirts of town when the sound of an explosion and a flame in the sky distracted him. Forget the reckless driver—it was clear that his services were needed elsewhere. About a half mile up the hilly road he found the source of the commotion. There, roughly 150 feet in front of him in a gully, Zamora saw an egg-shaped object with four girder-like legs and, according to his statement given just hours afterward, "two people in white coveralls" standing near the vehicle. He also noticed an unidentifiable red insignia on its surface. Initially thinking it was an overturned car, Zamora radioed the sheriff's office and got out of his car to help. Then he heard another roar and saw smoke shooting out from beneath the object as it "slowly rose straight up."

Scared out of his wits and fearing an explosion, he ran off and ducked behind his car. Local lawmen soon arrived on the scene and

PROJECT 10073 RECORD CARD

1. DATE	2. LOCATION	12. CONCLUSIONS
24 April 1964	Socorro, New Mexico	☐ Was Balloon ☐ Probably Balloon ☐ Possibly Balloon

3. DATE-TIME GROUP	4. TYPE OF OBSERVATION	☐ Was Aircraft ☐ Probably Aircraft ☐ Possibly Aircraft
Local 1745 GMT 25/0045Z	☒ Ground-Visual ☐ Ground-Radar ☐ Air-Visual ☐ Air-Intercept Radar	

5. PHOTOS	6. SOURCE	☐ Was Astronomical ☐ Probably Astronomical ☐ Possibly Astronomical
☐ Yes Physical Spec ☒ No	Civilian	☐ Other UNIDENTIFIED ☐ Insufficient Data for Evaluation ☒ Unknown

7. LENGTH OF OBSERVATION	8. NUMBER OF OBJECTS	9. COURSE
Less than 10 minutes	one	Stationary,SW or West

10. BRIEF SUMMARY OF SIGHTING	11. COMMENTS
Sighting of landing by Lonnie Zamora. SEE CASE FILE.	Initially believed to be observation of Lunar module type configuration. Effort to date cannot place vehicle at site. Case carried as UNIDENTIFIED pending additional data.

ATIC FORM 329 (REV 26 SEP 52)

Project Blue Book's investigation categorized the Soccoro case as "unidentified."

UNCLASSIFIED

A diorama built by Project Blue Book investigators to re-create the scene Lonnie Zamora witnessed in Socorro.

found their fellow officer sweating and pale.

"Lonnie, you look like you've seen the devil," one patrolman said.

"Well, maybe I have," Zamora responded.

Gathering his senses, he led the other officers on a short hike to the area where he'd seen the flying egg, and together they discovered four small smoldering clumps of grass and four depressions in the ground. Whatever had been there had left its mark.

Based on the word of an honest cop and the physical traces left behind, the case caught the attention of not only Blue Book and other UFO investigative groups, but also the FBI. Its director considered Zamora a high-caliber witness, describing him in a memo as "sober, dependable, mature and not known to engage in flights of fantasy."

Hynek met with the officer several times during visits to Socorro and agreed with the FBI's assessment. Zamora simply gave no reason for investigators to mistrust him. Yet further research revealed little else to corroborate his statement: radar observers at nearby installations hadn't seen any curious blips; the weather was not extraordinary; Geiger counters detected no radiation; and a soil sample analysis offered no outer space results.

That said, investigators explored the possibility that the vehicle was indeed an actual spacecraft—one built right here on earth and tested at nearby Holloman Air Force Base. On the day Zamora saw the UFO, Holloman was conducting special tests at the north end of the White Sands Missile Range, south of Socorro. The testing involved a helicopter carrying the Surveyor lunar landing craft, designed in preparation for the Apollo program's moon missions. Its manufacturer, Hughes Aircraft, might have had a logo on the side, and white coveralls would be a perfect fit for its technicians. However, a landing so far outside White Sands and so close to a populated area seems unlikely. The egg shape Zamora claimed to have seen would also seem to be a poor description of a helicopter carrying a lunar lander. Both White Sands Missile Range and Holloman agreed, and they assured investigators they had no object that would compare to the one Zamora described.

So was it a hoax? The idea was floated at the time, but Hynek ruled it out, believing a man of Zamora's character participating in such a ruse seemed "extremely unlikely."

But what if he was instead the victim of a hoax? That's what the era's chief skeptic, Donald Menzel—an astrophysicist and director of the Harvard Observatory—and his collaborator, Lyle Boyd, suggested to Hynek in a February 19, 1965, letter. Zamora gave out a lot of speeding tickets, which led Menzel and Boyd to think that perhaps a few angry recipients, namely teenagers, coordinated the UFO event and led the officer right to it just to mess with his head.

"Any bright youngsters, possibly juniors or seniors in high school, could dream up this plan," Menzel wrote. "Perhaps the hoaxsters have two or three simple hydrogen-filled balloons. They put up the flare-producing device, whatever it was, with a small balloon and wait for a signal from their confederate in the speeding car."

The scientist offered various ways in which clever teens could have concocted the whole thing. "You may well object that our hypothesis is far-fetched," he added. "However, much more elaborate hoaxes have been perpetrated in the past, in many fields."

Hynek never bought into any iteration of the hoax theory. "A hoax generally leaks, and a successful hoax is just too good a thing to be kept quiet for many years," he wrote to another skeptic, Phillip Klass, in 1967. "Somebody, sooner or later, talks."

Just a year later, someone did—though it wasn't discovered for decades. In 2009, UFO researcher Anthony Bragalia unearthed a curious 1968 letter written by chemical engineer Dr. Linus Pauling to the then president of Socorro's New Mexico Institute of Mining and Technology, Stirling Colgate. It included a question about the Socorro case: "What's the NMIMT feeling about this incident?" Pauling had an interest in UFOs, and his letter had been archived along with other personal documents and publications at the Special Collections of Oregon State University. Stirling offered a handwritten response: "I have good indication of student who engineered hoax. Student has left. Cheers, Stirling." Bragalia reached out to Colgate asking if he still believed this had been a prank. According to Bragalia, the answer was *yes*. Colgate added that he'd never commented publicly about it.

The school's geology lab had all the necessary pyrotechnics and equipment, along with the white lab suits, to concoct an extravagant and mischievous deception. The college kids who perpetrated the hoax—assuming they did—would have had good incentive to keep quiet. "When you're a college student, and your little afternoon prank on the local constabulary turns out to mobilize not only the Feds but half the branches of the armed services, some of whom work with your professors, and you'd rather graduate than spend the rest of your life at Fort Leavenworth, you tend to zip your lip," wrote Brian Dunning, executive director of Skeptoid Media, on Skeptoid.com in 2017.

To date, Dunning believes the student hoax theory is "the only complete explanation anyone has proposed that neatly checks all the boxes, fits all the descriptions, and requires no alien intervention."

Of course, there are those who still believe alien intervention is an equally possible conclusion. Extraterrestrials would allegedly intervene again later that year—in ways of far greater consequence than scaring a police officer.

When Nuclear Powers Became Powerless

By the mid-1960s, if any of the thousands of UFO sightings in the U.S. were in fact extraterrestrial, the visitors appeared to be friendly. Not one had overtaken or destroyed our planet or attacked Lonnie Zamora. Several witnesses from the air force believed that, if anything, their intentions might be benevolent, based on a simple message that their purported actions made unmistakable: *quit playing with nuclear weapons.* By allegedly striking down or disabling U.S. nukes in multiple facilities, alien technology had seemingly been warning us that the Atomic Age might be humanity's last.

Numerous books have been written on this subject, but in October 2021 I visited the National Press Club in Washington, DC, to listen to four retired air force officers give personal accounts of UFO involvement at nuclear weapons facilities. A few dozen reporters and ufologists joined me in the small thirteenth-floor conference room as each gave their presentation.

According to retired air force first lieutenant Robert Jacobs, the extraterrestrial effort to prevent a global disaster became perfectly clear during the launch of a dummy nuclear warhead aboard an Atlas D missile on September 14, 1964, at California's Vandenberg Air Force Base (now a Space Force base). Jacobs was in charge of providing photographic documentation of the test using a 2,400-inch telescope camera system. The goal of this particular mission was to release radar chaff from the missile's nose cone to distract Russian antimissile firings from a nuclear warhead that would be released simultaneously. "Our little warhead would fly over and obliterate Moscow," Jacobs said. "That was the game we were playing. Horrifying to think about it in retrospect."

Two days after the seemingly normal launch, Jacobs's commanding officer, Major Florenze J. Mansmann, called Jacobs into his office to play back his film of the test. Two unfamiliar men in gray suits stood by as the major and Jacobs watched the film, which showed the missile flying at 8,000 miles per hour and releasing its chaff and warhead.

"Suddenly, we saw an object come in from the same way we were going," Jacobs recalled of the video. He described this strange craft as being "shaped like a saucer, with a Ping-Pong ball on top." It then fired beams of light from four separate angles before zipping off-screen from the same direction it entered, while the warhead tumbled out to space.

Major Mansmann shut off the film and asked if Jacobs and his team were responsible for creating the unusual sighting. Jacobs denied any hijinks, and simply said, "It looks to me like we got a UFO." According to Jacobs, the major didn't appreciate the quip, replying: "You are never to say that again. As far as you're concerned, this didn't happen."

Mansmann escorted Jacobs out of the office, then leaned in close—ensuring he was out of earshot of the mysterious men in almost black—and quietly said, "Lieutenant, if you are ever tortured in the future, if somebody has you up against the wall and they're frying your privates with fire, you tell them this, just to get out of it, just tell them it was laser tracking."

As Jacobs noted, laser tracking didn't exist in 1964. "We are not alone," he said confidently. "That thing was up there. I saw it. It was on film." Jacobs believes the other men were from the CIA and took the film, snipped out the portion that showed the encounter, and then returned what remained to Major Mansmann.

Jacobs kept quiet as instructed for seventeen years before finally sharing the story on a local late-night talk radio show in California. He's since received threatening phone calls, had his mailbox blown up, and lost a teaching job at the University of Maine for "telling tall tales."

"We've been shut up and silenced, we've been ridiculed, we've had our lives disrupted, we've been treated like imbeciles," he said, imploring all of us listening to share his story. "This is a real thing that's happening to us. That UFO knocked one of our dummy nuclear warheads out of space. It shot it down. To me that looks like a superior force saying, hey, knock it off. . . . This is about the possibility of our survival."

> "If these creatures, from wherever they are, whatever time they are, whatever place they are, get mad at us enough, they can annihilate our entire species just like that. They have technology and power we can't even imagine. Their science to us is like magic."
>
> —ROBERT JACOBS, speaking at the National Press Club in Washington, DC, on October 19, 2021

David Schindele, a former air force launch control officer, followed Jacobs at the conference. In September 1966, just two years after the Vandenberg incident, Schindele believes a UFO interfered with ten nuclear-tipped Minuteman intercontinental ballistic missiles (ICBMs) at Minot Air Force Base in North Dakota. The night before he and his commanding officer were scheduled to relieve a two-man crew at the underground control room, an eighty- to one hundred-foot-wide disk-shaped object with "bright flashing lights" silently hovered about a hundred feet outside the facility. Witnesses watched it glide closer until it positioned itself almost directly above the launch control capsule located sixty feet below ground.

When Schindele arrived at the base, he heard about the unusual event. When he descended to the control room, he was shocked to see that all ten missiles at the site—positioned miles apart in underground silos—were "off alert" and unable to launch. Each showed a status indicating a "guidance and control system malfunction."

"At other times during crew changeover at launch centers, we might note one or two missiles down for scheduled maintenance, but never had we seen a situation like this," Schindele said.

The morning after his shift he asked the head security guard about what he'd seen, but was told everyone had been instructed not to talk about it. "We were to forever keep our lips zipped," Schindele stressed. "We were never questioned, interrogated, or debriefed about the incident."

His lips remained sealed for nearly forty years, till 2001, when he found a story online describing a similar incident experienced by air force captain Robert Salas.

"When I saw that, I said, 'Oh my god, it's been verified,'" Schindele said. "I experienced just a joyful freedom and I was finally able to tell my wife my secret."

Salas was next up at the Press Club and offered vivid details regarding an incident at Malmstrom Air Force Base in Montana on March 24, 1967, about six months after the Minot episode. Serving as a first lieutenant at the time, Salas was on duty as a deputy missile combat crew commander in the nuclear missile control room deep underground. The site's flight security controller called him from above ground to report an object in the sky making strange, seemingly impossible maneuvers. Unable to explain what the controller had seen, Salas shrugged it off. But shortly after, the controller called Salas again. This time he was in a full panic.

"He was shouting into the phone, screaming and saying that there was this lighted object about forty feet in diameter, looked like an oval shape but he couldn't be sure because of a red-orange light pulsating,"

Salas recalled. "Guards were out there with their weapons drawn. He wanted me to tell him what to do next. At that point I thought we were under some kind of an attack."

Alarms and indicators at the underground concrete-lined commander's console then showed that the site's ten missiles had been disabled, and they remained inoperable for the duration of his shift. According to Salas, the missiles ran on independent systems, making a complete shutdown essentially impossible. Like Schindele, Salas was given no explanation and ordered to keep quiet. The only information he got came from his commanding officer, who told Salas that the same thing had happened eight days earlier. It allegedly took nearly a day to get the ICBMs online once again.

"UFOs disabled twenty nuclear missiles within the span of eight days, there's no question about this," Salas said. "In my opinion, UFOs are simply reminding us that we should seriously try to eliminate these weapons."

The retired air force captain has been vocal about what happened at Malmstrom for decades, and Congress appears to finally be listening. During the May 17, 2022, congressional hearing on unidentified aerial phenomena, Wisconsin representative Mike Gallagher asked Scott Bray, the deputy director of naval intelligence, and Ronald Moultrie, the undersecretary of intelligence, if the UAP Task Force was familiar with the Malmstrom incident and if it could comment on the accuracy of the case. Bray answered that he had "heard stories" but had "not seen the official data" on it, nor had the task force attempted to look into it.

"Well, I would say it's a pretty high-profile incident," Gallagher responded. "I don't claim to be an expert on this. But that's out there in the ether. You're the guys investigating it. I mean, who else is doing it?"

"If something was officially brought to our attention, we would look at it," Moultrie said.

"I'm bringing it to your attention," Gallagher responded. "It's pretty official."

For Salas, the hearing was a long-awaited success. Nearly sixty years later, the government is expected to finally take a serious look into his report and others regarding the presence of unidentified objects over nuclear sites. "Those incidents are now part of the official record of the hearing and there has been an official request for DoD analysis of them," Salas told me in an email days after the open session. "They will only be able to conclude they happened because of our testimonies and documentation."

The Condon Report Closes Project Blue Book

Whether at missile bases or elsewhere, UFO sightings continued through the sixties and beyond, but with the closing of Project Blue Book in 1969, the government stopped investigating reports. Rather than listen to witnesses, it listened to a 1,485-page document commissioned by the air force and headed by a former physics professor at the University of Colorado named Edward Condon.

This mountain of paper, known as the Condon Report, cost half a million dollars and took two years and the help of thirty-seven scientists to produce.[†] It includes fifty-nine case studies, most of which it claimed fell into the categories of hoaxes, pranks, naïve interpretations, and misinterpretations. One photograph of a flying saucer was explained as being nothing more than a Leica camera lens cap suspended from a thread just outside a truck window. Another case included a man whose wife's grandfather had immigrated to America from the Andromeda galaxy more than two million light-years away (it turned out he didn't). Hoaxers and kooks aside, Condon noted that "in our experience, the persons making UFO reports seem in nearly all cases to be normal, responsible individuals." Of those reports, like Project Blue Book's studies over the decade, several were left unexplained.

Case Study 21, for example, involved a UFO that reportedly followed an aircraft and veered away just as the plane landed. "This must remain as one of the most puzzling radar cases on record, and no conclusion is possible at this time," the report stated.

---

† Technically the Condon Report's full title is: *Scientific Study of Unidentified Flying Objects: The Complete Report on the Study Conducted by the University of Colorado Under Research Contract Number F44620-67-000035 with the U.S. Air Force*. It's a bit of a mouthful and, as some ufologists might argue, more thorough than the study itself.

HYNEK'S CLOSE ENCOUNTER WITH SWAMP GAS

Over the course of his career as the air force's chief scientific advisor, Dr. J. Allen Hynek cited many natural explanations for UFO sightings. Swamp gas, however, was one theory people found as unbelievable as flying saucers.

The sightings in question occurred in areas of Michigan beginning on March 14, 1966. More than a hundred witnesses reported glowing objects drifting and zigzagging across the sky and hovering above swampy hollows near Ann Arbor and Hillsdale over the course of several nights.

"We come over that knoll just this side of the swamp and there it was, about eye-level with us, no more than five hundred yards away," Washtenaw county deputy David Fitzpatrick told the *Detroit Free Press*. "It had a blue light in front, and in the back a light that kept changing from red to white, like it was rotating, like the light on a police car."

Despite many similar reports, the Detroit Air Defense Sector said it had "no unusual sightings" on its fourteen radar installations. Regardless, Hynek spent three days interviewing witnesses in the nervous community and exploring the locations of the sightings. Having gathered as much information as possible, he addressed a press conference attended by more than sixty reporters eagerly awaiting his evaluation.

"A dismal swamp is a most unlikely place for a visit from outer space," Hynek announced. "It is not a place where a helicopter would hover for several hours or where a soundless secret device would likely be tested."

Hynek explained that springtime thawing released trapped gases resulting from "rotty vegetation." In other words, the illusion of saucers was created by swamp gas. "I emphasize . . . that I cannot prove in a court of law, that this is the full explanation of these sightings," he acknowledged. "It appears very likely, however, that the combination of the conditions of this particular winter—an unusually mild one in this area—and the particular weather conditions . . . were such as to have produced this unusual and puzzling display."

Needless to say, witnesses did not take kindly to Hynek's assessment. Officer Robert Hunawill, who saw four objects over a farm, gave a statement to the press that spoke for the community: "It's not marsh gas. My reaction to Dr. Hynek is the same as the rest of the people around here. He made us look like fools."

Even Kenneth Arnold, the father of the flying saucer, chimed in from Boise: "To come up with such an unscientific explanation as swamp gas is completely idiotic."

Hynek later admitted his gaffe, but insisted his comment wasn't intended to explain all the sightings in the area, just the ones over the swamp. But "swamp gas" had quickly become a household term and, as Hynek put it, "a standard humorous synonym" for the government's squelching of flying saucers. "Had a UFO been reported at that time from the Sahara Desert, I think it would have been attributed to swamp gas," he wrote in his 1972 book, *The UFO Experience*.

The "swamp gas" comment, however, didn't just affect Hynek's reputation. It led to Michigan representative and future president Gerald Ford's call for a congressional inquiry into the matter. Irritated at the lack of effort by the air force to better explain the sightings, Ford told the press on March 26, 1966: "At week's end, the Air Force explained away the UFO's as a product of college-student pranks, swamp gas, the rising crescent moon, and the planet Venus. But the Air Force has been explaining away UFO's for years, and I don't believe the American people generally are satisfied with its statements. For that reason, I have proposed that there be a congressional investigation of UFO's."

That investigation became the Condon Report, which led to 1969's Congressional hearing on UFOs and the closing of Project Blue Book.

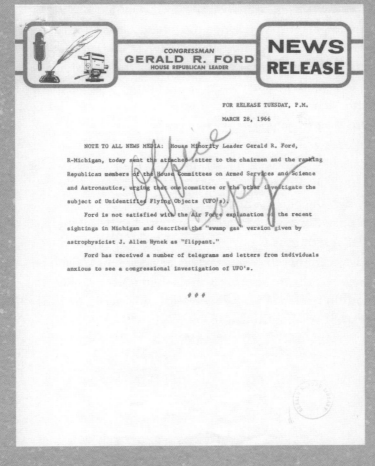

This March 28, 1966, news release was one of several from Michigan representative and future president Gerald Ford about his push for a congressional inquiry into UFOs following Dr J. Allen Hynek's "swamp gas" explanation for local UFOs.

Then there's Case 2, detailing a 1956 sighting at Lakenheath air base in England that also defied explanation. Radar detected unidentified objects flying at speeds as great as 2,000 or 4,000 miles per hour without creating a sonic boom. These speedy entities made right-angle turns while still moving at a hundred miles per hour. When fighter planes were sent in pursuit, they had no luck making contact. One pilot had an object in radar gunlock, but the UFO circled to the jet's tail and followed it despite the fighter's evasive maneuvers. The report didn't rule out conventional or natural explanations such as "abnormal radar propagation," but acknowledged it was highly unlikely and that "the probability that at least one genuine UFO was involved appears to be fairly high."

On the heels of the report—and that significant phrase, "genuine UFO"—physicist and UFO researcher James E. McDonald highlighted this case in his 1969 lecture, "Science in Default," saying it represented the type of UFO sighting that should have been investigated thoroughly when the events occurred, considering the fact that the observations all came from military sources. To him, the failure to do so emphasized the "dearth of scientific competence in the Air Force UFO investigations over the past twenty-two years."

Laying out the case as meticulously as possible, McDonald asked, "Doesn't a UFO case like Lakenheath warrant more than a mere shrug of the shoulders from scientists?"

But shrug they did. Despite the many unexplained cases within the incredibly long report, Condon ultimately concluded that "further extensive study of UFO sightings is not justified in the expectation that science will be advanced thereby"—at least, as he added, not based on the available evidence. Still, if there are things flying around that are unidentified, shouldn't science seek to understand them—whether they're extraterrestrial or something else entirely?

Fortunately, there are modern scientists looking for answers, as we'll see in Chapter 4. Yet for decades most members of the scientific community steered clear of the UFO enigma. They didn't want to be associated with flying saucers, or the people who claimed to have not only seen them but met their occupants and been aboard them—either willingly or by an otherworldly force.

CHAPTER 2

CLOSE ENCOUNTERS

Alien Contactees and Abductees

> "Perhaps some of what they're doing is to make adjustments or to figure out how to make us more adaptable as we continue to toxify the planet. But maybe we're somebody's graduate experiment gone horribly wrong and they want a better grade and they've come back to make do."
>
> —PETER ROBBINS, investigative writer who specializes in UFOs, speculating on why aliens might be visiting and abducting select humans, in a November 2021 interview with the author

When Klaatu arrived on earth after traveling 250 million miles from Mars, he planned to deliver a warning to the planet about its developments in atomic energy. Tall, thin, and perfectly human in appearance, he was shot at immediately upon exiting his spaceship. But by the end of the 1951 film *The Day the Earth Stood Still*, Klaatu recovered and finally made his announcement on behalf of Mars and the rest of the solar system:

> So long as you were limited to fighting among yourselves with your primitive tanks and aircraft we were unconcerned. But soon one of your nations will apply atomic energy to spaceships. That will create a threat to the peace and security of other planets. That of course we cannot tolerate. . . . Live in peace or pursue your present course and face obliteration. We shall be waiting for your answer.

Klaatu (played by Michael Rennie) warns earthlings of the dangers of atomic energy in 1951's *The Day the Earth Stood Still*.

The movie reflected the Cold War fears in post–World War II America, but also aligned with—and in some cases quite possibly inspired—the consistent messaging of a vocal group of so-called contactees throughout the fifties. According to their tales, they'd made contact with numerous aliens from various planets in our solar system (frequently Venus) who were on a mission to save us from ourselves. As Klaatu warned, the Atomic Age threatened to destroy us all and disrupt our planetary neighbors. And while no one could deny that the potential destruction of earth was bad, the contactees' outlandish stories of extraterrestrial encounters ultimately succeeded only in building a sturdy stigma that continues to hover over any mention of the terms *UFO* or *flying saucer*. Admitting to seeing one—much less being contacted or abducted by one—might result in being labeled a crackpot or nutcase. It's why many people kept quiet over the decades, including pilots who feared sharing their sightings with officials and the public. If they had spoken up, they might have been considered as odd as Daniel W. Fry, who was the first man to claim that he not only saw a flying saucer but flew in one as well. Throughout this chapter we will explore the outrageous adventures and earnest messages of the contactees and question whether there is more validity to abductee stories than meets the eye.

Daniel W. Fry: The World's First Flying Saucer Passenger

While most Americans were celebrating Independence Day in 1950, Daniel W. Fry climbed aboard a flying saucer in the White Sands Proving Ground in New Mexico and flew to New York City and back in a half hour, traversing the skies at an astounding 8,000 miles per hour. At least, this is what he told the world four years later.

Fry was a technician working for a California-based rocket and propulsion manufacturer called Aerojet. His job often involved work at the New Mexico missile-testing site. According to his 1954 book, *The White Sands Incident*, it had been a hot night and a broken air-condition-ing unit had left his room unbearably stuffy, so he went for a walk in the desert.

On the outskirts of the base he noticed a flying spheroid object decelerating toward him and preparing to land. Curious, Fry approached the silvery craft, which he described as having a highly polished metal surface and an estimated thirty-foot diameter. Initially he thought it might be advanced Soviet technology, but he quickly determined the intelligence behind it was beyond Soviet capabilities or those of any other foreign power on earth. As Fry took a lap around the strange craft, he noticed it had no seams and no apparent opening. So he did what anyone not terrified of a mysterious unexplained spaceship would do: he touched it.

"Better not touch the hull, pal, it's still hot!" a voice bellowed.

Startled, Fry jumped and fell backward in the sand. A friendly voice chuckled and said, "Take it easy, pal, you're among friends."

When the technician gathered his composure, he suggested that perhaps the voice could've warned him in a gentler manner. "Sorry, but you were about to kill yourself and there wasn't time to diddle with controls," the disembodied voice responded. As the voice would later reveal, the ship was remotely controlled, and communications were being transmitted telepathically from nine hundred miles above the earth's surface where the being sat on the "mother ship."

The voice also explained that the term *hot* best described the condition of the extraterrestrial field surrounding the hull: "Your physicists would describe the force involved as the 'anti' aspect of the binding energy of the atom. When certain elements such as platinum are properly prepared and treated with a saturation exposure to a beam of very high energy photons, the binding energy particle will be generated outside the nucleus."

Fry soon learned that these brilliant space travelers had "eliminated the reasons for conflict and misunderstanding among our own people" thousands of years ago. They were here to warn us that conflicts on earth could lead to its destruction. "If any one of the nations that dominate one or more others on your planet were to achieve conclusive scientific superiority over the other, then under present conditions, a war of extermination would likely follow."

After that dire warning, Fry accepted an invitation to take a joyride and settled into one of four empty seats in the bare metal ship. The simple cabin stretched about nine feet deep and seven feet wide, offering Fry luxurious legroom for the flight (clearly this thing was designed by advanced beings). The craft ascended, accelerated at a rate of ten g's, and off to New York City Fry went.

As he grew chummier with the alien, Fry was told its name was Alan (spelled in his language as A-Lan). Though he was not of the earth, he explained that his ancestors were, dating back thirty thousand years. These early earthlings were the last survivors of a war that destroyed civilization. Their bombs were "a thousand times greater than that of the Hydrogen bomb which threatens your race today." Political differences between two powerful empires—one of which was the continent of Atlantis—led to the annihilation.

With all the radiation spewing across the planet, the sole survivors had no choice but to escape in their "aerial crafts" to Mars. Back then, Alan explained, the Red Planet was a perfectly fine place to live. These ancient space-faring scientists eventually became independent of planets and roamed the solar system in their spaceships and scavenged worlds for raw materials. In the case of Alan, his special visit had been granted to offer his cautionary tale in hopes of preventing a second destruction of civilization.

It was a message Fry took seriously. Over the following decades, he produced a monthly magazine called *Understanding*, with the goal of "bringing about a greater degree of understanding among the peoples of earth and making available to them more of the higher understanding of those who are not of earth."

The lecture circuit gave him another platform that sometimes offered up to 250 speaking engagements a year. People flocked to hear his outlandish stories. But if he was going to make a real dent and set things right for the course of humanity, he'd need more than books, magazines, and lectures. He needed power. So in 1972, he ran for vice president of the United States on the Universal Party ticket with Gabriel Green, a fellow believer in flying saucers. Green, who had first made a bid for the presidency in 1960, did not win. For more on this blip of American political history, transport yourself to the sidebar on page 86.

AMERICA NEEDS A SPACE AGE PRESIDENT

IF YOU WANT...

★ Progress instead of prattle.
★ Principles instead of personalities.
★ Answers to problems instead of only talk about them.
★ Results instead of promises.
★ Ideas instead of double talk and ballyhoo.
★ Solutions instead of stalemates.
★ Survival instead of annihilation.
★ Peace instead of pieces.
★ Morality instead of moral degeneration.
★ Issues instead of smears, sneers, and jeers.
★ Abundance for everyone instead of poverty and waste.
★ A better tomorrow instead of no tomorrow.
★ Inspired leadership instead of rule by political opportunists.
★ Leadership by enlightened direction rather than by popularity polls and pressure groups.

★ A workable Plan for Peace rather than directionless confusion.
★ Hope and national purpose instead of apathy and hopelessness.
★ Government by moral and universal law rather than by military expediency and special interests.
★ Competition for the minds of men with new ideas instead of bombs and bullets.
★ Economic security and true freedom instead of economic slavery.
★ Everyman a Richman tomorrow in relation to his effective purchasing power today.
★ A Passport to Paradise on earth instead of oblivion.
★ The true Stairway to the Stars instead of missile-fizzles and launching-pad-blues.
★ What may be your last chance for a real choice.

then VOTE for GABRIEL GREEN

YOUR WRITE-IN SPACE-AGE CANDIDATE

(HIS HEART IS WITH THE PEOPLE)

For Independent Non-Partisan President of the United States

★ If you are "fed up" with the same hypocritical promises offering you a welfare state and plenty for everybody, but they can't tell you how to pay for it without raising your taxes or the national debt beyond our ability to pay—
★ If you want adequate school rooms and unlimited education for all: medical and dental care, better housing, highways, and transportation; more jobs and shorter work hours; better wages and more profits; retirement from work without reduction in living standard; and 100% distribution of all that our advanced technology is capable of producing—
★ If you want all these things for all our people without taxing them to pay for it—
★ If you want to eliminate vested interest in inefficiency so that machines and automatonic industry can be permitted to do the laborius work of man, and still distribute the abundance produced by those machines to the people who need it—
★ If you want more new freeways instead of traffic jams, free energy instead of

costly smog-producing power, full employment for all who are willing and able to work, and full production without surpluses and layoffs—
★ If you would like to see abundance where there is want, happiness where there is misery, true freedom where there is oppression and economic slavery—
★ If you want real peace in the world and not just lip service to peace as a substitute—
★ If you want a nation without discrimination by reason or race, color, or creed, and a nation where HUMAN rights are superior to those of the state—
★ If you want to see the people told the truth rather than kept in planned ignorance of the most vital information in all history—
★ If you want America to fulfill her sacred destiny to lead the nations onto the pathway of true peace, security, and righteousness—
★ If you want The World of Tomorrow today, and UTOPIA now,
THEN VOTE FOR, AND WORK TO ELECT GABRIEL GREEN FOR PRESIDENT OF THE UNITED STATES OF AMERICA in 1960.

ACT NOW! TOMORROW MAY BE TO LATE!

★ Learn the answers to mankind's problems before it is too late.
★ Be sure to hear **GABRIEL BLOW HIS HORN** for a better way of life for all people, at the Second National Convention, **AMALGAMATED FLYING SAUCERS CLUBS of AMERICA, SHRINE AUDITORIUM**, August 13 and 14, 1960, 10.00 a.m. to 5:00 p.m. Admission $1.00 per day. Buy tickets at door. Don't be late.

Open to the public. Don't miss it!

This ad sponsored by:
AMALGAMATED FLYING SAUCER CLUBS OF AMERICA
2004 North Hoover Street, Los Angeles 27, California. U.S.A.

Mail to:
GABRIEL GREEN FOR PRESIDENT CLUBS
2004 N. Hoover St.
Los Angeles 27, Calif.

I would like more information on how the above needs of our people, nation, and the world can be accomplished, and how I can help to elect a Space Age leader capable of effectively dealing with these needs.

Please mail to me your free 16 page public information booklet on "Prior Choice Economics," the key to a greater America.

Please type or print plainly.

NAME
STREET
CITY   STATE

This ad for Gabriel Green's presidential campaign ran on August 11, 1960.

GABRIEL GREEN:
THE ALIEN CONTACTEE WHO RAN FOR PRESIDENT

Anyone with a basic knowledge of American politics could tell you that John F. Kennedy defeated Richard Nixon in the 1960 presidential election. But lesser known is the fact that another candidate hoped to take the White House that year—with the help of men from outer space.

His name was Gabriel Green and he hailed from the same town as Richard Nixon: Whittier, California. Green served as the president of the Amalgamated Flying Saucer Clubs of America and in 1959 claimed to have seen more than seventy-five spaceships in the Los Angeles area. He met his first spacemen when they attended his club's convention that year. Like so many 1950s contactees, Green claimed the aliens looked just like earthlings.

By 1960, at the suggestion of the spacemen, Green organized the Space-Age ticket in an attempt to overtake Nixon and Kennedy for the presidency. Fellow UFO advocate and flying saucer passenger Daniel W. Fry served as campaign chairman.

Green explained that spacemen from Mars, Venus, and Saturn are interested in helping humans solve our problems because they solved theirs long ago. They had given him solutions, and allegedly offered the same quick fixes to other heads of state around the world, but none of them chose to take the extraterrestrials' advice.

"They could at any time take over our earth between breakfast and lunch and make robots out of all of us," Green told the press in August 1960. "But this would be against their universal laws and against their principles. They are here to help us help ourselves."

After promises of better wages and "Utopia now," Green withdrew from the race by October 1960 and endorsed Kennedy. In a press release, he announced that the "space people" approved his decision and said he believed that "a Kennedy administration would be more receptive to the new progressive ideas and programs which are needed in order to improve conditions for all the people of the land."

Kennedy did indeed build a space program that landed men on the moon in 1969, but Green sought still more progress. In 1972 he ran for president once again, this time with Fry as his running mate. Earning less than two hundred votes, the presidential hopeful once again found little success.

Other Sensational Tales of Flying Saucer Hitchhikers

The Klaatus of the universe continued to identify humans to spread their messages of good will. Take ham radio operator Richard Miller, for example, who made contact with an alien while tuning his dial in October 1954. After hearing an "unusual sounding thing," Miller arranged a meeting near Detroit with whatever was communicating with him. The 150-foot craft he encountered appeared to be made of "something similar to aluminum of magnesium" and caused a "tingling sensation, like a mild electric shock" when he stood beneath it. A ramp lowered, much like the one from Klaatu's spaceship, as an invitation to board. The ship's commander and electrical engineer greeted him and explained that a cosmic cloud was threatening all life in the solar system. By 1957, all those on earth would suffer mental and coronary diseases. Luckily for Miller and all humankind, the friendly aliens were surrounding our planet with their spaceships to shield us from most of the harmful radiation.

George W. Van Tassel, an aircraft mechanic working in Giant Rock, California, announced that he rode in a flying saucer in his 1952 publication, aptly titled *I Rode a Flying Saucer!* His book's introduction, however, quickly acknowledges the "stupidity" of such a proclamation: "You see, I don't claim to have been aboard a flying saucer; the intelligences that operate the saucers, claim I was aboard." Spacemen from a place Van Tassel called the "realms of Schare" frequently shared information telepathically with him, continuing the theme of warnings about nuclear weaponry. For example, an April 19, 1952, message from Kerrull of the 64th projection, 2nd wave, 4th sector patrol of the realms of Schare claimed that "due to inaccurate calculations, many of your fellow beings will suffer prolonged illness from an experiment to be conducted next week. This folly in the use of atomic power for destruction will rebound upon the users. Discontinue."

Aboard a Flying Saucer

by TRUMAN BETHURUM
Non-Fiction—A True Account of Factual Experience

My Flight to Venus

DANA HOWARD

ROUND TRIP TO HELL IN A FLYING SAUCER

By CECIL MICHAEL

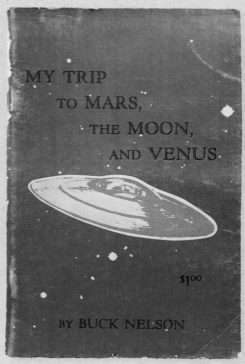

MY TRIP TO MARS, THE MOON, AND VENUS

$1.00

BY BUCK NELSON

In addition to spreading their messages through lectures and UFO conventions, many contactees wrote all about their extraordinary adventures and the aliens' missions to save earth.

George Adamski:
The Man Who Met the Man from Venus

As unbelievable as these claims of experiences aboard UFOs were, they were all one-upped by the tales of best-selling author George Adamski who claimed to have met a Venusian on November 20, 1952, near his home in Palomar Mountain, California. The event was the culmination of numerous saucer sightings since October 1946, when Adamski—also a restaurateur, occult enthusiast, and avid stargazer—first spotted a "gigantic space craft" during a meteor shower.

At the time he suspected it might be an experimental military craft, until later that night when he heard a radio broadcast discussing the "large cigar-shaped space ship" that he'd seen. The strange craft had hovered over San Diego and allegedly led to hundreds of reports regarding its mysterious nature. Adamski remained skeptical until several weeks later when six military officers stepped into his café and overheard his chatter with customers about the unusual event. According to Adamski's retelling of the story in his 1953 book *Flying Saucers Have Landed*, they didn't offer details, other than to assure the customers that "the ship [they] had seen and were discussing was not of this world."

From that moment on, Adamski spent his evenings staring at the stars hoping to catch a glimpse of another interplanetary visitor. In August 1947, his patience paid off. Scores of lights began zipping through the night sky in a single-file line, "but appeared to be moving in squadrons of thirty-two." He soon counted a whopping 184 flying objects—which didn't include the many he'd spotted before he began his tally. Adamski was hooked. By 1949 he'd snapped his first photos of cigar-shaped UFOs and began lecturing on their presence.

On that fateful November day in 1952, after hearing about numerous flying saucer sightings in the desert areas near Palomar Mountain, Adamski gathered six friends, including a curious anthropologist, Dr. George H. Williamson, and hit the highway on a quest to see more than any human ever had. Out on the open road, they encountered a "gigantic cigar-shaped silvery" mother ship "without wings or appendages of any kind" that seemed to hover motionless above them before

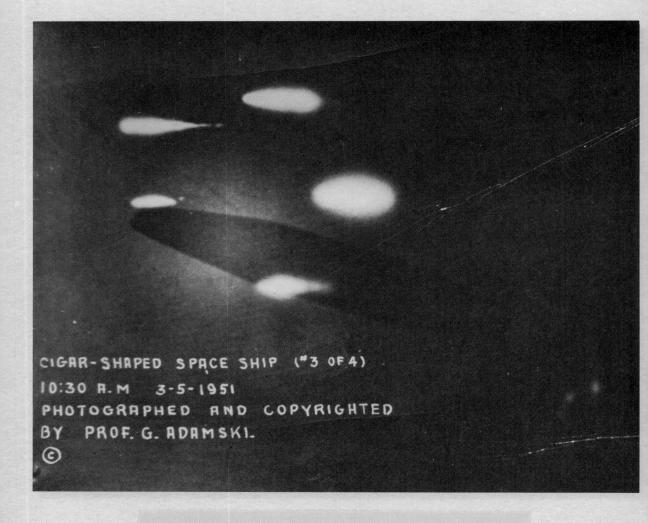

CIGAR-SHAPED SPACE SHIP (#3 OF 4)
10:30 A.M 3-5-1951
PHOTOGRAPHED AND COPYRIGHTED
BY PROF. G. ADAMSKI.
©

One of four telescopic photos George Adamski took on March 5, 1951, showing
an alleged cigar-shaped mother ship releasing multiple flying saucers.

flying off and disappearing over the crest of a mountain.

Adamski and his crew pulled over, grabbed their cameras, and looked up in hopes of an encore appearance. Sure enough, within five minutes a flash lit up the sky and a smaller ship began descending between two mountain peaks. Adamski snapped his shutter rapidly. But his big day was just beginning, because standing at the entrance of a ravine about a quarter mile away, the presumed occupant of the craft gestured for Adamski to walk toward him. Naturally, he did. As for his friends, they were inexplicably content to stay behind and give him all the glory of becoming the first man to make extraterrestrial contact.

After a short jaunt across the desert, Adamski found himself face-to-face with "a man from space" dressed in a tight-fitting one-piece suit who physically looked just like a human, only better. "The beauty of his form surpassed anything I had ever seen," Adamski remarked. He was particularly smitten by his hair, noting that it was "sandy in color and hung in beautiful waves to his shoulders, glistening more beautifully than any woman's I have ever seen."

> ## "If we are created in the image of God, there's no reason why intelligent inhabitants of other planets shouldn't be created in the same image."
>
> —GEORGE ADAMSKI, when asked in 1965 why people from other planets look just like us

Ufologists later nicknamed this brand of humanoid alien the "Nordics" for their Scandinavian appearance, and some believe they originate from the Pleiades star cluster, located about 444 light-years away. But when Adamski greeted his visitor and conversed through gestures and telepathy, he learned his beautiful new friend had taken only a relatively short jaunt from Venus. Their people were concerned about the development of atomic weapons on earth. Adamski was also told the Venusians, as well as other visiting spacemen, didn't want to announce themselves because they feared hysteria and thought extraterrestrials would probably "be torn to pieces by the Earth people, if such public landings were attempted." Apparently news of Orson Welles's panic-inducing *War of the Worlds* radio broadcast in 1938 had spread throughout the solar system.

Throughout this groundbreaking experience, Adamski's camera had been sitting on the ground, lonely and forgotten. When it finally occurred to him to use it, the visitor objected and Adamski respected his wishes. So his remarkable encounter went undocumented, aside from his own words and notarized witness statements from his friends watching from afar. If only they'd joined him to play the role of paparazzi.

Adamski hoped to extend the meeting by hitching a ride aboard the spaceship, but the Venusian rejected his request. Not even a simple peek inside was allowed. "I was a little disappointed," Adamski wrote.

As indicated by the title of his next book, *Inside the Space Ships*, his disappointment didn't last long. By February 1953, he was invited not only to board the Venusian scout ship but to ascend to the cigar-shaped mothership hovering forty thousand feet above earth. Two months later, he took another joyride in a ship piloted by a Saturnian. Top that, Daniel W. Fry.

Fantastic as Adamski's stories were, he had his believers who helped his books fly off the shelves. He'd clearly built a readership excited about his revelations and ravenous for anything UFO related. Adamski even secured an audience with Queen Juliana of the Netherlands in 1959. Though her cabinet pleaded with her not to entertain him, she insisted. Arriving at the palace in a royal limousine, Adamski regaled the queen with tales of his space-faring adventures, and even mentioned a woman he knew who eloped with a Venusian. The queen listened intently, proving to be an interested and gracious host. The Dutch air force chief of staff, Lieutenant General Heye Schaper, was less enamored, telling the press, "the man's a pathological case."

Adamski also attracted the attention of science fiction writer and

George Adamski stands in front of a painting by Gay Betts depicting the Venusian he allegedly encountered in California's Mojave Desert on November 20, 1952.

THE SAUCERS SPEAK

GEORGE HUNT WILLIAMSON

author of 'Secret Places of the Lion'
'Road to the Sky' etc. . . . .

This 1963 edition of *The Saucers Speak* features alleged communications from beings across our solar system, as transcribed by Dr. George Hunt Williamson.

futurist Arthur C. Clarke, who wasn't buying any of his otherworldly yarns. Clarke, who boasted a bit more of a scientific background, debunked Adamski's photographs in the March 1954 issue of *Journal of the British Interplanetary Society* by noting the "uncanny resemblance (of the 'scout ships') to electric light fittings with table tennis balls fixed underneath them" and that "the pictures seem to be of small objects photographed from very close up and not of a large object seen through a telescope." Theories also suggested that a tobacco humidor and an ordinary chicken brooder formed the rest of the craft.

If that, and a general sense of incredulity, wasn't enough to debunk Adamski's wild stories, some of those who were with him on November 20, 1952, eventually confessed that things weren't quite as he described. According to James W. Moseley, editor of *Saucer News*, several people connected to Adamski acknowledged he was rather liberal with the truth. The October 1957 issue stated that at least one of Adamski's witnesses admitted to seeing nothing that afternoon. Numerous others told Moseley they had been misquoted in *Flying Saucers Have Landed*, and several friends and colleagues stated that Adamski's alien encounters had been planned in advance.

Dr. George Hunt Williamson, however, was not among those who came clean. He not only stuck to Adamski's story but built on it with his own series of extraterrestrial exploits in his 1954 book *The Saucers Speak*. The book collects messages from a host of alien visitors communicating via automatic writing and "International Morse Code through radiotelegraphy" dating back to August 1952—just before Williamson's journey to the desert with Adamski and just days after the perceived UFO invasion of Washington, DC.

Howard Menger Marries a Venusian

Not to be outdone by Adamski and Williamson, Howard Menger of New Jersey took things a step further. A sign painter by trade, he claimed to have not only met Venusians and traveled in their bell-shaped spaceship but also married a curvaceous Venusian who, yes, looked just like an earth woman. He said he first encountered her during a sighting in 1932 when he was just ten years old and later met her again in 1946.

During one of Menger's spaceship flights in 1956, the Venusians projected a 3D image of their world for their guest to explore. The planet, as he described it, flowed with foliage, mountains, bodies of water, huge dome-shaped buildings, and spaceships zipping through the air. "If there was a Garden of Eden, this was it," Menger said afterward. "It was beautiful."

These Venusians in paradise were vegetarians, devoutly religious, and capable of living for up to a thousand years. And like missionaries on earth, they claimed they were simply here to help us. "They are not hostile but they are holy people who want us to know what we are and who we are," Menger said. "The earth is the lowest planet in vibration frequency around the sun and they feel that with their higher understanding of life and its meaning they can help us."

One might wonder why, if the Venusians really wanted to do good, they didn't spread their message directly to a broader audience. Why stop at Adamski, Menger, and a few other lucky souls? According to Menger, mass landings could only happen when us humans could handle such an event without panic. Once again, the *War of the Worlds* broadcast was scaring all our interplanetary neighbors away.

In addition to these revelations, the sign painter also learned he was a Saturnian reincarnated as baby Howard on earth. His real name was Alyn. Together with his five-hundred-year-old Venusian wife, Marla (whose real name was Connie and was, by all other accounts, a much younger earthling woman), they produced books about their space lives together and recorded an album titled *Authentic Music from Another Planet*, featuring Menger on the piano—which he claimed aliens taught him to play. These records were available for purchase to the thousand attendees at a 1958 space convention the couple hosted together.

Barker, Bender, and the Men in Black

Even if alien acquaintances weren't truly made, a few bucks clearly were. Many contactees capitalized on the nation's extraterrestrial mania with the sale of books, albums, and lecture tickets. It was a per-

Contactees, like Howard Menger, often lectured about their experiences and beliefs. Small cards announcing upcoming events were mailed to their followers.

SATURDAY NOVEMBER 2ND AT 8 P.M.
LECTURE BY
HOWARD MENGER
COME AND HEAR ALL ABOUT
FLYING SAUCERS AND SPACE VISITORS
QUESTION AND ANSWER PERIOD
AT THE
CHAPEL OF TRUTH
New Age School
1410 WALNUT ST.
ADMISSION DONATION 1.25
BRING THIS CARD FOR DOOR PRIZE

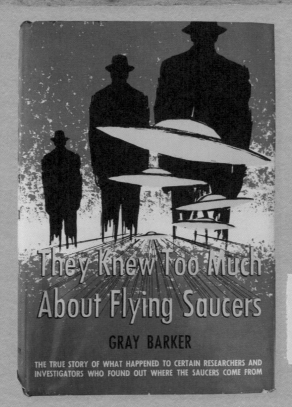

Gray Barker introduced the Men in Black into the public consciousness in his 1956 book.

fectly human thing to do. Many of them even had their own clubs—or cults, depending on your point of view.

Among their unusual but firmly held beliefs, some members of these groups were convinced that if they learned too much about the aliens, a visit from the mysterious Men in Black would follow. The term first appeared in Gray Barker's 1956 book, *They Knew Too Much About Flying Saucers.* Unlike Will Smith and Tommy Lee Jones, these Men in Black weren't erasing memories with a quick zap to the head. They were instead implanting self-destructive devices in brains, as Barker described with the case of Albert K. Bender.

Bender, a World War II veteran and UFO enthusiast, had successfully launched the International Flying Saucer Bureau—a civilian group dedicated to studying sightings and communications with aliens—from his Bridgeport, Connecticut, home in 1952. Within months, the IFSB gained several hundred members from branches in twenty-seven states and numerous countries—making it truly international.

On March 15, 1953, Bender organized World Contact Day with the goal of having members collectively send out a telepathic memo to spacemen. "Perhaps such a message might get across, particularly with so many minds concentrating on the same message," he wrote years afterward. The message called out to all "occupants of interplanetary craft!" and invited them to make an appearance on earth: "Your presence before us will be welcomed with the utmost friendship." After a third contact attempt from his home, he felt chills, suffered an excruciating headache, and partially lost consciousness. Suddenly he opened his eyes and found himself hovering three feet above his bed. At that moment, he received a telepathic message: "Please be advised to discontinue delving into the mysteries of the universe. We will make an appearance if you disobey."

Bender abruptly shut the IFSB down a year later after a visit from "three men in black suits with threatening expressions on their faces."

"They don't want you to tell anyone else what you know," Barker wrote about the Men in Black. "After they got through with you, you wished you'd never heard of the word 'saucer.'"

Based on his experiences, Bender claimed the MIB were not secret government agents but mind-manipulating extraterrestrials. They implanted a device in the IFSB's founder that promised to disintegrate him if he spoke of the secrets he knew. Nevertheless, Bender managed to write about it in his 1962 book *Flying Saucers and the Three Men* and lived to sell the tale.[†]

Today, some believers still fear the men dressed in black, but whether they exist or not, the mere mention of the Men in Black threatens us all when the theme song from Will Smith's movie gets stuck in our heads.

Dwight D. Eisenhower: Five-Star General, Thirty-Fourth President of the United States, Alien Contactee?

If you were to believe every word of UFO lore, you'd think President Dwight D. Eisenhower's entire administration revolved around aliens— even before his inauguration. According to documents unearthed in 1984, the president-elect received an official briefing on November 18, 1952, about the military's retrieval of a crashed flying saucer at Roswell and four dead bodies "badly damaged due to the crash trauma, action by predators and exposure to the elements." These long-lost papers belonged to a secret elite committee of twelve eminent military leaders and scientists appointed by President Harry Truman in 1947, coinciding with the establishment of the CIA. The group was called the Majestic 12, and they were tasked with retrieving and studying spaceships and their occupants.

This revelation excited many, but it didn't take long for skeptics to proclaim it a hoax, based on a few key details. Truman's signature, for example, was photocopied onto his memo, and the format used for the date of the Eisenhower briefing did not match the format used by the military. The mysterious documents weren't even physical—they were images on an undeveloped roll of 35-millimeter film mailed to a

---

† Despite the threats of the Men in Black, Albert Bender not only didn't disintegrate, he lived to the ripe old age of ninety-four, passing away in 2016.

film producer in an envelope with an Albuquerque postmark from an unknown sender. Though some ufologists believe the documents are genuine, others share the skepticism and wonder if they were created and sent as part of a government-orchestrated disinformation campaign.

"You don't have the paper, you don't have the watermark that you can look at in the paper, and you can't analyze the ink in that respect, like you can with an original document," UFO researcher and historian David Marler said during one of my research sessions at his archive. "These are simply images of purported documents, and all of these things that are now coming out quoting MJ-12 become more lurid and convoluted and spurious with each and every telling."

Eisenhower's timeline of conspiratorial deeds continued on the night of February 20, 1954, when he unexpectedly went missing from his Palm Springs vacation for several hours. The Associated Press jumped the gun and released a story stating he'd died of a heart attack, but quickly retracted it. The next morning the press was told that Eisenhower made an emergency visit to a dentist for a chipped front tooth suffered while chomping on a chicken wing at a dinner. UFO conspiracy theorists don't buy it. Instead, they believe the dental story was a cover-up for a secret meeting with aliens that conveniently took place at nearby Edwards Air Force Base.

This is in part due to a particular letter written shortly after the event by local metaphysical community leader Gerald Light to his colleague Meade Layne of the Borderland Sciences Research Foundation. In it, he described a two-day visit to Edwards during which he witnessed five "separate and distinct types of aircraft" and met their extraterrestrial occupants. Light, a known occultist and clairvoyant who allegedly was present with other community leaders to help test public reaction to the presence of aliens, also wrote, "President Eisenhower, as you may already know, was spirited over to Muroc one night during his visit to Palm Springs recently. And it is my conviction that he will ignore the terrific conflict between the various 'authorities' and go directly to the people via radio and television—if the impasse continues much longer. From what I could gather, an official statement to the country is being prepared for delivery about the middle of May."[+]

Clearly this official statement was never given, so the public was never told about these humanoid aliens. As the lore goes, in the early 1970s William Cooper, a member of the Naval Intelligence briefing team for the commander of the U.S. Pacific Fleet, gained access to classified documents and revealed that the extraterrestrials offered to give Eisenhower the secrets of their advanced technology if he'd end the country's nuclear program.[++] The atomic threat was a consistent theme with extraterrestrial visitors in the fifties, but at least in this case they went straight to the man in power, instead of the random mouthpieces discussed elsewhere in this chapter.

"They were afraid we might blow up some of our nuclear technology, and apparently that does something to time and space and it impacts on extraterrestrial races on other planets," Dr. Michael Salla, a former professor at American University, told the *Washington Post* in 2004 after writing about the fiftieth anniversary of the purported Eisenhower-extraterrestrial summit.

As Salla explained, Ike respectfully declined the aliens' offer. However, later that year, the professor claims, the president caved in and signed a treaty with another group of spacemen, the "Grays," that stated aliens wouldn't interfere with human affairs, and the government wouldn't interfere with theirs—with a few exceptions. This humanoid species, often portrayed in pop culture with large heads, large black eyes, small noses, thin limbs, and their namesake gray skin, supposedly offered us superior technology in exchange for letting them abduct a few people to experiment on (and return safely with no memory of the event). Plus, they were free to mutilate the occasional cow (more on that gruesomeness on page 168).

Aliens, however, weren't done offering Eisenhower their help. According to Dr. Frank E. Stranges, founder of the National Investigations Committee on Unidentified Flying Objects, the president was visited

---

[+] Edwards Air Force Base had been called Muroc Air Force Base until December 1949. Perhaps Light wasn't used to the change yet.

[++] William Cooper was known as a conspiracy theorist who also alleged that John F. Kennedy was assassinated to prevent his announcement of the arrival of aliens. But he didn't just spread ideas about otherworldly visitors; he also claimed AIDS was a human-made disease designed to decrease the population of minorities.

again in 1957 by a Venusian named Valiant Thor. Like Ike's earlier visitors in 1954, Thor was humanoid in appearance. He stood about six feet tall, weighed 185 pounds, and had dark, slicked back hair, which indicates he did as much homework on men's grooming in the fifties as he did on politics.

When Thor landed on March 16 in Alexandria, Virginia, two police officers spotted him and immediately whisked him away to Washington, DC. The secretary of defense took him into his custody and escorted the man from Venus to the Oval Office for meetings with POTUS and Vice President Richard Nixon. Despite the face-to-face conference and what would be three years spent in Washington, Valiant Thor achieved nothing. For all his superiority, he fared no better than a typical politician.

"His efforts to bring about an end to the sickness and disease that plague this planet were met with pathetic refusal," Stranges wrote in his 1967 book, *Stranger at the Pentagon.* "He was told over and over that his presence and his ideas were a threat to the political and economic structure. Certain religious leaders were also fearful of losing a grip on the people in the event that his presence was admitted on an official level."

Stranges claimed that Valiant Thor returned to his ship in Alexandria exactly three years after his arrival and launched himself back to Venus as a transfixed crowd watched. But the mission was hardly over. Valiant Thor allegedly came back numerous times over the following decades to help humankind solve its problems.

All of these fantastic claims sound like the plots of science fiction movies, yet Laura Eisenhower, the president's great-granddaughter, supports the idea that contact was made. At a 2012 MUFON meeting in Los Angeles, she told attendees that she's been in touch with aliens but doesn't discuss extraterrestrial business with the rest of the Eisenhower family. "I am the only one who is speaking about the treaties and agreements with the shadow government," she said. "The family has been infiltrated by the dark side."

If mid-century aliens were guiding us toward peace, giving free tours of their spaceships, patrolling our skies, and maybe even crashing in Roswell, they all seemed to be fairly innocuous. But then something changed. Extraterrestrials got extra touchy-feely—and extra creepy. As we entered the 1960s, these alleged visitors began abducting people, poking and prodding them aboard their crafts, and even implanting devices in them.

These were no longer the friendly Venusians or Martians who looked just like us. According to many abductees, these were entirely different types of beings, from Grays to giant praying-mantis-like creatures who seemed to want to study us, track us, and, in some cases, mate with us. A new era of our relationship with extraterrestrials had begun.

The Abduction of Helen Robbins

On a quiet and clear morning in June 1961, fourteen-year-old Peter Robbins and his twelve-year-old sister, Helen, were playing in the front yard of their small-town home in Long Island, New York. No cars raced down the streets, no neighbors were out and about. It was just the two of them—and five flying saucers watching from across the street. Silvery white, metallic, and elliptical in shape, they sat above a neighbor's home in a precise V formation, close enough for Peter and Helen to see detailing along the edges.

"All of a sudden I'm confronting the unknown in a way I could've never imagined," Peter Robbins said, describing what he and his late sister experienced on *The Richard Dolan Show* in 2021. Shocked, he began to mentally process what he was—or wasn't—seeing. "My conscious mind literally ticked off: these are not planes, helicopters, kites, balloons, blimps, dirigibles, flotsam and jetsam, string shaped clouds, birds. What am I looking at?"

He and Helen said nothing. Finally, Peter ran for his front door. But in his mad dash, he found himself moving in slow motion as if "running through molasses," then he blacked out on the front walkway. Sometime later, perhaps minutes or a half hour, he awoke. The flying disks were gone, and so was Helen. He wandered inside, saw his mother was cooking lunch, and found Helen looking out her bedroom window into the backyard. The two didn't speak of what they'd just seen.

This 1975 painting by Peter Robbins was his second UFO-related artwork. He created it immediately following his first conversation with his sister about their childhood sighting. "In fact we had seen five of them, not six, but Helen was unsure until she saw the painting," Peter explained in an email to me. "I had painted it with an extra craft bottom left and held my hand over it when I first showed it to her, then removed my hand. We both remembered an even 'V' formation and she immediately agreed that it had been five."

Artwork created by Helen Wheels, depicting her experience aboard a spaceship.

about 6 ft. tall - THIN
communicated by telepathy

met this particular being numerous times

seemed to move by gliding

showed me around 'control' room
LET ME SIT IN THE STARCHAIR
BLUE/SILVER METALLIC suit w/ no visible closures

whitish-gray skin
wraparound solid black eyes

shape of rooms

room with complex looking dials, monitors and star chair...

I enter the ship VIA LIGHT BEAM through here

8 or 9 identical

my size (about 3')
gnay white skin
SOFT LOOKING

didn't communicate
scared me
DID MEDICAL EXAMINATION

OPERATING ROOM

Wheels '93

Peter told his mother, but otherwise kept it quiet. At fourteen with overactive hormones, his biggest concern was girls at school thinking he was a crackpot. "I'll be a joke," he thought to himself. "I'd be in Siberia in junior high school."

Peter and Helen stayed close as they grew into adulthood and began making names for themselves in New York City. By the mid-1970s, Peter had followed his dream to become an artist and found himself rubbing elbows with the likes of Andy Warhol and Roy Lichtenstein, while Helen discovered her voice as a poet and a performer in the burgeoning punk rock scene. Under the name Helen Wheels, she was writing songs for Blue Öyster Cult and opening for soon-to-be-legendary bands like the Ramones, Blondie, the Talking Heads, and Iggy Pop.

In the fourteen years since their shared experience, Peter had thought little of it. During an LSD trip in the late sixties he painted a series of watercolors featuring a boy and girl taken aboard a flying saucer. He filed them away, forgot about them, and eventually destroyed them years later, fearing they might one day tarnish his legacy as an artist. But by 1975, his memories of that most unusual day in 1961 began flooding back. Peter reached out to Helen to ask if she remembered it as well. Without hesitating, she told him she hadn't forgotten anything. To her, it wasn't a terrifying experience. It was a moment, she told her brother, that made her think she was special. Without taking her eyes off the saucers, Helen had noticed Peter run off. A blue beam of light shot out from beneath one of the objects and lifted her off the ground just as Peter blacked out.

"You went down, and I went up," she had told him, as Peter explained on Dolan's show. "I guess I knew at a certain point if something happened I'd fall and I would die, but I was just fascinated. This was the most interesting thing that had ever happened to me."

Once inside the spaceship, Helen recalled "a bunch of little beings with big heads and big black eyes" walking her down a curved metal hallway. A taller alien communicated with her telepathically. "I felt no anxiety, just curiosity," she explained to her brother. "Next thing I know I'm on a metal table and they're all around me and I have no clothes on and it's not an issue."

According to Peter, they had assured her they wouldn't harm her and that they'd see her again. Although Helen was amazed by the experience, the violating examination did cause her pain. Peter believes this ruined the aliens' relationship with her for the rest of her life. Surely an abduction and upsetting experiments would cause trust issues.

"My first thought was 'Oh, my god my sister's gone insane,'" he told Dolan. "It only lasted a moment or two because I was able to catch myself saying 'Ah, but six seconds ago it was perfectly okay for five fucking flying saucers to be hanging over the Parkers' house close enough to see windows?'"

Peter believed his sister, and from that moment on his life forever changed. His pursuit of art took a backseat to his drive to learn more about the extraterrestrial phenomenon he'd personally experienced. He has since researched, written, and lectured on the subject and continues to do so today.

In 1987 the siblings came out in public and shared their story on *Geraldo*, where Helen expanded on the examination and the aftermath: "They stuck a probe up my nose and then they covered my face in some kind of cold jelly. I'm not sure what else was done. But I do know that for about six months—and my mother has corroborated this—that I had awesome nosebleeds all the time. And I never had this before or after. My nose was cauterized several times and my theory is that there was some kind of implant which I either sneezed or blew out."

The alleged implant exited through her nostril into a tissue with a splash of blood. Helen saw it was the size of a BB. Grossed out, she wadded it up and threw it away. The incident, however, finally spurred a visit to an ear, nose, and throat specialist. According to Peter, the doctor asked if she'd ever stuck a sharp pencil up her nose. She hadn't.

"Well, you must have stuck something up your nose," the doctor told her, convinced something had to have worked its way up high enough to have created the indentation left behind. "He basically—like medical people used to do with kids— passively called her a liar," Peter told me during a visit to his central New York home. "'You must have done it because that's all that could account for it.'"

Just three months after the Robbinses' 1961 encounter, another abduction occurred. Unlike theirs, this one did not stay quiet for decades.

America's First Known Abductees: Betty and Barney Hill

As a middle-aged interracial couple in the early 1960s, Betty and Barney Hill were already an unusual pair. But on the night of September 19, 1961, they became far more unique after a drive home to Portsmouth, New Hampshire, from their Niagara Falls vacation led them on an unexpected detour aboard a spacecraft. Forget that Barney was Black and Betty was white, or that both were respected in the community for their advocacy of civil and human rights—from the moment the news of their story broke, they became known as America's first documented alien abductees.

The Hills' harrowing experience began around 11:00 p.m. as the couple headed south in their '57 Chevy on Route 3 through the White Mountains and noticed an unusual bright light moving amongst the stars. Barney suspected it was just a distant plane or a satellite, but Betty wasn't so sure. Like every other state, New Hampshire had had its share of flying saucer reports in recent years, and this, she believed, may be another. Barney pulled off the desolate two-lane highway several times so they could stop and attempt to take a closer look with their binoculars. Each time it seemed as if the craft was getting closer and following them. No other vehicles had passed on the road. The Hills were all alone, watching the night sky—and seemingly being watched from it.

When the object maneuvered itself over a clearing just off the road, about a hundred feet above the ground, Barney braked again to investigate. Unlike Betty, he'd been skeptical of UFOs and thought perhaps the object was some type of military craft messing with them. Still, to be safe, he grabbed a gun that he'd kept in the vehicle for protection, along with the binoculars, and headed toward the hovering craft as Betty waited inside.

According to Barney, the UFO appeared to be about sixty to eighty feet wide and shaped as flat as a pancake. Fins at each end blinked red and a double row of windows stretched across the width and curved around the perimeter. He claimed that as he peered through his binoculars, he saw at least six living figures dressed in black uniforms and black caps, staring right back at him with piercing eyes unlike any he'd seen before. Several of them moved about and appeared to be busy at a control board, while one remained at the window. At that point, the craft descended even lower as a ladderlike contraption emerged from its underside.

Still in the car, Betty screamed at Barney to come back, but despite the silence of the craft he didn't hear her. Perhaps he was too lost in the moment, and under the spell of the peculiar beings in the windows. But as he continued gazing into their intense eyes, his curiosity finally turned to fright. Believing he was about to be captured "like a bug in a net," Barney dashed back to the Chevy, and they sped off. Betty looked out the window in search of the craft, but it had disappeared into the night.

After a short distance, their strange journey grew stranger when a series of mysterious beeps came from behind the vehicle, causing it to vibrate. The couple kept driving. The rhythmic beeps faded, but soon returned: *Beep. Beep. Beep.* Not knowing what the sounds were or where they came from, the Hills just stayed the course.

Betty and Barney finally arrived home at 5:00 a.m., but as they would realize months later, they should've been home by 3:00. Somehow two hours had been lost and could not be accounted for. The next day, the Hills found more to be puzzled by: there were inexplicable scuff marks on the tops of Barney's shoes; the rear of their car had a series of circular polished spots that wouldn't wash away; both their watches had stopped and refused to start again; and Betty's dress was torn and stained. Though Barney didn't want to think about the sighting any longer, Betty wanted answers. She started by reporting the event to nearby Pease Air Force Base.

After an extensive phone interview with Major Paul W. Henderson and a subsequent report that acknowledged radar had detected an unidentified object in the area that night, the case was submitted to Project Blue Book. Its brief investigation cited "insufficient data" in its conclusion and suggested that the sightings by radar and the Hills were "probably due to conditions resulting from the strong inversion which prevailed in area on morning of sighting." Therefore, it stated, the objects were due to "natural causes" and that the lights had "all the

UFO AS SEEN BY BETTY HILL
IN FIRST ENCOUNTER. FROM
SKETCH BY BETTY HILL.

Figures at
control panel

Figure that
grinned

Leader

UFO AS SEEN BY BARNEY HILL SHOWING
FIGURES, "FINS," & RED LIGHTS. FROM
SKETCH BY BARNEY HILL.

SKETCH OF "LEADER" DRAWN BY BARNEY
HILL WHILE UNDER HYPNOSIS (COPY).

Sketches of the UFO and alien by Betty and Barney Hill, as
seen in a NICAP investigation folder at the International
UFO Museum and Research Center in Roswell, New Mexico.

characteristics of an advertising searchlight." The lack of data is understandable, but advertising searchlights in the middle of nowhere at 11:00 p.m. seem unlikely, as do "natural causes" for Barney's description of humanoid beings hovering above him.

About ten days later, more details emerged in Betty's mind when she began having nightmares about the encounter. Over the course of five nights, she relived what seemed to have occurred during those missing hours: an abduction and physical examinations by their captors. Of course, they were just dreams. Regardless, Betty wrote them down to preserve the memories—whether they were imagined or not.

With the air force and Project Blue Book offering little help, Betty looked to NICAP—a civilian UFO research group—for a more thorough investigation. By October 19, exactly a month after their experience, the organization sent scientific investigator Walter Webb to meet with the Hills. Skeptical at first, he was eventually won over by the couple and their impressive account. "I cross-examined them together, separately, together, requestioned them again and again," he said following his meeting. "I tried to make them slip up somewhere, and I couldn't; I simply couldn't. Theirs was an iron-clad story."

The Hills may have been pleased with Webb's confidence in them, but there was still the important matter of understanding their two hours of amnesia. They attempted to revisit the site of the encounter several times over the next year, but it triggered no memories. Finally, by the beginning of 1964, they sought the help of Dr. Benjamin Simon, a distinguished psychiatrist and neurologist in Boston, to regain their memories through hypnotic regression.

Over the course of six months, Betty and Barney's fantastic story of abduction emerged with vivid detail and genuine emotion. It began, as Barney explained under hypnosis, after the UFO sighting when he mysteriously strayed from Route 3 and found himself on a "brightly lit" secondary road blocked by a group of men signaling to him to stop. Maybe there'd been an accident and they needed help, he thought. But there was no accident.

"They came and assisted me out of the car," Barney told Dr. Simon, according to transcriptions published in John G. Fuller's 1966 book, *The Interrupted Journey*. These figures escorting him from his vehicle were described as being humanoid in shape, about five feet tall with gray skin, and having elongated almond-shaped eyes that stretched to the sides of their heads, flat noses, and thin slits for mouths. "I felt very weak, but I wasn't afraid," Barney said. "And I can't even think of being confused. I am not bewildered, I can't even think of questioning what is happening to me. . . . I think my feet are dragging. . . . And I am not afraid. I feel like I am dreaming."

Though Barney's eyes stayed shut as the beings dragged him along in a somnambulistic state, he eventually sensed he was being led up a ramp and taken aboard the craft. Betty, too, was taken into the craft by its occupants. She'd been shouting at Barney to wake up, but to no avail. An alleged alien, who spoke English, tried to alleviate any fear Betty was experiencing.

"He said, 'Don't be afraid. You don't have any reason to be afraid,'" she said in one of her early sessions with Dr. Simon. "'We're not going to harm you, but we just want to do some tests. When the tests are over with, we'll take you and Barney back and put you in your car. You'll be on your way home in no time.'"

When Barney finally awakened he found the humanoids standing beside him as he lay on a table in what he described as a pale blue, spotless hospital operating room.

"I thought someone was putting a cup around my groin, and then it stopped. And then I thought: How funny. . . . If I keep real quiet and real still, I won't be harmed. And it will be over. And I will just stay here and pretend that I am anywhere and think of God and think of Jesus, and think that I am not afraid. And I am getting off the table, and I've got a big grin on my face, and I feel greatly relieved."

While aliens were seemingly withdrawing a sperm specimen from Barney, others had undressed Betty in a separate room on the ship and were poking her with a cluster of needles at various points across her body to check her nervous system. One examiner swabbed her ear, plucked a few strands of hair, clipped a nail, and scraped some skin cells from her arm. The samples were all neatly preserved. He then grabbed a longer needle, about four to six inches, and inserted it into her navel for what he said was a pregnancy test.

"I didn't want them to do it," she told Dr. Simon. "I said it would hurt, and the leader said it wouldn't. When his hand went over my eyes, the pain stopped."

Ufologists have since likened the procedure to an amniocentesis, which was hardly a common practice in 1961, and likely not one Betty would have been familiar with.

Afterward, Betty got dressed, but Barney was still being attended to. While she waited for them to finish probing him, she wisely requested a souvenir—something to offer as proof to others that she had truly been abducted. The spaceship didn't have a gift shop, but the attendant granted Betty's wish and allowed her to take a book, filled with unusual characters that looked unlike any other language. Next, the being walked across the room and touched the wall to activate a hologram-like map of their corner of the galaxy. The chart showed a cluster of nickel-sized dots and smaller dots connected by curved lines.

"He said that the heavy lines were trade routes," Betty explained. "And then the other lines, the other lines, the solid lines were places they went occasionally. And he said the broken lines were expeditions."

The alien asked if Betty knew where she was on the map. When she laughed and replied that she didn't, he said there was no point showing her where he was from. Barney's examiner then rushed in to exclaim his surprise and confusion over the earthling's dentures. Despite their having mastered English and intergalactic travel, dentures proved quite confusing to the visitors. So did the concept of age, which Betty had to explain as she described the need for false teeth. To the examiner's credit, Barney was only thirty-nine, so dentures were indeed a bit unexpected (they were due to a mouth injury).

By then, the visitors were all set with their experiments and guided the Hills back to their car, but not before one of them confiscated Betty's souvenir book, denying her the undisputable proof she desired. She protested, but was told they'd never remember the experience anyway.

Back in their car, the Hills watched the "beautiful bright ball," as Barney described the UFO, take off, presumably headed back to wherever it came from. As they drove home, Betty asked her husband if he believed in UFOs now. "Don't be ridiculous," he told her. "Of course not."

Once in the safety of their own home, as Barney described to Dr. Simon, he was anxious to examine his groin for proof that something unusual had happened, but he found nothing. Yet several months later he developed itchiness in his genitals and developed a circular pattern of wartlike growths in the area. Three minor operations were needed to remove them. "The growths were, in all probability, psychosomatic in origin," Webb wrote in a 1965 update to his initial NICAP report, believing Barney had repressed feelings about the alleged extraterrestrial groin cup the visitors subjected him to.

Following their sessions, Dr. Simon acknowledged that the Hills had witnessed some sort of craft, though it may have been terrestrial rather than alien. As for the abduction story, the psychiatrist alleged that the experiences stemmed from Betty's dreams, and that Barney heard them so much, he eventually accepted them as truth. "There seem to be indications that a great deal of the experience was absorbed by Barney Hill from Betty, in spite of his insistence that this was his own," Simon noted after a session.

As Dr. Simon wrote in the foreword to Fuller's book in regard to what hypnosis reveals from its subjects, "The truth is what he believes to be the truth, and this may or may not be consonant with the ultimate non-personal truth. Most frequently it is." Ultimately, he believed the Hills believed they were telling the truth, whether the abduction truly happened or not.

As for Webb, he understood how Simon reached his conclusions. Though Webb found the couple to be intelligent and honest, he saw Betty as "dominating and possessive," whereas he described Barney as "passive, highly suggestible, and full of repressed anxieties and fears." As a Black man living in Betty's white world, he never knew what prejudices he might face.

Webb, having researched UFOs far more than Simon, was willing to believe the craft was extraterrestrial. That gave him reason to be more open to the idea of the abduction. "The dream theory has not eliminated all doubt from my mind as I had hoped it would," he wrote. "Unlike most UFO 'contact' claims, the Hill case is particularly hard to explain because the first encounter appears to be true, and if the first encounter took place, then I feel we cannot positively rule out the possibility, however remote, that the second encounter did in fact occur. Dr. Simon admits he cannot prove the dream hypothesis is correct but, on the other hand, spaceship abduction cannot be proven either."

Simon and Webb may have finished their work, but the Hill story was too big to end there. Although the couple insisted that their case remain confidential, it was leaked to the *Boston Traveler* in 1965 and captured the public's imagination. After all, in the nearly twenty years since UFO mania began, people had never heard a tale like this one. If they were hungry for a next chapter, they got one in 1966, thanks to an Ohio schoolteacher and amateur astronomer named Marjorie Fish. A drawing of Betty's star map reproduced in Fuller's book left her wondering if she could test its accuracy. This was no small task. But three years later she got a little help after new astronomical data offered positions for about a thousand stars within seventy-two light-years of the sun. Using this data, Fish built a model based on Betty's map that seemed to align with the Zeta Reticuli system—a nearly 230-trillion-mile trek from earth. Her work attracted the attention of Stanton Friedman, who persuaded *Astronomy* magazine's editor, Terence Dickinson, to publish her findings in 1974.

The article sent scientists swirling over the legitimacy of Betty's drawing from an alien spacecraft recalled under hypnosis. Carl Sagan, for one, wasn't convinced. Though he'd met the Hills years earlier and found them perfectly earnest and sincere, in 1979 he wrote, "A close examination shows it to be not much better than the 'star map' which would be produced if you took an old-fashioned quill pen and splattered a few blank pages with ink spots."

Dickinson, however, didn't waver. "The fact that all of the stars did not fall into place until the 1969 catalog positions were published rules out a hoax," he wrote in 1980. "No one on Earth back in 1961 knew where some of those stars would appear on such a map. Coincidence, however, cannot be totally rejected, as unlikely as it might seem. And, given that possibility, we can only say the Zeta Reticuli star map is provocative evidence—not proof—that extraterrestrial intelligence is visiting Earth in the twentieth century."

The magazine's staff leaned more toward Sagan's side. In the years that followed, the subject within the publication's halls was referred to as "The Zeta Ridiculi Incident." Even Fish apparently changed her mind. According to her 2013 obituary, she eventually found that newer data showed the stars were too close together to support life and, "as a true skeptic," stated that she "now felt that the correlation was unlikely."

Whether or not aliens captured the Hills, their story undeniably captured America's attention. By 1965 they were lecturing on UFOs and attracting hundreds of attendees. That year they were even invited to the inauguration of President Lyndon B. Johnson. Soon after, Barney shared his story on an episode of *To Tell the Truth*, and in 1975, their experience was adapted into a television movie, *The UFO Incident*, starring Estelle Parsons and James Earl Jones (just before he landed another role in a galaxy far, far away as the voice of Darth Vader).

As much as the Hills' case penetrated pop culture, it's worth asking if it was influenced by pop culture as well. Sure, sci-fi movies about aliens were a dime a dozen in the decade preceding the couple's abduction, but as writer Martin Kottmeyer first noted in 1990, Barney's description and sketch were provided during a hypnosis session on February 22, 1964, which happened to be twelve days after ABC aired an episode of *The Outer Limits* called "The Bellero Shield," featuring an alien that finds its way into a scientist's laboratory. The creature has wraparound eyes and a flat nose—eerily similar to the creatures Barney described. There were other similarities, too, in the dialogue. The scientist's wife asks the alien if it can read her mind. "No, I cannot read your mind. I cannot even understand your language. I analyze your eyes. In all the universes, in all the unities beyond all the universes, all who have eyes have eyes that speak. And all speak the same language.... I learn each word just before I speak it. Your eyes teach me."

As Barney recalled the occupants of the UFO before they led him aboard their spacecraft, he told Simon, "They won't talk to me. Only the eyes are talking to me. I—I—I—I don't understand that. Oh—the eyes don't have a body. They're just eyes . . ."

Cue the *Twilight Zone* theme (since no one remembers the *Outer Limits* theme).

"The discovery of this pseudomemory will not shock hypnosis experts," Kottmeyer wrote. "They have long been aware of the danger

Betty and Barney Hill holding a copy of John G. Fuller's 1966 book chronicling their experience, *The Interrupted Journey*.

Barney Hill was played by James Earl Jones in 1975's *The UFO Incident*.

of confabulation in regression work. There was no reason to expect *The Interrupted Journey*'s narrative to be immune from such contamination."

Betty later claimed neither she nor Barney had ever heard of the show. Even if he had, she added that he worked nights and would not have been home to watch it.

As the years went on, Betty became a frequent speaker at UFO conventions and claimed to have continued seeing flying saucers. She remained a staunch believer until her last day on earth in 2004. Barney, sadly, had passed away decades earlier in 1969 after suffering a massive cerebral hemorrhage at just forty-six years old.

Their niece, Kathleen Marden, who was a young teenager at the time of the alleged abduction, has continued to research the case. Among her findings are inconsistencies with Betty's notes about her dreams and her full hypnosis transcription, leading Marden to believe Simon's dream explanation doesn't sufficiently explain the incident.

She's also done extensive testing on Betty's dress. After returning home, Betty placed the torn garment in the closet and left it untouched for three years. In 1964, after finally removing it, she discovered that it was coated with a strange pink powdery substance and several stains. Unfortunately, according to Marden's account of the story in her book, *Captured!*, Betty took the dress outside to her clothesline and the pink powder blew away, perhaps back into the cosmos from which it came. Marden sent swatches of the garment to several chemical analysts, who determined the pink stains were caused by an unusual biological substance that did not originate from Betty, and only some of which may have originated from Barney. "Betty's torn dress has highly anomalous laboratory findings that point to the accuracy of Betty's statements," Marden said in an email to me.

As for Barney, Marden scoffs at the idea that he was suggestible. "That's totally false," she told attendees at the 2022 MUFON International Symposium. "I was a witness to that over and over again, where he said, 'Betty, don't be ridiculous!' He had a mind of his own."

ROBERT SALAS:
FROM THE AIR FORCE TO THE SPACE CRAFT

I met retired air force captain Robert Salas after his talk at the National Press Club in October 2021 about the 1967 incident at Malmstrom Air Force Base (see page 71). As we stepped away from the crowd of attendees and sat down to discuss his experience, I asked if he'd had other UFO-related encounters since then. Sure enough, he had. One such example occurred in 1985, nearly twenty years after Malmstrom, while he was living in California's Manhattan Beach and thriving in a new career in real estate.

Married with two small children, Salas was enjoying a normal life. And then the aliens returned. This time, they weren't after missiles or trying to send a warning about our possible self-destruction. No, this time it seemed they were solely focused on collecting sperm in the middle of the night. Salas claims that a strange blue light coming from his living room stirred him from his sleep, so he woke up his wife and told her he was going to investigate. As he explained to me, here's what happened next:

As I try to get out of bed I'm paralyzed. I can't move. And I remember, this was not a dream. I remember struggling, struggling to get any momentum back. Finally, exhausted, I see this figure in the doorway of the bedroom with a hood on. I don't recall the appearance of the face, at least at this point I don't recall. It had a hood on. Then I remember sensing there were small children in the room. They seemed like small children to me. They weren't children, but they were small.

Next thing I know I'm being lifted off the bed horizontally and escorted toward the bedroom window, which I'd locked the night before. I thought to myself, "These children don't know how to unlatch that." They took me right through the window. I know that sounds ridiculous, but this is what I recalled through hypnosis—hypnotic regression. Took me right through the window.

Next thing I know I'm on a steel bed in the belly of an aircraft. I'm being shown a needle. A very large needle. It was being held by fingers, they placed it in front of my eyes, they wanted me to see it. They were telling me, telepathically, they were going to insert this into my groin area. They didn't tell me why, but said it wouldn't hurt. But they're going to insert it down there. But when they started that, it hurt like hell. So, that's why this was not a dream. I remember that pain, it was excruciating. When I communicated that to them the pain stopped almost immediately. The pain just stopped. Pain gone.

After that, I was seated on a bench that was kind of built in, circular interior. They sat me down there. Two of those small children on either side of me. Then they took me to another cubicle. And this guy, swear to God, had a white smock on, a white kind of uniform on, he turned me around and he poked his fingers down my spine. That's all I remember of that. Then they escorted me through this curved tunnel to a bright light, then I was back in my bed.

The next morning, like Betty and Barney Hill, Salas had no memory of the event. Neither did his wife. Twenty-two years later, a speaker at a UFO conference jogged their memory when describing a personal abduction experience that began with a similar blue glow illuminating a room.

"I turn to my wife who was sitting next to me and said, 'Do you remember a blue light in the bedroom, way back long ago?'" Salas recalled. "And she looked at me and said, 'Yes, I do!' So that also convinced me this was not a dream. This really happened, because she remembered. My wife doesn't lie."

It was at that point that he began hypnotherapy sessions to recover his memories. Over the course of five years with multiple hypnotherapists he consistently produced the same story.

THE SEVENTEENTH-CENTURY ABDUCTION OF ANNE JEFFERIES

Betty and Barney Hill may have been the earliest documented American case of an alien abduction, but if extraterrestrials have been visiting us humans throughout our existence, are there examples of much earlier abductions that were simply reported through the terminology, beliefs, and folklore of the time? As God and angels in Biblical times, and demons and fairies in the Renaissance? As UFO researcher and scientist Jacques Vallée proposed in his 1969 book *Passport to Magonia* and other writings, the commonality between these types of beings, along with ghosts, cryptids, and other unusual sightings throughout the human experience, could be evidence of another reality or dimension existing alongside the one we live in.

Take the story of Anne Jefferies, for example, who was plucked from her garden in Cornwall, England, in 1645 by beings that she called fairies.

"I was, one day, knitting of stockings in the arbour in the garden, and there came over the garden-hedge, of a sudden, *six small people*, all in green clothes, which put me into such a great fright, that was the cause of this my great sickness," she said, according to an account published in 1732.

Another telling of her story adds that these little green men or women whisked her off to "some distant place, flying through the air," to a beautiful land with temples and palaces made of gold and silver. Jefferies wished to stay in this utopia forever but was soon "whirled through space" and found herself back in the garden surrounded by a small crowd who'd been witnessing her suffering from convulsions.

The fairies continued to visit Jefferies over the next year, though no one else around her saw them. "They were just gone out of the window!" she'd often cry to her caretakers. "It was really so, although you thought me light-headed."

These strange beings offered her food (the bread was reportedly *delicious*) and the power to heal the sick. Despite the fairies' seemingly good nature, once word got out the church decided the little creatures were demons and Anne was briefly imprisoned as a witch. Many ufologists believe that Jefferies' experience represents an early alien abduction and that these fairies in green clothes were in fact little green men who took her on a brief tour of their home planet.

Is Hypnotic Regression Reliable?

Ever since the Betty and Barney Hill case, aliens have seemingly been having a field day abducting people. By 1992, the front page of the *Wall Street Journal* reported that 3.7 million Americans may have been abducted. These tales are frequently recovered through sessions of hypnotic regression. Therapists put their subjects in a trance and guide them back through time to explore details of experiences not in the conscious mind. The process often results in the recall of extraordinary information that is, without question, rather unbelievable. How reliable this recovered information is may depend on how the hypnotherapist conducts the session.

"If the hypnotherapist isn't using impeccable language skills, you can create false memories," Holly Holmes-Meredith, a doctor of ministry and a marriage and family therapist who's worked with more than a dozen abductees, explained to me. She noted that in some cases the experiences retrieved could be screen memories—or, in other words, false memories that mask a true traumatic childhood event.

"Maybe they were sexually abused, and they confabulate through their psyche that it was an alien because it's a lot a lot easier to handle that than it is their father sexually abused them," Holmes-Meredith said.

She also believes it's possible that memories from past lives are bleeding through. "Maybe they think they were abducted in this lifetime, and it didn't happen this lifetime," she says, or perhaps they were "an alien themselves in a previous lifetime." Memories, it seems, can take on many forms. Add to that the possibility that their memories are intertwined with all the information that we're exposed to on a daily basis, from the shows we watch to the news we read to the conversations we have with others. Some might argue that the combination of it all manifests as the abduction stories that regression brings forth. Others might say that's exactly what the aliens are counting on people to think.

In the late 1980s, Robert Baker, a psychology professor at the University of Kentucky, proposed that abductees are simply victims of "fantasy-prone" personalities. Not crazy or neurotic, just "a little different than the rest of us." As such, he didn't believe regressions could uncover real experiences.

"There's currently no way even the most sophisticated hypnotist can tell the difference between a memory that is real and one that's created," Baker said. "If a person is hypnotized and highly suggestible, and false information is implanted in his mind, it may get embedded even more strongly."

Fantasy prone, suggestible, or perhaps even perfectly honest, let's meet a few other abductees, starting with two fishermen who got caught: Charlie Hickson and Calvin Parker.

The Fishermen Who Got Caught: The Pascagoula Incident

On the evening of October 11, 1973, two shipyard workers named Charlie Hickson and Calvin Parker were hoping to reel in a few keepers from Mississippi's Pascagoula River when the tables were unexpectedly and drastically turned. Hickson and Parker heard a loud noise, then spotted a "fish-shaped" spacecraft emitting a bluish haze approaching them. Before they knew it, a trio of crab-clawed aliens snatched them right off the pier.

"Three things came out of [the spacecraft]—and they didn't touch the ground—just floating, you know, slowly, a couple of feet off the ground," Hickson told officers at Keesler Air Force Base in Biloxi the next day, where they were checked for radiation exposure. (The tests came back negative.)

"I was paralyzed right there," Parker added. "You know, just like if you walk outside and step on a rattlesnake. Think how you feel. That is just how I felt. I would rather it had been a rattlesnake."

Venomous rattlesnakes would've been a welcome surprise compared to the three "things" that emerged from the craft and seized the two fishermen. In addition to clawlike hands, the creatures were described as having wrinkly reddish skin, pointed ears, eye slits, sharp noses, and holes below their noses. Aboard the UFO, the aliens placed the men on a glass examination table and began a thorough study of

Hickson and Parker using a strange machine they described as resembling a giant eye. "It went all over my body," Hickson said. "Up and down."

Fortunately, the extraterrestrials practiced their own version of catch and release when they apparently had enough of whatever they needed. Following the ordeal, the Jackson County sheriff said the two abductees were "scared to death and shaking all over" while reporting the incident. A polygraph determined they were not lying about the experience. Lie detector tests aren't infallible and there's no technology that's 100 percent accurate, but when multiple people produce similar results on the same questions, the credibility increases.

Dr. J. Allen Hynek, along with Dr. James Harder, a professor from the University of California and member of the Aerial Phenomena Research Organization (APRO), further investigated the case with their own questioning and hypnosis session. In Hickson and Parker's defense, Hynek said, "They're not crackpots. There was definitely something here that was not terrestrial of this earth." Harder agreed, and later told Hickson, "Charlie, if anyone doesn't believe you and Calvin, they are a damn fool, and you may quote me on any news media in the country."

Decades later, there are those who continue to believe Hickson and Parker experienced something truly unusual. UFO researcher Ray Stanford is one of them. The director of Project Starlight International, who has been using cameras and electronic instruments to capture meaningful data on the phenomenon since 1954, met with Hickson extensively following the event and found his story to be credible. "I would bet my life on it," Stanford told me during a phone discussion. "I've interviewed many, many people who make claims about UFOs. Many sincere, many of them absolutely liars. But I have never encountered anybody that impressed me as being so forthright, and genuine and absolutely sincere, as Charlie Hickson. Now that's a personal interpretation, of course, by me, but I have a lot of experience."

Skeptics, however, believe Hickson may have imagined the whole thing during a hypnagogic "waking dream state," and that Parker, who claimed to have passed out at the start of the alleged experience, may have simply absorbed what Hickson told him. Or maybe they did expe-

CAPTURED

Last October at Pascagoula, Mississippi, Charles Hickson and Calvin Parker were paralyzed, while Hickson was *floated aboard a UFO* and examined. A lie-detector test vindicated the bizzare account.

HEAR CHARLES HICKSON TELL OF HIS TERRIFYING EXPERIENCE ABOARD A UFO!

8 P.M. Thursday, September 26
Town Hall in Hancock Center
Admission: $2.50   Students: $1.50

UFO researcher Ray Stanford, who created this flyer, had extensive contact with Charles Hickson after the Pascagoula incident and helped him share his story with the public.

rience something truly unusual—and entirely terrestrial.

Writer and ufologist Nick Redfern thinks they may have caught a whiff of a powerful hallucinogenic blown over from nearby Horn Island. Following World War II, this long strip of land was considered as a possible location for testing chemical and biological warfare—the types of mind-altering drugs used in the MKUltra program.[†] Redfern points out that the plan was cancelled since winds could carry aerosol-based hallucinogens to populated areas. Still, secret testing may have continued into the early 1970s.

"Might the 'UFO' actually have been a helicopter and not a UFO?" Redfern asks in an article on MysteriousUniverse.org. "Could the references to the aliens having mask-like faces, and clawed hands, actually have down-to-earth explanations: full-body protection suits, helmets, and thick gloves, worn by the abductors and seen by two men rendered into states of mind in which hallucinations were running wild?"

Budd Hopkins and the World's First Abductee Support Group

Budd Hopkins wasn't an abductee, but one might think he would've been an excellent candidate—an impressive trophy to return to a home planet with. Aside from being a ufologist, he was an accomplished Abstract Expressionist painter and sculptor who made his name in the 1960s New York art circle that included Mark Rothko, Franz Kline, and others. Hopkins's work appeared in such distinguished institutions as the Metropolitan Museum of Art, the Museum of Modern Art in New York, and the British Museum.

Hopkins's interest in UFOs began after he personally witnessed a flying saucer in 1964 at Cape Cod. He, along with his first wife and a friend, were en route to a party when they spotted what he described as a "darkish, elliptical object" that was about "two car-lengths long"

---

† The CIA's Project MKUltra experimented with LSD and other psychoactive drugs on humans to develop interrogation techniques using brainwashing and psychological torture. Watch your step as you make your way down this rabbit hole.

Portrait of Budd Hopkins at his New York City art studio, taken in the summer of 2010 by Peter Robbins.

sitting eerily still in the sky as the wind blew clouds past it. Just as he stopped the car so they could step out and watch, it took off and disappeared into the night sky. When they shared their story at the party later that night, others claimed to have seen a similar object. Confused and curious, Hopkins became hooked on UFOs.

He began devouring books on the subject, including Fuller's *The Interrupted Journey* about Betty and Barney Hill. "Who can believe such foolishness?" the artist asked himself. But as he read voraciously and saw that even scientists generally accepted the existence of extraterrestrial intelligence, that "foolishness" became believable. (As we'll see in Chapter 4, a notable astronomer had announced thousands of possible intergalactic intelligent civilizations just a few years earlier.)

"By the time the Pascagoula abduction occurred in 1973, I was able to accept the idea of 'human sample-taking' as quite plausible, within the context of the thousands of worldwide UFO sightings," Hopkins wrote in *Missing Time*, his book profiling abduction cases. "The crucial reason for my ability to accept these accounts as true was the central issue: if these events did not occur as reported by the witnesses, then what caused their recollections?" He could find no other satisfying answer.

As fascinated as Hopkins had become by the early seventies, he didn't fully dive into the world of UFOs until November 1975, when a routine trip to the liquor store across the street from his Chelsea art studio led him on what would be become the first of many investigations. George O'Barksi, the shop's quiet seventy-two-year-old proprietor, had been selling Hopkins wine for years. But during that night's visit, O'Barski was visibly troubled from arthritic pain and muttered about disgruntlement with the world. He went on to tell his longtime customer that a strange thing had happened to him as he was driving home earlier in the year—something came "down out of the sky" and terrified him. Naturally, Hopkins had to hear more. *What* came down from the sky?

O'Barski assumed his story was too bizarre to be believed and hesitated to continue. But Hopkins convinced him otherwise. It all began in January, the wine seller explained, while he was driving to his home in North Bergen, New Jersey, just across the Hudson River, and static suddenly overtook his car radio. As he attempted to adjust the dial, something passed directly overhead, veered off to the left, and landed in a field behind an apartment complex. O'Barski followed slowly. Keeping his distance, he witnessed a saucer-shaped craft, about thirty feet long, with a group of small humanoid figures descending from a ladderlike plank. Each appeared to be roughly three and a half feet tall. Between their diminutive size and their one-piece hoodies, O'Barski likened them to "kids in snowsuits." However, there was no snow on that unusually warm January night. The little visitors scooped up samples of dirt, put them in containers, then climbed back into the spaceship and shot off toward the stars.

"I've been held up in the store lots of times by men with pistols and knives, and I've been plenty scared, but nothing like this, ever," O'Barski told Hopkins.

The liquor store owner's son traveled to the site the day after O'Barski's sighting and, similar to the Socorro case, found holes in the ground from what appeared to be the landing gear. By the time Hopkins heard the story in November and began to investigate, the impressions had been filled in with soil—but grass no longer grew in those specific spots. A doorman from the apartment complex came forward as another witness who shared O'Barski's fear and confirmed his story.

This was Hopkins's first big case—and he wasn't about to keep it to himself. He pitched and sold an article to New York's *Village Voice*, and soon began hearing from others who'd experienced not just sightings but abductions. The overwhelming response eventually led him to start the first known alien abductee support group, with sessions of eight to twelve people talking about their encounters in the privacy of his living room. Peter Robbins, who served as Hopkins's assistant in the group, believes the meetings were successful because both men truly cared and created a unique environment of mutual respect. The other key ingredient, according to Robbins, was "an absolute understanding that whatever goes on and is said in that room goes no further." Any guests to the group had to be agreed upon unanimously.

Among the members was Linda "Cortile" (a name Hopkins gave her to protect her identity), a mother of two who claimed to have been abducted at 3:15 a.m. on November 30, 1989, from her twelfth-floor Manhattan apartment. Several witnesses observed her float right outside her window in her nightgown, accompanied by three short humanoid beings within a blue beam of light. They entered a glowing UFO hovering in the sky and took off toward the Brooklyn Bridge. Two of the helpless onlookers were New York City police officers parked under the FDR Drive, there to provide added security for UN Secretary-General Javier Pérez de Cuéllar, who also allegedly witnessed the event.

As Hopkins listened to hundreds of stories and discussed abductees' cases, he uncovered an undeniable pattern. Like the Hills' experience, these occurrences tended to happen at night and involve a flash of light, an empty road (Cortile being an exception), elevation into a spacecraft, and chunks of unexplainable missing time. Under hypnosis, that missing time was typically filled with big-eyed and bigger-headed grayish aliens on a mission to poke, probe, and pilfer eggs and sperm.

Robbins found that the subjects overwhelmingly "seemed sincere and rarely seemed to have an ulterior motive." Only on rare occasions did he and Hopkins catch people lying. These attention seekers typically fantasized that their tale would go from Hopkins's ears to Hollywood's dollars. "Otherwise, I honestly don't remember any fakes," Robbins told me. "I remember a lot of interesting people."

Hopkins's belief in their sincerity and the results of hypnosis—which he began conducting himself after eight years of watching professionals—led him to believe the visitors were trying to crossbreed with humans in hopes of saving their own declining race. Despite his clout as an artist, his ideas were not easily accepted by the general public or by the scientific community. At the beginning of 1990, however, he found support from an unexpected advocate at one of academia's most prestigious institutions: Dr. John E. Mack, head of the department of psychiatry at Harvard Medical School.

Mack met Hopkins through a colleague who convinced the professor to sit in on an abductee support session. Mack found himself utterly drawn in. He, too, saw seemingly normal people sharing incredible stories, with equally incredible similarities.

"What the abduction phenomenon has led me (I would now say inevitably) to see is that we participate in a universe or universes that are filled with intelligences from which we have cut ourselves off, having lost the senses by which we might know them," Mack wrote in the introduction to his 1994 book, *Abduction*. Like Hopkins, Mack eventually began conducting hypnotic regression sessions with people who'd had alien encounters.

During his robust studies he interviewed more than two hundred self-proclaimed abductees. As a distinguished professor and Pulitzer Prize winner devoting time to such a taboo subject, he faced not only ridicule but also an investigation by a committee of his Harvard peers. Yet he didn't let any of it stop him. Mack just wanted answers.

"No one has been able to come up with a counter-formulation that explains what's going on," the professor said in 1992 in regard to alien encounters. "But if people can't be convinced that this is real, that's okay. All I want is for people to be convinced that there's something going on here that is not explainable."

The Probing of Whitley Strieber: An Author Gets the Story of a Lifetime

Of all those who sought guidance from Hopkins, perhaps the most well-known was *Communion* author Whitley Strieber. In the 1987 book, he claimed that "nonhuman beings" abducted him from his cabin in the woods of New York's Hudson Valley in 1985 on the day after Christmas. Strieber's best seller recounted the events and his experiences with hypnosis in his quest to understand what had happened to him. Strieber had previously written science fiction novels (take what you will from that).

Several of his captors were about three and a half feet tall with "two dark holes for eyes and a black down-turning line of a mouth"; he described another as being "about five feet tall, very slender and delicate, with extremely prominent and mesmerizing black slanted eyes" and "an almost vestigial mouth and nose."

According to Strieber's account, the beings took him from his home and whisked him up over the trees and into the sky, where he suddenly found himself in a round room. More specifically, it appeared to be an operating room.

"The next thing I knew I was being shown an enormous and extremely ugly object, gray and scaly, with a sort of network of wires on the end. It was at least a foot long, narrow, and triangular in structure. They inserted this thing into my rectum. It seemed to swarm into me as if it had a life of its own. Apparently its purpose was to take samples, possibly of fecal matter, but at the time I had the impression that I was being raped, and for the first time I felt anger."

Strieber goes on to discuss psychological tests he took in the aftermath to check his sanity, as well as a neurological examination and a lie detector test. He passed them all; there were no anomalies to suggest some sort of natural or alien-imposed brain malfunction. Hypnotic regression helped unearth the details of his abduction from his mind. The extracted story was hard to swallow, even for him. In a 1987 interview with a reporter following the release of *Communion*, Strieber claimed to have never even believed in UFOs before being swept up into one.

"I would have laughed in the face of anybody who claimed contact," he said. "But now I know how some people must have suffered. I have shared their sensations. I understand that they have been reluctant to come forward because they were frightened not only of what happened to them, but of other people, their friends and even close relatives laughing at them and dismissing it all as stupid nonsense."

Hypnotherapist to Thousands: Barbara Lamb

John E. Mack suffered an untimely death in 2004, and Budd Hopkins passed away at the age of eighty in 2011, but others have continued performing regression therapy to help people who believe they've been abducted. Barbara Lamb, a psychotherapist, hypnotherapist, and regression therapist based in San Diego, California, has helped more than two thousand individuals since 1991 to fill in missing time and relive their abduction experiences.

"The wonderful thing about regression is that even if somebody knows, or suspects, that they may have had this kind of experience, the subconscious part of our minds has recorded everything," Lamb explained to me in a phone interview. Once she begins the hypnotic regression, she claims she's able to access those recordings and recover the entire experience.

Lamb's clients describe experiences consistent with those of Robert Salas, Whitley Strieber, and the subjects seen by Hopkins and Mack—from the flash of light to levitation to finding themselves aboard a spacecraft. Many also wake up with unusual bruises, straight line cuts, or even pinprick marks in the shape of a square, a triangle, or a perfect ring.

"There are a lot of markings that people find on their back or someplace where they could not have even reached, you know, to put the markings there themselves. And they know that nobody during the night came and stuck them with pins or scooped out skin or did anything—they would've awakened," Lamb said. "So a lot of people will have those markings. And they'll live with them for years. And wonder about them."

One of her subjects even had a small lump in his arm that was about the size of a BB, which eventually led him to wonder if it was an alien implant. When people with these physical anomalies finally decide to work with Lamb, they often uncover what appear to be extraterrestrial experiences. But their recovered experiences don't always involve invasive medical exams. In fact, Lamb claims that the encounters can be surprisingly positive.

"Some people come back from this experience and feel that they've learned something of value, or something that maybe changes their life for the better," the therapist said. "They had a very strong impression that they needed to be doing some sort of healing, or maybe some sort of spiritual work with people." That said, she's seen her share of people who've been poked and prodded on the exam table by what she calls "self-serving" aliens: "The little gray beings seem to be very, very interested in learning about our bodies."

Lamb's clients come from all walks of life, including artists, musicians, and engineers. Some of them, she believes, are taken because their talents pique the extraterrestrials' curiosity. In other instances, the aliens appear to be tracking genetics through a family line or selecting people as part of a hybridization project to salvage a dying race—as Hopkins had suggested.

Lamb arrived at this conclusion after working with numerous women who mysteriously became pregnant, then just as mysteriously lost the pregnancy months later. Some of them were unmarried and hadn't had a sexual partner in a long time—at least, not a terrestrial one. As Lamb explained, aliens will add their genetics to an embryo and implant it in a woman. Once removed, it's "put into a tank of special fluid on the spaceship and is gestated for the full gestation period."

No mother wants to lose her child, but according to Lamb some women grow proud of their hybrid babies. "They're kind of glad that they're contributing in this particular way. Some of them really get to know the hybrid children by being taken on the spaceship."

As much as these mothers might like to bring their half-alien kids home, it's simply not safe. Hybrids have been described as having square heads with big eyes or oversized heads atop thin bodies. Such kids would likely endure incessant teasing at school and a nonstop media frenzy, but the real concern is the one that killed the Martians in *The War of the Worlds*: bacteria. "They wouldn't survive here," Lamb explained.

Kim Carlsberg, *Baywatch*'s Mother of Hybrids

Not only do some mothers get to visit their hybrid children aboard spaceships, as Barbara Lamb claims, but in the case of Kim Carlsberg, a meeting happened right at her home. I learned this after making contact with her at the 2022 MUFON International Symposium.

She was selling a book at one of the vendor tables, *The Art of Close Encounters*, which led me to ask if she'd had one herself. Carlsberg didn't hesitate to tell me she'd had many—often during her time working as a camerawoman for *Baywatch*. Her first experience was in 1988 at her beach house in Malibu, California, where she saw a "huge" glowing orb over the horizon "too low to be a star and too high to be a boat."

AFRAID OF BEING ABDUCTED BY ALIENS? THERE'S INSURANCE FOR THAT.

If you're concerned that someday a beam of light may pull you into a spacecraft and turn you into the next Betty or Barney Hill or Whitley Strieber, you can get insurance to cover yourself.

The St. Lawrence Agency in Altamonte Springs, Florida, has been selling alien abduction policies since 1987. Its motto: "Beam me up, I'm covered."

Lifetime coverage costs just $19.95 with a $10 million policy—paid in increments of $1 a year over 10 million years. However, the policy includes double indemnity coverage if the alien wants conjugal visits or refers to the abductee as a "nutritional food source."

The policy's creator, Mike St. Lawrence, came up with the idea after listening to a Larry King interview with *Communion* author Whitley Strieber. He decided to have fun with the UFO craze and wrote the policy.

"I started selling them right away," St. Lawrence told me during one of our several conversations about his humorous insurance endeavor. "It happened to be during the Christmas season. It's a unique gift. Most people don't buy it for themselves—they buy it for someone else and make themselves the beneficiary."

In fact, St. Lawrence won't even sell the policy unless the buyer understands it's a joke. In the thirty-six years he's been in business, he's

sold more than 12,000 policies and only refunded one elderly man who apparently missed the humor.

"He didn't really read it till ten years later and realized it wasn't what he thought it was," St. Lawrence said. "He got his twenty bucks back."

Two customers, however, have submitted claims and had them approved. In 1990, a New York policyholder believed that an alien abducted him and left an implant in his body. According to St. Lawrence, an MIT professor analyzed the implant material and determined it was not from this planet. "I sent him a dollar a year for eight or nine years and then lost track of him, which suggests he may have been abducted again."

The other claimant sent in his form with a Polaroid from the inside of the UFO he supposedly had been aboard. "You couldn't see much, but he indicated 'This side up' in the margin," St. Lawrence said. Amused, he decided to approve the payout. A check for $1 is sent each year on April 1.

While the insurance policy began as a gag, recent UFO-related events like the navy "Tic Tac" video (see Chapter 5) have led St. Lawrence to believe something is indeed happening out there.

"Reality is changing right in front of us, is the way I look at it," he said.

It doesn't mean he's worried about having

to pay out more policies, but he's realizing that many of the people he's spoken to over the years may have actually experienced something. And whatever that something may have been, the policy has helped them deal with it.

"They have this thing going on," he said. "And they like the idea that I have this product that kind of takes the edge out of it. So they can talk to their friends about what's going on with them. It's an icebreaker."

Abducted or not, for those policyholders the laugh might be worth far more than a $1-a-year payout.

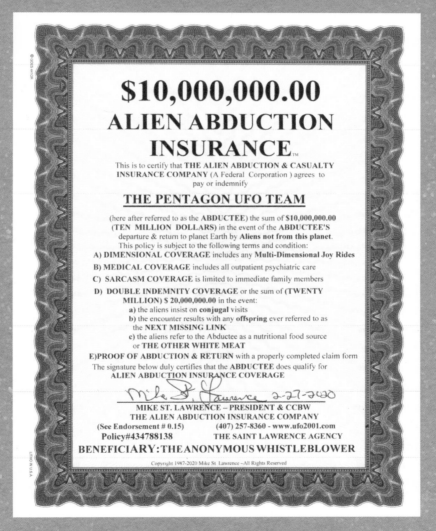

$10,000,000.00

ALIEN ABDUCTION INSURANCE™

This is to certify that **THE ALIEN ABDUCTION & CASUALTY INSURANCE COMPANY** (A Federal Corporation) agrees to pay or indemnify

THE PENTAGON UFO TEAM

(here after referred to as the **ABDUCTEE**) the sum of **$10,000,000.00** (**TEN MILLION DOLLARS**) in the event of the **ABDUCTEE'S** departure & return to planet Earth by **Aliens not from this planet**. This policy is subject to the following terms and condition:

A) **DIMENSIONAL COVERAGE** includes any **Multi-Dimensional Joy Rides**

B) **MEDICAL COVERAGE** includes all outpatient psychiatric care

C) **SARCASM COVERAGE** is limited to immediate family members

D) **DOUBLE INDEMNITY COVERAGE** or the sum of (**TWENTY MILLION) $ 20,000,000.00** in the event:
    a) the aliens insist on **conjugal** visits
    b) the encounter results with any **offspring** ever referred to as the **NEXT MISSING LINK**
    c) the aliens refer to the Abductee as a nutritional food source or **THE OTHER WHITE MEAT**

E) **PROOF OF ABDUCTION & RETURN** with a properly completed claim form
The signature below duly certifies that the **ABDUCTEE** does qualify for **ALIEN ABDUCTION INSURANCE COVERAGE**

Mike St. Lawrence 2-27-2020
MIKE ST. LAWRENCE – PRESIDENT & CCBW
THE ALIEN ABDUCTION INSURANCE COMPANY
(See Endorsement # 0.15)   (407) 257-8360 - www.ufo2001.com
Policy#434788138   **THE SAINT LAWRENCE AGENCY**
BENEFICIARY: THE ANONYMOUS WHISTLEBLOWER

Copyright 1987-2020 Mike St Lawrence –All Rights Reserved

The St. Lawrence Agency sells insurance policies to cover alien abduction. This policy was created in honor of the Pentagon's recent UFO studies.

As it moved along, Carlsberg claimed it hovered over Johnny Carson's house at the furthest point in Malibu, then in an instant appeared just feet from her window. "I could see two entities staring at me through this window and there was no kind of communication," she said. "It just hovered and looked at me. And so after a while it just decided to take off, and it went straight up."

She got back to work and thought little more of it until a week later when she woke up and found herself naked and paralyzed in what seemed to be an elevator. Several Grays then pushed her into a large round room with "a hundred little tables filled with human beings." Next, Carlsberg said, she was anesthetized and eventually awoke on a table in a small dark room where two beings monitored her, including a woman who she would later realize was a hybrid.

"She said to me, telepathically, 'Stop being such a big baby, this will be over with soon enough.' The next thing I know, I'm back in my bed. And that was the beginning. Like, seriously, I was taken probably three times a week for eight years." She claimed this included contact with seven different species. After each abduction, Carlsberg alleges that the military found her and brought her to underground bases in search of details. The experiences only stopped when her friend Darryl Anka (Paul Anka's cousin) intervened. Anka (Darryl, not Paul) claimed to have been channeling an alien entity called Bashar for decades. Sitting with Carlsberg at her house in Malibu, he went into a trance to summon the being.

"All of a sudden this energy started going down Darryl's crown chakra into his body, down his arms and his legs, and where our knees were touching, I started vibrating for ten minutes," Carlsberg explained. Anka was vibrating too, as Bashar came through him and gave Carlsberg a preventative mantra to repeat every night. In addition, Anka told her that her "frequency was changed." This, he claimed, thwarted the extraterrestrials' ability to locate her.

During the eight-year experience, Carlsbeg says she mothered many hybrid children who exist in another dimension. One of her sons visited her home in Sedona, Arizona, in a UFO she described as a huge iron shape, filled with lights spanning "every color of the rainbow." So where was this camerawoman's camera? Carlsberg says her profes-

Illustration of an alien cradling its hybrid child by Christine "Kesara" Dennett.

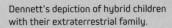

Dennett's depiction of hybrid children with their extraterrestrial family.

sional equipment stays locked in a closet, and though she wanted a photo, her attempt to retrieve a camera and lens was taking too long. By the time she ran back to her living room emptyhanded, her son was seated on the sofa. He appeared human and communicated telepathically during their half-hour visit. "He said to me, 'Every moment of every day around every corner is a new opportunity to be of service.' And I was like, wow, that was pretty cool. Pretty profound for a little hybrid guy."

So did all of these abductions affect her work? The *Baywatch* cast was well aware of Carlsberg's experiences, and David Hasselhoff would ask her about them. Her stories inspired the 1993 episode "Strangers Among Us" which ends—spoiler alert—with an abduction.

Are Aliens Just Sleep Paralysis Demons?

If the memories retrieved through hypnotic regression can't be accepted as proof of actual occurrences, could something else be going on? In 2019, a team of scientists from the Phase Research Center in Moscow wanted to find out. They looked for an explanation that exists not in the realm of outer space, but rather in the realm of sleep— where many stories of abductions originate.

"When sleep paralysis occurs, unpleasant and incomprehensible hallucinations often also occur," the researchers explained in the *International Journal of Dream Research*. "Therefore, people who experience sleep paralysis might seek out nonmedical explanations, including those that tap into supernatural beliefs."

The team experimented with 152 volunteers by having them fall into a state of lucid dreaming, meaning a dream state in which the person retains consciousness and a degree of control. Subjects were asked to summon alien and UFO encounters and then report what they experienced. People often find that whatever the mind creates during lucid dreaming feels quite real. Of the group, 75 percent of them succeeded in encountering aliens. One volunteer described two blue creatures, one on each side of him:

> Each one had one huge oval eye, arranged vertically. They had no
> limbs; they were only pulsating bodies that levitated 5 cm above the
> floor. Both aliens gazed at me as they kept making sounds, which I
> heard even outside the door. After 8–10 seconds, a lot of thin tentacles
> reached me from the body of one of them. It was very creepy.

Aliens reminiscent of the kinds found in sci-fi movies and books, like these blue tentacled blobs, were common. Some spoke with the extraterrestrials, had physical encounters with them, or both, and a few even flew on a spaceship.

"It appears that bedtime alien and UFO encounters (as well as alien abductions) can be emulated based on one's will and deliberate actions," the researchers' report states. So while they recognize that not all abductees are necessarily lucid dreamers on a mission, their results do show that "ordinary people might spontaneously enter phase states, unintentionally have an alien or UFO encounter, and confuse it with reality.... Extraterrestrial civilizations, if they exist, better escape seeing us from bedrooms, for not being confused with dreams."

There are no certain answers, especially in the case of abductions that don't rely on sleep or hypnotic regression. Like in the case of David Huggins, who believes that he's been helping breed a race of aliens for decades.

The Otherworldly Art and Experiences of David Huggins

According to artist David Huggins, his encounters with aliens began in 1951 when he was an eight-year-old boy growing up in rural Georgia. "I was playing at the base of a tree and I hear this voice say, 'David, behind you,' and I turned around and there's this little hairy guy with large glowing eyes coming straight toward me," he said in the 2017 documentary *Love and Saucers*. "I thought it was the bogeyman. I didn't know what to think of it." Huggins ran to a nearby barn, and as he glanced back, he saw the little hairy fellow run back into the woods.

Over the next few months, insect-like aliens and Grays stalked him as he played outside. Eventually they took him aboard a spacecraft and one of them inserted a rod into his nose before returning him to his home. Huggins described the act as being tagged, like one might do to track an animal.

By the age of seventeen, Huggins's encounters reached a new, far more personal level when an extraterrestrial woman called Crescent met him under a tree in the woods. He's described her as having long black hair, large oval black eyes, a pale face, a small nose, a pointed chin, and a curvaceous human female body.

"I become very aroused sexually," Huggins recalled. "I couldn't get my pants down fast enough." At that moment, Huggins lying naked on the ground, Crescent mounted him and took his virginity. It wasn't exactly how he'd imagined that moment would occur.

Two years later, Huggins left for New York to pursue a career in art and design. But while he'd escaped the farm in Georgia, he did not break free from his otherworldly friends. Crescent followed, and their sexual encounters continued for decades in the context of what Huggins described as a warm, loving relationship. During this time, he says he fathered hundreds of alien-human hybrid children.

In 1987, after reading about similar extraterrestrial sexual acts in Budd Hopkins's *Intruders*, all of his memories began flooding back. As they did, Huggins picked up a paintbrush and recorded them in more than 125 cathartic paintings depicting his relationship with Crescent, the other visitors, and their experiences together. They hearken back to his first encounters as a scared child and his sexual exploits with Crescent, and they include his visitations to the hybrid babies.

In one painting he stands before an incubator holding dozens of children awaiting his human touch to bring them to life, while in another he teaches one of the babies to breastfeed. Apart from capturing his memories on canvas, Huggins has an entire archive of journals and sketchbooks that frequently reveal his desire for Crescent, his loneliness, and a sadness that surrounds his experiences—none of which needed to be surfaced through hypnosis.

Aside from the physical meetings Huggins claims to have experienced, he has also visited with the various beings in the realm of sleep

David Huggins created artwork to represent his various
experiences with otherworldly beings over multiple decades.

and by stepping through portals that he says appear in his bedroom and lead him to spacecraft, the moon, or even possibly Mars—though he's never quite sure where exactly these places are.

Huggins has no explanations for why these beings have chosen him to visit and breed with, nor does he know where they come from. What he does know is that the experiences are not simply dreams. "You wanna say they're interplanetary, fine. They're intergalactic, fine. Another universe, fine. Another dimension, I don't know," Huggins said in *Love and Saucers*. "It doesn't really matter to me. I know they exist, I know they're real. And that's enough for me."

Those close to him attest to that sentiment. "I fully believe that David is speaking his truth," Joseph Villari, a friend and confidant, told me. "There's not an ounce of him saying anything that isn't his experience."

Huggins, who is also the father of one wholly human child with his earthly ex-wife, has said that if the visitors offered to take him with them and never return to earth, he would go. To this day, he remains at home in Hoboken, New Jersey.

Travis Walton's Five-Day Abduction

Like Huggins, Travis Walton retained memories of his abduction without undergoing numerous sessions of hypnotic regression. Unlike Huggins, he fathered no hybrids and had only one experience—though it quickly became one of America's best-known abduction cases. In November 1975, the twenty-two-year-old logger was allegedly snatched from a wooded area in Arizona for five days before being plopped back down to earth and left cold, hungry, and frightened.

Walton and six friends had been driving through a forest after work when they spotted a glowing UFO hovering over a clearing just off the secluded road. They pulled over for a closer look, but not close enough for Walton. He jumped out of the truck and ran directly beneath the craft. As he stared up in awe at what he described as looking like "two soup plates on top of each other," a bolt of bluish light shot down and zapped him to the ground. Whether in shock or in fear of being zapped too, his friends panicked and fled the scene. Within fifteen minutes they had calmed down enough to return for their fallen friend, but by then Walton was gone. Mystified by the entire event, the woodcutters headed to the police and filed a missing person report.

Search parties scoured the area, but there was no sign of Walton. Some began to suspect his friends of foul play, but that theory fell apart after Walton suddenly reappeared on a roadside near the spot of his disappearance five days later. Dazed and confused, he managed to call his brother from a pay phone for help. The young logger's fantastic story of being taken aboard the craft and prodded by several five-foot-tall humanoid creatures with big eyes and no hair was soon shared with the press, and Walton became a national media sensation. He described being disoriented and in pain when he found himself lying on an elevated surface in the saucer, surrounded by extraterrestrials. The shock of seeing them gave him a jolt of adrenaline that allowed him to push a few out of the way and jump off the table.

"They were coming toward me as I was backing up and screaming threats, trying to seem as dangerous as I could," Walton recalled at the online 2021 International SkyFire Summit.

Though he fended them off momentarily, it took him nearly a week to be released. Ultimately, he decided they weren't looking for a fight or anything particularly malicious. "If they were really out to harm me, they never would've returned me at all," Walton said.

Upon his return, Walton set out to prove he wasn't crazy. After a series of psychiatric tests, his examiner, Dr. Gene Rosenbaum, issued a press release stating: "Our conclusion, which was absolute, is that this young man is not lying, that there is no collusion involved."

A drug test showed he wasn't high, either. Not a trace of drugs was found in his urine. "So it was not a drug hallucination," Walton emphasized at SkyFire. "To me, that was a really lame way to try to explain it away. Because seven people are not going to have the same drug trip. No drugs in my body. Period."

His defense was further bolstered when he and five of his friends all passed lie detector tests (the sixth's test was inconclusive). Dr. J. Allen Hynek and APRO's Dr. James Harder examined the results and were both impressed, with the latter announcing that "the evidence is as valid as any that would be accepted in an American criminal court."

Harder happened to also be on the *National Enquirer*'s Blue Ribbon panel, which rewarded Walton and his crew with a $5,000 prize for offering solid proof in a UFO case.

Not surprisingly, skeptics weren't buying it (and surely the tabloid's endorsement didn't help). A separate polygraph test arranged by the *Enquirer* didn't warrant the same rave reviews from its examiner, John J. McCarthy. He believed Walton showed "great deception" during the test by "attempting to distort his respiratory pattern." Drastic changes in blood pressure and a slowing of heart rate raised suspicions.

"In my opinion, Walton was perpetrating a hoax," McCarthy told reporters. "He has not been on any spacecraft."

UFO debunker Philip Klass agreed, adding that Walton had been fascinated by UFOs before his capture and had expressed a desire to ride in one some day. This didn't prove he made the whole thing up, but as Klass also noted, Walton had admitted that he'd watched the Hills' movie, *The UFO Incident*, which aired just weeks before his own incident. It's not unlike the theory that Barney Hill had been subconsciously inspired by *The Outer Limits* airing before one of his hypnosis sessions.

Then there was the question of Walton's urine test, which seemingly passed with flying colors but, as Klass pointed out, was absent of acetones. This didn't add up: if Walton had gone five days without food as he claimed, his body would've begun breaking down its own fat and excreting acetones as waste in his urine—meaning his urinalysis would've shown their presence. Finally, Klass was surprised by the lack of surprise Walton's mother showed about beings from outer space kidnapping her son. Either these facts, for whatever reason, were not shared with the *National Enquirer*, or it didn't care. Given the tabloid's reputation, the latter isn't hard to imagine—especially if it wanted to believe Walton's story.

On the other hand, those who believe in Walton's case also tend to believe that Klass was on government payroll and instructed to spread disinformation. Believers also point to the fact that aside from the one inconclusive polygraph test, all of Walton's friends passed. There's room for error in one test, but five additional tests dramatically decrease the odds. "Statistically, you're looking at a one in millions of billions chance that they were not being truthful on the relevant question—meaning 'Did you see a UFO, and did this event happen with your friend?'" UFO researcher and TV host Ben Hansen, explained to me in a phone interview.

Believers also point to peculiarities discovered years later at the alleged abduction site. The trees nearest to where the craft had descended were growing at an usually fast rate. "The calculations show that these trees were producing wood fiber at thirty-something times the rate they had in the previous eighty-five years," Walton said, citing testing conducted by experts in the 2015 documentary *Travis: The Travis Walton Story.* "Other trees exhibited the same kind of changes, and the effect is diminished the farther you got from that spot."

In addition to the documentary, Walton's story was depicted in the 1993 movie *Fire in Sky* starring D. B. Sweeney and has been featured in a variety of other UFO-related programs. One of them was *Fact or Faked: Paranormal Files*, hosted and investigated by Hansen. It's where he first met Walton in 2011. During the taping, they visited the forest site together and Hansen had a chance to hear Walton's story firsthand and see his reactions in the very place it all happened.

"I was just observing his behavior, and I saw something in him that was like a PTSD, almost like someone who had been abused," Hansen said. "He was legitimately afraid when the sun went down. He didn't want to be up there. He wasn't putting on a show for us. He's a very humble, down-to-earth guy, and when you hear him speak and meet him, you just get a feeling this guy wasn't in it for money or fame. And he's been consistent all these years, and something really did happen to him. So combining everything together, that's what convinced me he's telling the truth."

D. B. Sweeney played Travis Walton in 1993's adaptation of his story, *Fire in the Sky*.

Journalist and *Edge of Reality Radio* host Lee Speigel hasn't been abducted, although he did witness a UFO at close range in 1975 during an investigation for Dr. Hynek (more on that in the next chapter) and has reported on the phenomenon since the early seventies. I first met Speigel while writing for AOL Weird News from 2009 to 2011. He invited me to the SkyFire conference, where he was a speaker on the "Investigator Panel." Like Hansen, Speigel believes Walton's story, along with those of other abductees.

"I have a feeling that the powers that be, whether in America or in other countries, know about these UFO abduction cases and probably feel that the public shouldn't be told more about it," he explained to the online audience. "It is, after all, a pretty terrifying thing that people are reporting. And nobody really knows how to prevent it."

Speigel added that for the U.S. government to admit that such experiences are happening would be to admit that it can't stop them. "I don't think they can prevent this ongoing experiencer culture that we're now living in," he said. "How do you tell the public that 'Yes, we are aware that many people around the world are having experiences with something—some kind of beings or creatures or intelligence. Sometimes they just take people out of their cars, something they take people out of their beds at night while they're sleeping and bring them to a place where they do a variety of experiments or medical examinations.' How do you tell the public that? How do you acknowledge that without freaking everybody out? These are not just people making these stories up. . . . We depend on the air force, the army, the navy, our doctors, our leaders; we depend on them to protect us on this planet, and if they're telling us that can't really protect us, where does that leave us all?"

To date, it's left us with countless instances of alleged alien contact and abduction that remain unexplained. And without the government offering an explanation to the public, people have resorted to finding their own. The question is, have they found answers or just complicated the mystery?

CHAPTER 3

THE PHENOMENON CONTINUES

Mass Sightings, Conspiracies, and Flying Triangles

> "The witnesses I interviewed could have been lying, *could* have been insane, or *could* have been hallucinating collectively—but I do not think so. Their standing in the community, their lack of motive for perpetration of a hoax, their own puzzlement at the events they witnessed, and often their great reluctance to speak of the experience—all lend a subjective reality to their UFO experience."
>
> —DR. J. ALLEN HYNEK in his 1977 book *The Hynek UFO Report*

The good news about aliens is that if they're here, we still are too. They've haven't destroyed us, and despite the many reports of abductions since the 1960s, they're not all scheming to scoop us up and experiment on us. Harmless yet curious UFO sightings have continuously been reported around the globe by everyone from military officials to schoolchildren to celebrities to large groups of witnesses. Oftentimes, as we'll see in this chapter spanning the 1970s through the early 2000s, these flying saucers were actually flying triangles—giants ones hovering quietly above cities. And through it all, conspiracy theories grew in scope and popularity. It all gave those who believe and those wanting to believe compelling evidence, particularly via several international incidents of alleged UFO landings that have drawn comparisons to Roswell. Let's examine these cases to understand why, starting with a triangular craft that mentally transmitted binary code to an air force sergeant while parked in a forest.

The British Roswell:
An Encounter in Rendlesham Forest

As with many UFO encounters, the Rendlesham sighting began with a flash of light filling the sky: in this case, red and blue flickers over the forest in the wee hours of December 26, 1980. The light first caught the attention of Airman First Class John Burroughs during his patrol at East Gate in Woodbridge, one of two U.S. Air Force bases adjacent to England's Rendlesham Forest in Suffolk County (the other being Bentwaters). If something had crashed, it hadn't gone up in flames or even made a sound. Burroughs found it unusual enough to report to his sergeant, Bud Steffens, and they in turn alerted Sergeant Jim Penniston and Airman First Class Edward Cabansag. A check with the control tower at Bentwaters confirmed radar had picked up an unknown object about fifteen minutes prior. With Steffens staying on patrol, the other three officers headed into the forest to investigate.

Deep in the woods, their radios began malfunctioning. The officers decided to spread out and form a communications relay chain, with Cabansag staying put as the first link in contact with the base. As Penniston and Burroughs delved forward, things got stranger, as sudden jolts of static electricity made the hairs on their arms and necks rise. Soon their footsteps grew slow and heavy, as if they were trudging through water. With a clearing in sight just ahead, the officers saw a burst of light.

Penniston walked toward it, and here's where things get otherworldly. He claimed to have seen a small metallic triangular craft with tripod-like legs resting quietly on the ground. The object was roughly ten feet wide and just as tall and appeared to have a form of hieroglyphics running along its side. Penniston staggered cautiously toward it, withdrew his notebook, and sketched what he saw—including the strange symbols. He even got close enough to touch it gently. The craft, as he later recalled, was smooth like glass. His caress of the surface sent a low voltage racing from his hand to his forearm. The encounter lasted nearly forty-five minutes before a white light glowed at the apex and the object blasted off, disappearing into the dark of night.

By sunrise, the group had returned to headquarters and shared their

UFO tale, which, not surprisingly, was met with ridicule. Still, their commanding officer, Lieutenant Colonel Charles Halt, advised them to make a note of it in the security blotter as "unexplained lights." Despite the cloud of doubt around their story, Penniston and Burroughs led a team of investigators back to the clearing. Similar to the case in Socorro, New Mexico, they found three indentations in the ground along with broken branches and scorch marks left on the surrounding trees. It all seemed to correspond with the craft's landing and subsequent ascent.

The next evening, the on-duty police commander interrupted a family Christmas party at the base to inform Halt that "it" was back. According to Halt, the trusted officer was "white as a sheet" as he shared the news. "When he got excited, I was concerned," the lieutenant colonel explained to me during a phone interview. So he left the festivities to investigate the scene, fully expecting to find a logical explanation. However, when Halt and a small group of officers, including Burroughs and Penniston, arrived at the site, logic had evaded the situation. In addition to their examination of the same physical evidence remaining from the first encounter, Halt's Geiger counter detected an unusual blip in the radiation level. A report filed in the UK's Ministry of Defence states it was "significantly higher than the average background" reading. It wasn't enough to pose danger, but it did seem to indicate something strange had happened there.

As Halt began documenting the investigation on his tape recorder (he always carried one), he heard nothing but animals from a nearby farm making a ruckus. Then, as if having been warned by their cries, he and his men witnessed a bright yellowish-orange oval object with a dark center. It was about the size of a beach ball and appeared to be shedding sparks or particles.

"We watched it for maybe a minute or two," Halt recalled. "It actually came toward us. I said, 'That thing's under intelligent control,' and at first I thought it was ball lightning. I'd never seen ball lightning but I've certainly heard of it. It came into the forest and actually moved through it, horizontally bobbing up and down and zigzagging around trees. So it was obviously controlled somehow or another."

The object approached the group and they observed beams of light aiming toward the ground. "This is unreal," Halt said with a disbelieving laugh on his recording. It got to within about a hundred feet, and then, as they watched, it silently exploded into five pieces that all dispersed in different directions.

"We looked around in the field trying to find any evidence and all we found were cow pies," Halt said.

Afterward, the officers just wanted the whole situation to go away. "This was not career enhancing, believe me," Halt stressed. He wrote a memo dated January 13, 1981, with the subject once again listed as "Unexplained Lights." It offered a description of what had been witnessed over those late December days, but stopped short of calling it a UFO encounter. Little more was said by anyone at the time. Despite their wishes, however, Rendlesham has never gone away.

By October 1983, a small group of ufologists had learned about the incident and sold the story to *News of the World*, a popular UK tabloid. Suddenly, the forest sighting turned into a front-page headline: UFO LANDS IN SUFFOLK. AND THAT'S OFFICIAL. Believers, researchers, and skeptics have been looking for something truly official ever since.

Years later, more details began to emerge and the encounter became shrouded in controversy, earning it the label "the British Roswell." Halt, for example, learned his memo had been curiously sent the following day to CIA headquarters in Langley, Virginia. Shortly after the incident, Penniston, Burroughs, and several other officers involved were reportedly, as the lieutenant colonel put it, "debriefed" by government officials. Halt said they were "drugged and hypnotized and probably given screen memories." Penniston and Burroughs, he added, "have never been the same." Both servicemen have been denied access to their medical records from the Department of Veterans Affairs.

Other officers later admitted seeing something on those nights as well, including men stationed at the weapons storage area who, according to Halt, claimed to have seen a mothership with small objects dispersing from it. "You can't believe how many people from Bentwaters, after they retired, came forward and talked to me," Halt said. "We had cops that said they actually shot at one on a different occasion. They had emptied their M16 at it—with no effect, obviously."

Those testimonies, multiple sightings before and after the December 1980 incident, along with his boss at the base claiming to know "a

secret report
tells the facts

in exploding
wall of colour

from strange
glowing object

UFO LANDS IN SUFFOLK

And that's OFFICIAL

A UFO has landed in Britain—and that staggering fact has been officially confirmed.

Despite a massive cover-up, News of the World investigators have proof that the mysterious craft came to earth in a red ball of light at 3 a.m. on December 27, 1980.

It happened in a pine forest called Tangham Wood just half a mile from the United States Air Force base at RAF Woodbridge, in Suffolk.

NEWS OF THE WORLD INVESTIGATES

EVIDENCE DETAIL from Lt. Col. Charles Halt's confidential

Lieutenant Colonel Charles Halt at the edge of Rendlesham Forest in 2021, where he stood in 1980 and witnessed a mysterious glowing object in the field between him and the farmhouse in the distance.

whole lot more"—though what he knew has yet to be revealed—has led Halt to believe he was part of something truly out of this world.

"I think the origin is extraterrestrial, it's here, whatever it is," he told me. "There's still activity in that area. There's some kind of an attraction, some kind of a portal or there's some reason that that area has a lot of strange happenings."

For Jim Penniston, the strangeness graduated to downright bizarreness. In 1994, he visited a hypnotherapist for help with a sleep disorder. During a regression, he revealed that he'd received a series of numbers telepathically during his Rendlesham experience. But not from aliens. "They are time travelers—they are us," he said.

When describing the scene later, Penniston said that as he touched the craft, a message that what appeared to be in binary code entered his mind's eye. "The stream of ones and zeros ran relentlessly and I was unable to see my surroundings, I was scared, though I seemed to understand it was not harmful, but required," he said. "I am not sure how long this took place, this bright light with flashing of these ones and zeros. Seconds, or minutes, it seemed like a brief moment. Unable to pull my hand back, I finally had it release my hand. As quickly as the release of my hand from the triangle, the ones and zeros stopped." He allegedly wrote the digits in his notebook several days later—a miraculous feat of recall, if true—then set it aside.

It wasn't until 2010 when Penniston was at a documentary shoot about Rendlesham that he revealed those forgotten pages. A decoding led to the following message:

Exploration of Humanity 666 8100
52.0942532N 13.131269W
Continuous For Planetary ADVAN???
Fourth Coordinate Continuout UQS CbPR BEFORE
16.763177N 89.117768W
34.800272N 111.843567W
29.977836N 31.131649E
14.701505S 75.167043W
36.256845N 117.100632E
37.110195N 25.372281E

Eyes of Your Eyes
Origin 52.0942532N 13.131269W
Origin Year 8100

The coordinates appear to be latitudes and longitudes indicating places rich with UFO lore, including the Nazca Lines of Peru, the Great Pyramid in Giza, and Sedona, Arizona. "It's almost like playing buzzword bingo with New Age spiritual people's bucket lists," said Nick Pope in my phone interview with him about the case. The retired UK Ministry of Defence official previously investigated UFOs and is the author of *Encounter in Rendlesham Forest*. Of all the strange claims in the story, he acknowledges Penniston's binary code as the most controversial: "The whole thing sounds like something out of a sci-fi movie."

The sci-fi feel is especially strong in the final line that tells us Rendlesham Forest was visited by time travelers from the year 8100. As we've seen in other cases, the idea of time travelers may have been seeded in Penniston's head from a TV movie called *Official Denial*. It aired on the Sci-Fi Channel within a year of his hypnotherapy. The film involves a spaceship shot down by the air force, which lands in a forest and reveals inhabitants who are not aliens. "They're us," a character explains. "From the future. Our future."

Halt raised the same concern in an article he shared with me in advance of its publication in the *MUFON Journal*, noting that "many of the phrases Jim uses to describe 'them' appear to have come from the movie." He also compared the symbols Penniston saw on the craft to those Jesse Marcel Jr. claimed to have seen on the beams his father showed him during the Roswell case. "Possibly copied?" Halt asks. "Draw your own conclusions!"

British skeptic Ian Ridpath believes the extraordinary incident may have a remarkably ordinary explanation. The initial sighting, for example, coincided with the timing of an unusually bright fireball that streaked across the southern England sky on December 26. The flashes of light, Ridpath suggests, were likely from nearby Orfordness Lighthouse. This is supported by a 1999 letter in the Suffolk police archives online, in which an inspector (name redacted) offers information about the case to an inquirer (name also redacted), including the following statement: "I know from personal experience that at night, in certain weather and cloud conditions, these beams were very pronounced and certainly caused strange visual effects." Ridpath also notes that a Suffolk police report from the morning of December 26 states that the three ground indentations were of "no depth and could have been made by an animal." He adds that investigating foresters identified the tree markings as, well, cuts made by foresters. As for the radiation measurements, Ridpath claims they were nothing more than background levels, meaning they had no real significance.

"Confirmation that this was only background radiation comes from the fact that the same levels were also recorded over half a mile away from the supposed landing site, after they had crossed two fields beyond the forest," he said on his website. "At its most basic, the case comes down to the misinterpretation of a series of nocturnal lights—a fireball, a lighthouse, and some stars."

Halt acknowledged that they had seen the lighthouse beam while in the forest, but this was in addition to the mysterious lights that grabbed their attention. "It wasn't the lighthouse," he told me. "You ever see a lighthouse move through the forest?"

Over the years there have been claims of hoaxes, some of which appear to be hoaxes themselves. These include tales of a retired military cop playing a joke with police car lights, vengeful Special Air Service officers coordinating an elaborate orchestration of lights, flares, and remote-controlled balloons, and a secretive mind-control experiment involving sophisticated holograms and weaponized ball lightning. To Halt, these are "as ridiculous as can be."

Is it possible that this "British Roswell" case has an explanation similar to the U.S. air force's statement about Project Mogul? Pope believes it's at least a more likely theory. "I think the more plausible explanations are that this was some sort of military hardware, some secret prototype, aircraft or drone, or even some sort of counterintelligence operation," he said. Still, he admits it "doesn't quite sit" right. "But just applying Occam's razor, I guess you could say that that secret military prototype technologies should be your first port of call before aliens and time travelers."

As for Halt, his conclusion is one most can agree on: "The real answer is we don't know what it was."

Whatever you choose to believe, Rendlesham Forest now has an official UFO trail that leads to the areas associated with the sighting. Perhaps one day it will also lead to the truth.

The Strange, Smelly Creature of Varginha, Brazil

Sixteen years after "the British Roswell," Brazil had one of its own. The country was no stranger to UFOs, having had five hundred reports in 1995 alone. But it was a particular incident that took place on January 20, 1996, a few hundred miles northwest of Rio de Janeiro, in the coffee-producing city of Varginha, that captured the world's attention.

According to newspaper reports, the incident began with early morning sightings of a gray, submarine-shaped object the size of a minibus flying overhead. Shortly after, a "strange creature" was spotted near a forest. Firefighters responded to calls about the being and managed to find and capture it. It was so strange that they allegedly handed the living thing over to military officials who took it to a hospital for doctors to examine. It remained there for two days and then died.

Five hours after the firefighters' adventure, a second creature was spotted. This time the witnesses were a young pregnant woman, Kátia Andrade Xavier, and her two friends, Liliane Fátima Silva and her sister, Valquíria. While walking home, they passed through a vacant lot and encountered the bizarre being crouched in the weeds next to a wall. It looked to be about three to four feet tall and had oily brown skin, rubbery limbs, bulging eyes, and three horns protruding from an oversized forehead. It smelled as wretched as it looked and appeared to be in pain. After a brief and uncomfortable stare-down, the women fled in terror, fearing they'd just gazed into the devil's eyes.

"It wasn't a man or an animal—it was something different," said Xavier.

Rumors spread, the press caught wind of the story, and Varginha soon found itself firmly planted on the UFO map. The Brazilian hot spot made headlines in international newspapers and magazines, in-

THEY SAW A UFO AND SUED THE GOVERNMENT: THE CASH-LANDRUM CASE

Just days after the Rendlesham Forest incident, on December 29, 1980, Betty Cash, her friend Vickie Landrum, and Vickie's seven-year-old grandson Colby Landrum were driving home after dinner in Dayton, Texas, when they suddenly saw a giant, glowing, diamond-shaped light hovering around treetop level and emitting flames from its base.

Betty described the sighting in a taped interview at Bergstom Air Force Base on August 17, 1981: "On that country road, the lights were so bright, and the heat was so intense, I got out of the car. I don't know what my purpose was unless it was just normal instinct to think well, maybe I'd be safer outside than I would be inside. But tell you the truth, we thought the end of the world was coming. I mean I'd never in my life gone through such a situation. But I knew that there was no way we could go under it the way the fire was shooting out the bottom of it."

Vickie added that she'd assured Colby, who was frightened, that if he looked inside the craft and "saw a big man it'd be Jesus."

The UFO then ascended, and twenty-three helicopters allegedly appeared to either pursue the object or escort it away. Later that night, all three witnesses suffered a variety of ailments, ranging from swollen eyes and ears to vomiting to hair and nail loss. An examining doctor attributed the ailments to ionizing radiation.

By 1985, Betty, Vickie, and Colby sued the United States for twenty million dollars. The lawsuit claimed the government failed to warn them of the UFO and recklessly permitted it "to fly over a publicly used road and come in contact with the plaintiffs." The case was dismissed in 1986 due to the fact that the plaintiffs couldn't prove the helicopters belonged to the government. Every agency within the military denied having a helicopter fleet in the area or a diamond-shaped aircraft. As MUFON's lead investigator for the event, John Schuessler, told a reporter in 1999, "They would just pretend like it didn't happen."

cluding the *Wall Street Journal*, which noted "a troubling lack of physical evidence." Still, Xavier and the sisters were in such demand for interviews that they started charging $200 a pop.

All the buzz was enhanced by an element of Roswellian controversy. Ubirajara Franco Rodrigues, a lawyer and the director of the Brazilian Center for the Studies of Flying Saucers, spent months interviewing the firefighters and troops who'd handled the creatures. He allegedly obtained secret statements from soldiers confirming that two strange beings had been captured and that their bodies were whisked away in army trucks to a military facility in São Paulo. Soldiers and hospital personnel were told to keep quiet. Threats ensured they would.

Colonel Luiz Cesario da Silveira Leite, a spokesperson for Brazil's Eastern Military Command, told reporters the allegations were "absurd" and "ridiculous." The army trucks weren't delivering alien corpses; they were transporting military vehicles for maintenance.

Hospital administrators had a different story as well. They claimed the body in question was an exhumed corpse of a college student who committed suicide in prison after being jailed for robbery. The family had requested an autopsy.

Like Roswell and Rendlesham, the story has lived on and taken new twists and turns along the way. Further research by Rodrigues and other ufologists revealed that an object had first been seen flying over Varginha a week earlier than initially reported, on January 13. A driver claimed to have seen it pass over the highway, trailing smoke as it plummeted to the ground just outside the city. He pulled off the road to search for the crash and offer assistance, but found army and military police already surrounding the wreckage. The curious witness didn't see any bodies—alien or otherwise—though he didn't have long too look before being asked to leave. And to keep quiet.

According to an employee at the Varginha zoo, the fire department had also attempted to unload the captured creature within the facility before delivering it to the military. Weeks later, several deer, tapirs, and ocelots mysteriously died. The zoo's veterinarian performed necropsies on the animals and detected an "unidentified toxic-caustic substance."

The animals weren't the only untimely and inexplicable deaths.

Ufologists claim a twenty-three-year-old police officer, Marco Eli Chereze, had come into contact with the second captured creature and allegedly suffered from a peculiar infection as a result. Doctors removed a small abscess, but he then began suffering from a fever and complained of various pains. Chereze died shortly after, on February 15. His family struggled to obtain information about his health during his final weeks and never received an exact cause of death. However, as Rodrigo Cardoso reported in a 2021 article on the Brazilian news site *Istoé*, Chereze had a cyst under his left armpit and had planned to remove it surgically. Maurício Antonio Santos, then commander of the 24th Battalion of the Varginha Military Police, explained that the officer's death "occurred due to a strong hospital infection after the operation" and that he "was not involved in any incidents with extra-terrestrials."

In 2006, Xavier and the Silvas retold their story in a Brazilian TV interview and claimed that four months after the sighting, five shadowy men approached them at the sisters' house and offered them money to deny everything they'd seen and said. The girls didn't disclose a dollar amount, but Liliane acknowledged that it was enough to leave Brazil. Yet they turned it down.

Four years later, military investigators offered another explanation: rather than an alien who'd lost their way, the "creature" the girls saw might have been a mentally disabled man who was often seen crouched in the street and tended to be covered in mud, earning him the nickname "Mudinho."

"It is a more likely hypothesis that this citizen, being probably dirty, as a result of the rains, seen crouching next to a wall, was mistaken by three terrified girls for a 'creature from outer space'," wrote Lieutenant Colonel Lúcio Carolos Pereira as part of a 357-page Military Police Inquiry. Mudinho lived with his family near the area of the sighting, and happened to have a larger-than-normal head. The girls, however, felt confident they didn't confuse a strange man for a strange something else.

Following in the extraterrestrial footsteps of Roswell, Varginha embraced its unexplained experience. Shortly after the incident, the mayor vowed to host an international UFO conference and planned

In 2001, the city of Varginha built a sixty-five-foot water tower designed to resemble the UFO that residents claimed to have seen five years earlier. It glows purple at night for a bonus otherworldly effect.

to transform the city into a permanent home for extraterrestrial research. Today, a sixty-five-foot-tall water tank in the shape of a flying saucer stands in the center of town and glows purple at night for a touch of otherworldly pizzazz. Elsewhere, a statue of the creature described by Xavier and the Silvas stands proud in a city square; bus stops that resemble UFOs greet awaiting passengers for nongalactic trips; and alien décor enthusiastically adorns businesses.

A Recess Like No Other:
The Landing at Zimbabwe's Ariel School

If Rendlesham and Varginha were the Roswells of Britain and Brazil, the encounter at the Ariel School in 1994 might be Zimbabwe's version. On the morning of September 16, sixty-two children at the private elementary school in a rural area just outside of Harare, Zimbabwe, were playing at recess when a group of UFOs joined them for a recess of its own. The students were unsupervised when flashes of light and a high-pitched frequency caught their attention from just beyond the thornbushes, trees, and bamboo shoots that formed the perimeter of their playground. Clustered together, they began pointing and confirming with one another that they were seeing the same objects hovering just above the ground.

All of the teachers happened to be inside at a staff meeting and missed the entire event, which included the apparent landing of one of the strange, silver, oval-shaped vehicles and the emergence of several occupants. These creatures, according to the children's descriptions, stood about three feet tall, had big heads, scrawny necks, and large black eyes, and were dressed in what appeared to be black bodysuits. One eleven-year-old boy added that he saw two figures running around in the bushes with hair that "was a bit like Michael Jackson's." Many of the children stood in awe and wonder and fright just a few feet away, staring into the darkness of the extraterrestrials' eyes and mesmerized by their close encounter of the third kind.

"It was like nothing I've ever felt before," recalled Salma Siddick on

Martin Willis's *Podcast UFO* in 2017. "There was no fear. It was almost as though this being was looking into my soul. Like it knew me. Like it knew who I was. That is the best I can describe this interlocking of eyes for however long it was."

Eventually, Salma and her schoolmates snapped out of it, panicked, and raced inside to alert their teachers. By the time any of them bothered to investigate the situation, there was nothing left to see.

Not surprisingly, the teachers initially thought their students had imagined the whole thing, but the children clearly and confidently expressed what they had seen. The stories they shared were so consistent that teachers eventually acknowledged something truly unusual had occurred.

The news traveled at near light speed. A leak to the press along the way caused an instant media frenzy, including a story from Zimbabwe's BBC correspondent, Timothy Leach. He'd survived coverage of war zones and thought he'd seen everything, but suddenly found himself baffled. Within days Leach contacted local UFO investigator Cynthia Hind, who immediately visited the school and inspected the area with a Geiger counter. Unlike the object that visited Rendlesham Forest in 1980, whatever landed or hovered just above the ground outside the schoolyard vanished without a trace of radiation. Nor was any of the foliage trampled or pressed down by the alleged craft.

Hind suggested the students draw what they'd witnessed while it was still fresh in their memories. Most illustrated a classic UFO saucer and beings that matched their initial descriptions and were consistent with the other children's drawings. According to Hind, one little girl told her, "I swear by every hair on my head and the whole Bible that I am telling the truth."

Amazed at what they were hearing and seeing during their interviews, Hind and Leach called for reinforcements: alien abduction specialist and Harvard Medical School's head of psychiatry, Dr. John E. Mack, and his associate, Dominique Callimanopulos.

The Harvard dream team adjusted their schedules and by early December made the journey halfway across the world. As Mack wrote in his 1999 book, *Passport to the Cosmos*, their interviews with a dozen children resulted in "more or less the same story." Nothing about the young witnesses' recollections or their demeanors appeared dishonest or deceitful. There was no indication of an elaborate hoax coordinated by scores of first- through seventh-graders. These were a diverse group of children—racially and religiously—with a presumably limited awareness of UFOs. Some of the native African students who'd been present saw the beings not as aliens, but as tokoloshes (mischievous goblins of Zulu folklore) and ran off, fearing they would be eaten.

Whether goblins or aliens or something else, several children believed they had received telepathic messages about climate change, the dangers of technology, and not taking "proper care of the planet."

"I think they want people to know that we're actually making harm on this world and we mustn't get too technologed," said eleven-year-old Emma.

Playing devil's advocate, Mack asked if perhaps the children had seen something more mundane and terrestrial, like a plane with a few passengers getting off. Nathaniel, age eleven, said no. "If kids my age got dressed up in funny suits, then maybe. But it couldn't be adults. Unless they're dwarfs."

"It's definitely reality, and anybody can think that it's not true or that we're making things up," twelve-year-old Emily added. "But we know what we've seen, and we believe it."

The innocence and conviction of the children makes it an undeniably compelling case. But could they have seen something besides diminutive extraterrestrials warning rural schoolchildren about our planet being in peril? Skeptoid Media's Brian Dunning points out the fervor over strange lights and UFOs in the skies over the region in the two nights prior to the incident. Unbeknownst to those looking up in bewilderment, the lights above were the reentry of the Zenit-2 rocket from Russia's recent Cosmos 2290 satellite launch.

"The booster broke up into burning streaks as it moved silently across the sky, giving an impressive light show to millions of Africans," Dunning said on his *Skeptoid* podcast in 2020. "Many people answered ZBC Radio's request by calling in with all sorts of disparate UFO reports prompted by the reentry, ranging from one shooting star to a fleet of sixteen brightly lit spaceships. Zimbabwe was gripped with its own little wave of UFO mania."

Had the children already been hearing stories about the sightings? Were they familiar with pop culture despite their young age and rural location? They were, as Dunning noted, from affluent families able to afford the private school, and therefore they likely had some exposure to movies and television.

Dunning also questioned Mack's impact on the stories he collected during his interviews. The three-month delay gave the children time to converse among themselves, possibly causing the stories to evolve and align. The interviews marked the first time the telepathic environmental messages were revealed.

"Why? Because [Mack] prompted and suggested it, according to his existing beliefs," Dunning said. "In addition to being an alien visitation advocate, Mack was an antinuclear and environmental activist."

Though sixty-two witnesses are significant, there were more than one hundred fifty other students who didn't see anything. For Dunning, these factors point to several possibilities: "Maybe an alien spaceship did land there that day and communicate telepathically to this handful of children. Or, maybe a couple of strangers strolled through the nearby field, and maybe a stray party balloon floated past. We'll never really have any good idea of what did or didn't happen on that day, if anything happened at all—keeping in mind that 'nothing at all' is what three-quarters of the students reported."

Nearly thirty years later, many of those who were present continue to discuss that unusual day on podcasts, UFO conferences, and in Randall Nickerson's 2022 documentary, *Ariel Phenomenon*. As adults, they all maintain their conviction in what they witnessed. None have decided it was a stray balloon or a couple of strange folks.

"I believe in what I saw," Salma told Willis and his listeners. "Regardless of what everybody else thinks or may think. . . . It definitely opened up my mind to the fact that there was more than just us out there."

The Ariel students drew pictures for investigator Cynthia Hind.
Many depicted UFOs or aliens, and sometimes both.

CATTLE MUTILATION CULPRITS: ALIENS OR SATANISTS?

Tim Burton's 1996 sci-fi comedy classic *Mars Attacks!* opens with a herd of flaming cattle stampeding by a bewildered farmer. The film's Martian invaders had no intent of dissecting the bovines or draining their blood or harvesting their organs. For them, searing livestock and farms with heat rays was pure strategy: burn earth's food supply and the planet would fall to its knees. These were aliens with a clear plan, unlike the ones that have often been accused of mutilating cattle across the country for the past six decades—primarily in the 1970s—and continue to be accused today. Of all the wonders earth has to offer, what would make cow lips, ears, tongues, and udders a prize worth traveling light-years for?

Cases of cattle mutilation typically involve the removal of such body parts, as well as the sex organs, with surgical precision, yet leave no trace of blood, footprints, or vehicular tracks. As one farmer in the early seventies told a reporter, it was "as if the bodies were mutilated elsewhere and dropped to the ground via the air." These types of mysterious mutilations have given aliens a bad rap. In 1975—a year in which Colorado ranchers reported nearly two hundred cases between April and October—a report by the Aerial Phenomena Research Organization (APRO) exonerated interstellar visitors in at least one wave of murders.

The group's investigation covered hundreds of deaths in Kansas, Nebraska, Iowa, South Dakota, Colorado, and Minnesota. Many of the victims had been slain by earthly predators or died due to natural causes, but enough cattle "bore strange mutilations which could not be accounted for in a mundane manner." Perfect health at the animals' time of death and no signs of struggle raised questions and stirred imaginations.

"Blood was missing from the carcass and there were definite indications that certain organs had been removed with surgical skill," an APRO spokesperson said, regarding cases where simple explanations did not suffice.

If not aliens, hungry coyotes, or other beasts, what savage creature could be so cruel and precise? Apparently, humans. With the help of law enforcement and veterinarians, a cult of satanists was found responsible and apprehended.

They had wreaked their havoc under the cover of night and avoided leaving tracks by carefully walking over large pieces of pasteboard. The cultists then shot the animals with tranquilizer darts, withdrew their blood, and severed their organs. As Colorado's El Paso County undersheriff Gary Gibb explained to the *Colorado Springs Gazette Telegraph* in 1975, "They use the organs they take in satanic rites. A male member will eat the sex organ of the animal in order to better his sexual prowess." The same article reported that APRO believed the satanists might have also intended to provoke rumors of alien attacks with the hopes of unhinging locals and causing glorious chaos.

"What needs to be emphasized is the entire lack of what could be called UFO involvement," APRO stated in its March 1975 bulletin. "To this date no satisfactory evidence has emerged which links UFOs to mutilated animals."

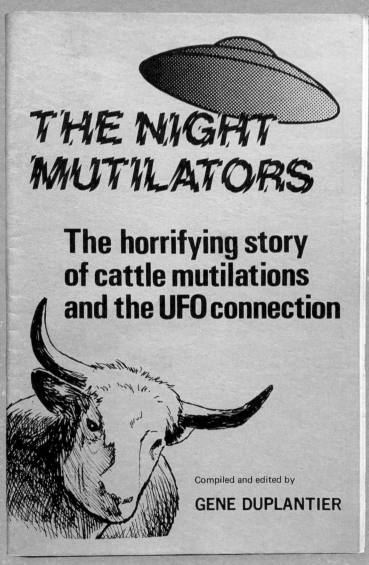

THE NIGHT MUTILATORS

The horrifying story of cattle mutilations and the UFO connection

Compiled and edited by

GENE DUPLANTIER

Ufology publisher Gene Duplantier compiled and edited stories of cattle mutilations across America in this 1979 booklet.

Mass Witnesses See a Flying Triangle: The Phoenix Lights

At 5:00 p.m. on June 19, 1997, Arizona governor Fife Symington called a news conference at the state capitol to announce "serious developments" in a months-old UFO sighting. Back on March 13, thousands of Arizonans looked up at the sky hoping to catch a rare glimpse of the passing Hale–Bopp comet, but instead saw a series of mysterious lights flying in a massive triangular formation.[+] It became known as the Phoenix Lights and is considered by some the most witnessed and most documented UFO sighting in modern history.

So people were eager to hear the governor's explanation—and not just Arizonans. After *USA Today* published a story the day before Symington's conference, everyone from *Today*'s Katie Couric and Matt Lauer to Peter Jennings on ABC's *World News Tonight* was reporting about it. The entire country was eager to find out what was happening in the Phoenix sky.

When the big moment arrived, Symington stood before the press and began his statement: "I'll ask Officer Stein and his colleagues to escort the accused into the room so that we may all look upon the guilty party. Don't get him too close to me, please."

On that cue, a man in a silver spacesuit with a bulbous head and big rubbery hands secured in cuffs was trotted up to the podium. Symington welcomed the extraterrestrial and told the press, "It just goes to show you guys are entirely too serious." He removed the alien mask to reveal one of his aides in the costume. Symington later said the joke was intended to avoid panic. Perhaps he'd just seen Independence Day and didn't want reality to imitate art. The Hollywood blockbuster had been released the previous summer and featured citizens chaotically fleeing their homes as similarly large UFOs obliterated cities across the world. The press conference broke out in laughter during the stunt, but as Dr. Lynne D. Kitei—author of *The Phoenix Lights*—assured me during a phone interview, the people of Phoenix were not amused.

+ Nearly two weeks later, thirty-nine members of the Heaven's Gate cult were found dead in a suburb of San Diego. They believed their mass suicide was their ticket aboard a UFO trailing the Hale–Bopp comet.

National media spotlight UFO sighting in Phoenix

— **NATIONAL,** *from Page A1*

Flanked by two Department of Public Safety officers, Symington described how the law-enforcement agency had solved the alien mystery by capturing one of them. Then, with most of his staff looking on, Symington aide Jay Heiler walked in wearing an alien suit.

Symington said he wasn't trying to ridicule Arizonans who believe in space creatures. But he doesn't believe the state has been the tourist destination for the alien world.

"I don't discount any more than Carl Sagan ... the fact that the universe is such a large place and so old that ... there may well be life out there," he said. "On the other hand, if this particular event were truly significant, I think you would probably have national security involved, the Air Force and everybody else working on it."

Pretty big doings for a story that began so long ago, on the evening of March 13.

Calls poured in that night, starting a little after 8 p.m. Callers from Phoenix, Glendale, Scottsdale and across the state reported sight-

Mike Rynearson/The Arizona Republic

With a wink and a nudge, Gov. Fife Symington, flanked by DPS officers and staff, welcomes the space alien captured by the law-enforcement agency. The alien is none other than Jay Heiler, a Symington aide, in an alien suit.

On June 19, 1997, Arizona governor Fife Symington held a press conference to discuss the Phoenix Lights mass UFO sighting. His costumed colleague, seen in this article from the June 20, 1997, edition of the *Arizona Republic*, made a mockery of the incident.

"Everyone took it seriously," she said about the anticipated gubernatorial announcement. "And I was thrilled. They found a solution or whatever it was. And then he made a mockery of the whole thing."

Kitei, a physician and health educator, was among the estimated 20,000 witnesses to the phenomenon. She filmed the event from the porch of her home overlooking the city. Five circular lights, each amber in color, formed a V shape with two additional lights trailing the triangle. Their eerily silent and slow movement perfectly relative to each other seemed to indicate they were attached to a singular craft. According to some of the observers, the object appeared to be several miles wide. Whatever it was, sightings began in Nevada and continued over approximately seven hours as the object made its way across the entire state of Arizona, demanding the attention of anyone looking up.

"They were coming directly at us," Charles Painter explained to the *Arizona Republic*. The retired train traffic controller was driving from Tucson to Phoenix that night. "They were much larger than airplane lights. We even pulled off the highway to listen for jet engines. We didn't hear any."

As cement truck driver Bill Greiner told *USA Today*, "I'll never be the same. Before this, if anybody'd told me they saw a UFO, I would've said, 'Yeah, and I believe in the tooth fairy.'" Greiner added that he'd seen three F-16s take off toward one of the orbs when the object was over the air force base, but it sped away before the pilots could've reached it. "I wish the government would just admit it. You know what it's like in this city right now? It's like having fifty thousand people in a stadium watch a football game and then having someone tell us we weren't there."

About a month later the military did admit something: that the Maryland Air National Guard ran a training exercise with eight A-10 planes southwest of Phoenix on March 13 and dropped heaps of high-intensity flares.

"Our guys did create, while they were up there, an event that this one colonel told me could be perceived as a hell of a light show," Captain Drew Sullins of the Maryland Air National Guard told the *Arizona Republic*. But he didn't exactly claim the flares were the light show thousands of people were paying attention to. "All I'm saying is, yes, we had aircraft flying in that area doing night illuminations. These guys were flying it. They were there. We can prove it. Whether people want to believe it was the mysterious lights, it's up to them."

Some did believe it. One man wrote a letter to the editor of the *Arizona Republic* to say that he'd witnessed similar flares during the Vietnam War and that the Phoenix Lights was nothing more than a bunch of hoopla. "This explanation is generally rejected by the public because it is incompatible with the preferred fantasy," he said.

Most people who denied the theory would attribute their doubt less to fantasy and more to fact, based on what they'd seen. The illumination flares were dropped from the planes with parachutes at about 6,000 feet in elevation, then fell slowly toward the ground. If the night was clear enough they could've been seen from 150 miles away. But the location of the flares didn't match witness accounts of the Phoenix Lights. Even if they did, falling flares emit smoke, leave visible trails, and don't fall in perfect unison.

Kitei called the Air National Guard, she told me, and expanded on this point. "You're trying to tell me that flares that cannot keep a formation traversed the entire state in a rock-solid equidistantly spaced mile-wide V for hours?" she asked the representative. "And [the representative] says, 'I have a call coming in. I'll get back to you.' I'm still waiting."

Even Governor Symington eventually rejected the flares as an explanation. By 2007, he finally acknowledged that despite his press conference shenanigans, he, too, had witnessed the Phoenix Lights—and that it was a solid structure. Symington admitted to sneaking out of the governor's mansion so he could drive around town to see what he'd been hearing about all evening. When he returned, he told his wife that what he'd observed was "breathtaking." And that he wasn't going to talk about it.

"I suspect that unless the Defense Department proves us otherwise, that it was probably some form of an alien spacecraft," Symington told CNN during his divulgence. "The lights were really brilliant. And it was just fascinating. I mean, it was enormous. It just felt otherworldly. You know, in your gut you could just tell it was otherworldly."

His status as a politician, not to mention a Vietnam air force veter-

"People were in wonder, they were curious—I can't tell you how many cars pulled off the road to watch it. And twenty-five years later, I still have people contact me to say that they just wanted to let me know that they still feel blessed that they had the experience. Now, let's be real, that doesn't happen with planes and helicopters and flares or whatever."

—DR. LYNNE D. KITEI, Phoenix Lights witness and author of *The Phoenix Lights: A Skeptic's Discovery That We Are Not Alone,* in a January 2022 interview with the author an, added credibility to the story. Ten years later, another high-profile witness publicly announced he'd seen the lights: actor Kurt Russell.

The movie star and licensed pilot had been flying his son to Phoenix to visit a friend when they both spotted the phenomenon. "I saw six lights over the airport in absolute uniform in a V shape," Russell said on a BBC talk show. He called it in to Sky Harbor Airport, but they were unaware of aircraft matching his report. "Okay, I'm going to declare it's unidentified, it's flying, and it's six objects." By definition, it was unquestionably a UFO.

Of course, an unidentified flying object could be just that, without being from another world. The air force began experimenting with V-shaped balloon configurations for high-altitude flights decades ago. John Powell of JP Aerospace has stated that his company has been working on such configurations for space travel for forty-two years.

"We were testing vehicles at the time of the Phoenix lights incident, however, I can absolutely say that JPA was not, nor [was] our equipment, involved," he told the *War Zone* in 2020. "There have been times where our vehicles have been sighted and confused for UFOs or other mysterious things. I have also seen images of great V-shaped objects in the sky that I can say for sure were not mine, but I could note perhaps the tech of a competitor. This is all speculation."

When he heard reports about the Phoenix Lights, the similarities made him believe that a competitor, or the air force, had been further developing the tech his company had been working on. Though why either would make experimental aircraft so visible—and remain so secretive—to thousands of people defies explanation.

So what if the explanation thousands of witnesses believe is the one that is correct? If the lights were indeed piloted by aliens, one can't help but wonder if they were merely conducting an experiment. What would happen if an entire community, rather than a few isolated witnesses, watched a massive aircraft drift right over their heads? Would it spark a sense of awe and curiosity or straight-up *Independence Day* pandemonium?

Whatever the lights were, they did indeed affect people. Mike Fortson, for example, witnessed the event with his wife of twenty-five years. "Other than the hand of God coming through space, nothing could have been more profound," he told reporters. The couple grew closer from the experience and began spending their evenings looking up at the sky and talking. "To be able to shut the TV off and talk, that's a great thing."

As for Kitei, the March 13 event wasn't her first. She'd seen three amber orbs in a similar triangle formation on February 6, 1995. "As I was staring at them—I did not admit this to a soul until two years later after the mass sighting—it felt like something was watching me. It just did. And going through my mind, I was thinking, who are you? What are you? Do know that I'm here? I'd love to meet you."

Kitei witnessed the lights again after 1997 but remained anonymous for seven years before sharing her experiences. She has pursued answers ever since and in the process has met with other witnesses who were inspired to join peace movements or environmental movements as a result of their experiences. Though much mystery remains, one answer is clear to her: "We are not alone in the universe." According to countless reports over the years, neither was this triangular variety of spacecraft.

Early Flying Triangles and the UFO Capital of the Northeast

Triangular-shaped UFOs have been spotted around the globe since at least 1950, when the occupants of a two-seater plane saw a pair of the crafts coasting below them in north central California. "At first I thought they were birds, but there was no wing motion," one of the passengers told reporters. "Then, suddenly they put on a terrific burst of speed."

According to the United Press, the air force looked into the case but "denied knowledge of any so-called flying saucer." In that mid-century golden age of the saucer, flying triangles were hardly in the vocabulary. Yet in the years that followed they made their presence loud and clear as we'll see in cases across the world, starting with another mass sighting of a silent, luminous pointy object in New York's Hudson Valley.

On March 24, 1983, hundreds of people in Westchester and Putnam counties stopped in traffic, pulled off roads, ran for cover, and lit up police switchboards after a giant and silent V-shaped vehicle slowly looped the area just above the treetops. According to one police officer, the appearance of the boomerang-shaped object may have simply been created by four or five pilots who regularly fly in close formation.

"I think they get a kick out of the [UFO] reports," he told a reporter. "I think that's what the idea is now, although I doubt they'd admit it." Several witnesses agreed, stating they could see separate fuselage shapes and hear engine noise. Still, many others argued that the object was flying too low and too quietly to be a group of small planes.

This particular incident was perhaps the largest mass sighting in the region, but it was hardly the first or last time locals saw something unusual in the Hudson Valley sky. Whitley Strieber, who was mentioned in the previous chapter, was allegedly abducted from the area just two years later. Other anomalous events have been observed since the mid-seventies, particularly in and around the quiet hamlet of Pine Bush. Its more than 25,000 reported sightings over the decades earned it the title of "UFO Capital of the Northeast."

In the early nineties, geologist Bruce Cornet made frequent visits to the small village and collected a series of photos and videos showing unusual lights and unnatural flight patterns. "I'd love these to be conventional planes," he told *Hudson Valley* magazine in 1997. "But they do loops, tiny figure-eights loops, zig-zag, go backwards, stop in midair, dive into the ground."

Some believe mineral deposits on the banks of the nearby Shawangunk Kill or the location's large deposits of magnetite and quartz attract aliens to the area. Or that unusually strong magnetic fields could be creating an interdimensional or intergalactic pathway to Pine Bush. Cornet went as far as comparing geographical data of the Pine Bush area to the Cydonia region of Mars, made famous by an image taken by a *Viking* orbiter in the 1970s that looked like a face on the planet's surface. For example, craters in both locations have a diameter of 2.3 miles and matching latitudes at 41 degrees, 36 minutes. "What is the probability of taking twelve geologic anomalies over a 200-square-mile area on one planet and have it correspond with those on another?" he asked. It led him to a theory that interplanetary links from ancient civilizations on both planets remain active. Others have proposed more terrestrial theories, such as Cessnas making local flights or, as is often the case, secret military projects.

Like in Roswell and Varginha, the Pine Bush population of about 1,800 have embraced their claim to fame with an annual festival and year-round imagery of aliens and saucers around town, from the front entrances of banks to restaurant windows to a local diner cleverly named the Cup and Saucer. In the summer of 2021, the celebration of local lore continued with the opening of the Pine Bush UFO and Paranormal Museum.

THE BERKSHIRE UFO INCIDENT:
THE ONLY UFO SIGHTING OFFICIALLY ARCHIVED AS HISTORICALLY TRUE IN THE UNITED STATES

Labor Day fell on September 1 in 1969, and just east of the Hudson Valley in Great Barrington, Massachusetts, families were out and about celebrating just like anywhere else. But by nightfall, what had been a normal holiday suddenly became most unusual, particularly for the Reed family.

Nine-year-old Thom was in the backseat of his mother's car as they headed home from their family diner in neighboring Sheffield. His younger brother, Matthew, was beside him, and his grandmother was in the passenger seat. As they drove slowly along a bumpy dirt road and across an old covered wooden bridge, Thom offered Matthew a fireball candy. His grandmother turned around to stop him for fear that the young boy would choke.

At that moment, she saw lights shining through the planks of the bridge and the gaps in its weathered covering, and then spotted a sphere of light rising from the banks of the Housatonic River. The thing was about three times the size of a car. Another one then appeared on the other side of their vehicle but stayed low to the water. Thom's mother saw a clearing ahead and pulled over so they could get a better look. By then the lights had vanished, but now a much larger object appeared in front of them, hovering over a marsh. This one seemed to be about a hundred yards wide, had a reddish glow, and was shaped like a turtle shell.

"We then felt like a pressure change, like we were deep underwater—there was, like, this almost suffocating feeling," Thom Reed recalled as he shared his experience at the 2022 MUFON International Symposium. "And we started to just look out at that craft, and everything just seemed muted. And then there was a flash, and an eruption of crickets, and katydids and frogs. Like someone flipped a switch and it all came back on."

That was the last memory Reed had of being in the car before suddenly finding himself in what appeared to be an airplane hangar. The open space was far too large to be a craft, he emphasized. Reed remembered hearing voices and seeing rows of tables, possibly autopsy tables, and apparatus coming down from the ceiling. Then, just as suddenly, he was back in the car. The ignition had been turned off and his grandmother and mother had mysteriously swapped seats. At that point, only his grandmother was conscious and she knew something was wrong. She turned the car around and headed back to town for help. By the time she arrived, she realized two and a half hours had passed since they'd left the diner.

Reed didn't remember being scared by the

strange event. "We had seen stuff in the area before but not as a family and not that close. There was a lot of activity in the area." They had first seen unexplained phenomena in the sky in 1966 and 1967. The latter sighting was reported by the *Berkshire Eagle* and described as "a big round glowing object" that hovered over the Great Barrington Airport.

This time, however, they weren't alone in witnessing the strange craft. Many holiday revelers were still outside that night and called the local radio station to share what they'd seen. No explanation has ever accounted for what the Reeds and other witnesses experienced.

"Does an alien know how to turn the key off on a Chevy station wagon?" Reed wondered. "But then you've got to ask yourself—because two and a half hours go by—did somebody else see the car running and turn it off to save the gas or whatever? So could someone else have intervened? Or was our government involved?"

As he looked back at the Great Barrington area in 1969, he pointed out that Sprague Electric, NASA, missile sites, and various manufacturing facilities were operating nearby—and magnesium used in the atom bomb was mined three miles from their diner. "So we have kind of adopted or believe that there was government involved in who extracted us from the vehicle."

In recent years, the Great Barrington Historical Society examined all the evidence in the case—including a 99.1 percent passing grade on a polygraph taken by Reed—and proclaimed that it believes what happened to his family is true. In November 2015, Governor Charles D. Baker signed a citation in recognition of the "off-world" incident, stating that it was "deemed historically significant and true by means of Massachusetts historians," thereby inducting it into the state's history.

The town erected a monument to the site, and supporters of the Reeds, including the families of B. B. King and Stevie Ray Vaughan, have sponsored benches in what's now become known as UFO Park. The 1969 sighting was also deemed worthy of an episode of the Netflix reboot of *Unsolved Mysteries* in 2020.

"There's no other case in the United States that has ever been formally and officially inducted as historically true," Reed told me at the MUFON event. "We are archived. We sit in history with the Boston Tea Party and Paul Revere."

The site of Thom Reed's 1969 UFO sighting in Sheffield, Massachusetts, is now known as UFO Monument Park.

The Belgian Wave of Triangles

In 1989, just as the Cold War was coming to an end with the fall of the Berlin Wall, V-shaped UFOs began dotting the skies of Belgium. The triangular objects first appeared in October and then put on shows almost daily for eight months to an estimated 10,000 witnesses. These included military and police officers, civilian pilots, air traffic controllers, meteorologists, aeronautical engineers, and scientists.

One of the most notable sightings took place in eastern Belgium on November 29. Among the hundreds of witnesses were several police officers. "It was like lights on a huge football field," recalled officer Heinrich Nicoll, who spotted the craft hovering near a meadow. "There was a huge triangular platform and underneath it, strong headlights, and in the middle was this blinking pulsating orange light. The whole thing was floating in the air." When he and his partner reported the event to their dispatcher in Eupen, they joked that "it might be Santa Claus trying to land."

Just minutes later, two other police officers a few miles north in the town of Kelmis saw it too. "We thought it was an American airplane or something," said officer Dieter Plumanns. "We had no other explanation for what it might be, but it was real. And it was above us."

Even if Plumanns didn't see an American aircraft, others might have. It's possible that over the months, citizens witnessed F-117 Stealth Fighters during night missions. The U.S. Air Force acknowledged the presence of F-117 flights over Europe, but offered no specifics on where they occurred. Other sightings were revealed to be hoaxes. Skeptics claimed it was a case of mass hysteria.

But these explanations account for neither all the sightings nor the unusual nature of so many of them—particularly considering that on March 30, 1990, a radar sighting concerned the Belgian air force enough to dispatch two F-16s to chase down whatever it was. The object accelerated from about 620 miles per hour to 1,120 miles per hour in seconds. The Belgian jets couldn't possibly keep up. "What the computers registered exceeded the limits of conventional aviation," a Belgian air force officer told reporters.

"We are not talking about 'lights in the sky' UFO reporting that could easily be explained away in conventional terms," wrote David

Marler in his 2013 book, *Triangular UFOs*. "These sightings appear to be what I would term 'unambiguous' UFO reports. Most eyewitnesses in Belgium described structured craft of immense size upwards of 300 feet in length. Misidentification, although possible, is not likely given the nature of the reports and corroboration by numerous witnesses."

The Highland, Illinois, Triangle UFO: "This Is Not a Joke."

Marler had personally investigated another case of flying triangles while he was living in Illinois and serving as MUFON's state director. These sightings began just east of St. Louis in the city of Highland at around 4:00 a.m. on January 5, 2000. The UFO seemed to be observing one of earth's underappreciated forms of amusement: a miniature golf course.

At the time, the owner of the course, Melvern Noll, was working an off-season side gig as a truck driver and decided to stop by his golf venue between deliveries. Suddenly, a light appeared in the sky and began moving toward him. Within minutes, it got close enough for Noll to realize the light was attached to a large metallic craft drifting slowly about a thousand feet above the ground. He said it was as big as a football field and appeared to have two levels, with bright white lights emanating from "windows" on both.

"I kept my eyeballs on it," he told the *St. Louis Post-Dispatch*. "It was all lighted and so low that someone could have waved at me out the window." The object eventually sped off without any little green men waving goodbye.

So Noll left too, and headed straight to the Highland police station to report whatever it was he'd just seen. The dispatcher contacted a neighboring police department in Lebanon, about fifteen miles southwest, to see if they'd had any similar sightings. The Lebanon dispatcher put out a call, and Officer Ed Barton responded. Not surprisingly, it was a rather odd exchange. Here's how it started:

> Dispatcher: (4:11 a.m.) Lebanon, this is a call from Highland PD in reference to a truck driver who just stopped in. And (he) said there was a flying object in the area of Lebanon. It was like a two-story house. It had white lights and red blinking lights, and it was last seen southwest over Lebanon. Officer, could you check the area?
>
> Officer Barton: (4:12 a.m.) It's a joke, right?
>
> Dispatcher: (4:12 a.m.) No. This is not a joke. I just got off the phone with Nancy at Highland PD.
>
> Officer Barton: (4:13 a.m.) Ten-four. Did they say if the truck driver was DUI or anything?
>
> Dispatcher: (4:13 a.m.) She said he was serious.

Soon enough, Barton saw the object himself, though what he witnessed was more of a narrow triangle with bright lights at each corner. Within the next half hour, three other police officers from other rural towns spotted the V-shaped UFO as well.

The sightings weren't far from Scott Air Force Base, though representatives responding to questions about the event said they knew nothing about it. The Federal Aviation Administration didn't have a clue either. A spokeswoman told the press that air traffic controllers "didn't see anything, didn't hear anything, didn't catch anything on radar."

According to the *Post-Dispatch*, two of the police officers said what they saw resembled a drawing of a stealth blimp designed by Lockheed Martin Skunk Works and published just months earlier in *Popular Mechanics*. So was the flying two-story house just new technology being tested? Or was it, as skeptic Philip Klass suggested, just a hoax or a balloon with bright lights or flares? "I would suspect this report is bogus," Klass told the press. Of course, ufologists hardly believed it was bogus. Not with four police officers witnessing the event in four separate locations.

Like the earlier triangle cases, the Highland incident remains unexplained.

UFO SIGHTINGS OF THE RICH AND FAMOUS

People who've seen UFOs haven't always found a receptive audience. Why should someone believe a random person's story with no proof? On the other hand, the general public is much more open to tales from people they know and love. Namely, famous people like Kurt Russell, who has discussed witnessing the Phoenix Lights (see page 170). And he's hardly the only celebrity who's claimed to have a close encounter.

Among the biggest, physically speaking, is NBA Hall of Famer Shaquille O'Neal, who shared his UFO sighting on *Jimmy Kimmel Live!* in May 2021. His experience happened in 1997 while he was on a double date in Madera, California.

"Right when we passed the fairground, by this big open lot, I could swear I saw this flying saucer come down with all the lights and it was spinning, and it took off," he told Kimmel. "Everything happened in less than five seconds. And we all looked at each other. I know that it was a UFO, I don't care what anybody says."

In July 2017, during an interview on the *Zach Sang Show*, pop star Kesha claimed to have witnessed five to seven UFOs during a visit to Joshua Tree National Park in southern California. "I was on nothing. I was a totally sober Sally, just a lady in the desert," the singer said. "I look up in the sky and there's a bunch of spaceships." She described them as "little balls of fire in the sky."

The experience influenced the prominent UFO cover art on her *Rainbow* album.

Fran Drescher, star of the '90s hit show *The Nanny*, told *HuffPost* in 2012 that she believes aliens abducted her when she was a teenager on the road with her father. A few years later she met her now ex-husband and learned he'd had the same type of experience.

"I think that somehow we were programmed to meet. We both have this scar. It's the exact same scar on the exact same spot," she said. Drescher's ex insisted that her scar must have come from a more mundane experience, but she disagreed. "I said to him, that's what the aliens programmed us to think. But really, that's where the chip is."

In an even more startling claim, UFO lore says that in February 1973, Richard Nixon showed avid flying saucer fan Jackie Gleason the bodies of four aliens "with small bald heads and disproportionately large ears" at the heavily guarded Homestead Air Force Base in Florida.[†] The story picked up steam years later when *The Honeymooners* star's ex-wife, Beverly, shared the tale while promoting her upcoming book on "The Great One." The tome was never released, but the legend lives on, with little to back it up.

A year after Gleason saw or didn't see dead spacemen, John Lennon saw a spaceship. It appeared in New York City on a Friday evening in

---

† Jackie Gleason's personal library included 1,700 books on UFOs, parapsychology, and the occult. He also built a home in Peekskill, New York, shaped like a flying saucer.

August 1974 after the legendary Beatles song-writer and his girlfriend at the time, May Pang, returned to their apartment from a studio session for Lennon's *Walls and Bridges* album.

"I was lying naked on my bed, when I had this urge," he explained in a 1974 issue of *Andy Warhol's Interview*, while insisting no drugs or alcohol were involved. "So I went to the window, just dreaming around in my usual poetic frame of mind, to cut a long short story, there, as I turned my head, hovering over the next building, no more than a hundred feet away was this thing . . . with ordinary electric light bulbs flashing on and off round the bottom, one non blinking red light on top."

It wasn't a helicopter or a balloon, he quickly determined. It was too silent for the former and didn't look like the latter. Its slow speed and low elevation didn't add up either. Excited and amazed, Lennon shouted for Pang to join him and the two witnessed the strange vessel together.

"John looked at me and he said, 'You're seeing what I'm seeing?' I said, 'It's an f-ing UFO!'"

Pang recalled in a Q104.3 interview in 2020. Windows were black all around them, indicating their neighbors on the block were away for the summer weekend. "I'm screaming like there's no tomorrow. So I'm thinking, God, if anything happened, nobody was coming up to us."

They tried taking pictures, but the film came back blank. According to Lennon, his photographer, Bob Gruen, tried to develop the roll but said it "looked like it had been through the radar at customs."

The UFO stuck around for about ten minutes and then drifted off toward the East River. A call to the *Daily News* the next day informed the Beatles frontman that two other reports were made, though it was unclear what had been seen.

Lennon recorded the event in the liner notes of *Walls and Bridges* with the message: "On the 23rd Aug. 1974 at 9 o'clock I saw a U.F.O." In the posthumously released song "Nobody Told Me," he continued the theme with the line, "There's UFOs over New York and I ain't too surprised."

The "Flying Dorito" over Lumberton, North Carolina

The Phoenix Lights is the most famous of the triangle UFO sightings, but a flurry of reports in 1975 that UFO researcher and historian David Marler has called the "first well-documented wave of triangular UFO reports" in the United States is equally as puzzling. It began at 1:45 a.m. on April 3 in Lumberton, North Carolina, when the sheriff's department received the first reports of a V-shaped craft drifting across the area.

Over a three-day period, at least thirty law enforcement officers and a host of civilians described seeing a triangular UFO with rows of red and white lights lining its sides and one or sometimes two spotlights beaming to the ground. It appeared to be roughly the size of a car and generally hovered at about treetop level but also zipped around the county, often taking sharp ninety-degree turns and zigzagging through the sky.

Officer Ernest Hagin was among the first witnesses and stared at the craft for about eight minutes before it sped off. "I never heard it make a sound, except when it turned, and made a SHHHHHHH type of noise," he said days after the event. "I'll tell you—I saw something out there, and I don't know what it was." As it took off, Hagin gave chase, but by the time he reached a hundred miles per hour, the flying V "just left real fast."

Following the initial reports, officials from the Federal Aviation Administration suggested the sightings were due to nothing more than training flights over nearby counties by a Boeing 737. Although these flights included low-altitude landing maneuvers, the first reports of the V-shaped craft were called in at least an hour before the 737 was in the air.

Ruling out conventional aircraft, sheriffs and highway patrol officers in the Lumberton area contacted America's flying saucer expert, Dr. J. Allen Hynek, at the Center for UFO Studies (CUFOS). Hynek was intrigued but wasn't available to make the trip to North Carolina immediately, so he asked fellow researcher Lee Speigel to go on his behalf.

"You're asking me to go to Lumberton to see a flying Dorito?" he said in response to Hynek's request. But thrilled at the prospect, off he went.

THE ROBESON COUNTY SIGHTINGS

© 2015 Dale Hendrickson. All rights reserved.

In 2015, after illustrator Dale Hendrickson heard about the Lumberton UFO, he contacted Lee Speigel for permission to create a painting of his sighting alongside law enforcement personnel. Artwork reprinted with Hendrickson's permission.

10 a

Large Spotlight

Flashing Red Light

1 or 2 Rows Red Lights Along outer Edge if wings

At 01:30 Policeman Ernest Haggin and two passengers were on a rural road north of St. Pauls when they spotted a flying V-shaped object. Haggin stopped and got out of the car. The outstanding features were a large white spotlight in front and rows of red and green lights along the edges. The altitude was estimated to be 200 feet; the distance to the object to be 500 feet. It appeared

Sketch and notes from Lee Speigel's 1975 CUFOS report on the Lumberton, North Carolina, UFO sighting.

By the time Speigel arrived at the Lumberton sheriff's department the next night, calls were already flooding the office. Wasting no time, he joined dispatcher Ronn Thompson for a drive in hopes of seeing the "Dorito" for himself. They followed the reports of the sightings from one location to another, but always arrived too late. Speigel saw a few pulsating lights at a distance, but later noted in his report that he "wasn't impressed or convinced." That soon changed.

Not long after midnight, as Speigel and Thompson continued their pursuit, a deputy radioed them to say the V-shaped craft was headed in their direction. Sure enough, lights appeared over the treeline across a nearby field. Thompson stopped the car and turned off the engine and lights, and they both stepped outside. Another officer and several other witnesses joined them as the object drifted closer and eventually hovered above the group. Shining brightly, it stayed silent and motionless for more than a minute as they gazed up in both awe and fear.

"My heart was pounding in my chest, I'll never forget that," Speigel told me during a phone interview. "I remember thinking, 'I feel pretty confident. Look, I'm surrounded by these guys and they've got their six-shooters, so yeah, no problem.' Then a moment later, I thought, 'What am I saying to myself? If this thing is here to eat us, or to take us away where no one will ever hear from us again, how safe and confident do I suddenly feel right now?'"

As he and the others watched the craft, a beam of light from its apex suddenly reached straight to the ground in front of them for two seconds and then shut off. Fortunately the UFO appeared to have no interest in eating or abducting them.

"The whole thing then turned an amber color and it very slowly turned in about a forty-five-degree angle, again making no sound, and it started to move off slowly and then shot away," Speigel said. Eager to keep after it and learn more, they all returned to their cars and chased it as far as they could.

Speigel's report to Hynek detailed observations from multiple witnesses, including the neighboring county's chief of police, Garry Moore, who'd seen the object just hours earlier. The bright light had lit up the entire cabin of his patrol car as he was driving, forcing him to pull over. He stepped out and grabbed a large flashlight and shined it up at the craft. "I blinked the light at it and the spotlight on the front of the object blinked back!" So Moore blinked twice. It blinked back twice, and then flew away.

Local air force officer Billy Cline told Speigel that no experimental craft were being tested in the area or in connection with other nearby bases. Even if they had been, FAA regulations would've forbidden maneuvers at such low altitudes in populated areas.

"These reports certainly don't describe anything that we have in the military today," Cline said. "I don't believe you'll find an aircraft that can slow down that slowly, stop, hover, and then speed off, unless it has rotor blades, which this object apparently did not have. . . . I think we're dealing here with something from another place . . . I don't know exactly where, but I don't think these objects are manufactured on this Earth."

By the time Speigel boarded a conventional aircraft to leave Lumberton, he agreed with Cline's assessment. Hynek and CUFOS expanded on the report but found no terrestrial explanation.

As an astronomer, Hynek was unquestionably one of the most vocal of scientists looking for answers to the UFO question in the latter half of the twentieth century. But just three years after his death in 1986, another voice spoke up. And to some, it might be loudest of them all.

Warning: Now Entering the Area 51 Section

If you've watched *Independence Day*, *Indiana Jones and the Kingdom of the Crystal Skull*, *The X-Files*, or countless UFO television shows, you've heard of Area 51. Maybe you even planned to storm it in 2019 along with a few million other Facebook users eager to break into the ultra-covert, top-secret, off-the-map, don't-get-too-close government facility. Area 51 resides in the desolate Nevada desert at Groom Lake, just north of Las Vegas, but had the authorities had their way, its location and very existence would never have made it into pop culture or conspiracy culture. Because like Vegas, what happens in Area 51 is supposed to stay in Area 51. Until a guy named Bob Lazar decided it didn't.

The entrance to Area 51 makes it clear you are not to enter.

Hungry UFO hunters heading toward Area 51 can stop for a Saucer Burger and Fries at the Little A'Le'Inn in the tiny town of Rachel, Nevada.

The thirty-year-old physicist began working at S4, a hangar located about nine miles south of Area 51, at the start of 1989. Technically, his position was with EG&G, a major defense-industry contractor working at the secret site. According to Lazar, getting to his new gig was a process as secretive as the facility itself. He and others met at EG&G, flew to Groom Lake, then got onto a bus with blacked-out windows and drove to S4. He wasn't entirely sure what he'd be doing, but he assumed it would involve advanced propulsion systems. It was a good assumption, considering the organization's history of success in that particular field.

Prior to 1989, Area 51 quietly went about its business of developing and testing advanced war machines, from military aircraft to other new technologies. The CIA and air force first opened its clandestine doors in 1955 to assess the high-flying U-2 Dragon Lady spy plane. Able to soar to an unprecedented altitude of 70,000 feet, it's no surprise the aircraft led to reports of UFO sightings. By the early 1960s, the complex was developing the A-12 Oxcart, capable of speeds reaching 2,300 miles per hour—five times that of any commercial plane. Over the course of six years, its 2,850 test flights around Groom Lake led to another spike in UFO sightings. The SR-71 Blackbird, the boomerang-shaped F-117 Nighthawk, and others followed. To all but the small team of scientists, engineers, and military personnel involved—and sworn to secrecy— these planes were indeed unidentified flying objects.

Upon Lazar's arrival at S4 he was given an overview document of the project he'd be working on. By his account, the word *extraterrestrial* showed up in the first paragraph. As he read on, the whole thing sounded unbelievable. "Was this just a test of my temperament and suitability to work in this environment, or was this reverse engineering of an extraterrestrial propulsion system a real work assignment?" he wrote, reflecting on his thoughts in his 2019 autobiography, *Dreamland*. Another file in the briefing explained that the spacecraft in question had arrived from the Zeta Reticuli star system, much like Betty Hill believed of her alleged abductors. Photos of a "humanoid organism" showed close-ups of body parts: a stub where an arm might be on a torso; a suggestion of legs protruding from a hipbone; but no head.

Not long after he'd begun work, he was taken to a hangar and shown

"It's the easiest
secret in the world to keep.
It's leaked out many times
before and no one believes it."

—GEORGE KNAPP, relaying to a coanchor at KLAS-TV
what Bob Lazar claimed he was told about flying saucers
by his superiors at S4

what few people on earth had seen—the alleged spacecraft from the distant star system. It resembled the classic flying saucer people had reported seeing since the late forties. In Lazar's words: "The familiar saucer shape of the craft, like an inverted soup bowl resting atop a second one, sat on the paved floor of the hangar. It had no landing gear or other structure that might have supported its weight while on the ground. From what I could discern, it was approximately fifty feet or so in diameter and was roughly twenty feet tall." He dubbed it the "sport model."

As he made his way around the metallic craft, he noticed it had no seams, no panel lines, and no welds. It's a description reminiscent of the UFO Daniel Fry claimed to climb aboard back in 1950. And like Fry, Lazar got to step inside. Three unusually small seats filled the cabin, but he saw no apparent control systems, dials, lights, or any types of displays.

"I was in awe of the technology behind this elegantly simple and purposeful execution of a craft designed to travel enormous distances, and with what seemed to me, to be based on the craft's construction, relative ease," he wrote.

After his tour, Lazar was debriefed further on the project and then taken back outside. There, he noticed the doors to the other bays in the facility were open, revealing eight other unique crafts. The craft he had just examined was now sitting in front of the hangar. Lazar heard a loud hiss, then witnessed the "sport model" lift off the ground with a wobbly motion, emitting a blue glow from beneath. The saucer rose thirty or forty feet as Lazar looked up "wide-eyed and mind-boggled." It descended, and then officials instructed him to get back to work.

As the days and weeks went on, Lazar grew frustrated with being followed by mysterious cars and having his calls tapped. Going public, he realized, might offer a little protection. He also felt people had a right to know what he knew—that whoever was running the show at S4 was deceiving the public and the scientific community. So Lazar reached out to investigative journalist George Knapp from KLAS-TV's *Eyewitness News* in Las Vegas, with the news that scientists at Area 51 were back-engineering alien spaceships with an antigravity reactor powered by a mysterious "Element 115."

Knapp, who wasn't a UFO guy prior to hearing about Area 51's secret saucer, spent months working with Lazar and checking his background. The schools he claimed to have attended, MIT and CalTech, said they had no records of him, as did Los Alamos National Laboratory representatives, where he claimed to have worked. Knapp, however found proof of Lazar's existence at the lab buried in a 1982 office directory. That didn't indicate what his position was, but it at least offered a shred of evidence to support that Lazar had been there in some capacity. Either Lazar invented and enhanced his own past, or someone went to great efforts to erase it. Believing the latter, Knapp felt confident Lazar was the real deal. And if there was ever breaking news, this was it. By November 1989, a series of interviews aired on KLAS.

"This came from somewhere else," Lazar told Knapp, as he described the ship that he saw. "I mean as bizarre as it is to believe, it's there, I saw it, I know what the current state of the art is in physics, and it can't be done."

As Knapp reported, polygraph tests yielded inconclusive results. Some experts felt Lazar passed, and others believed they indicated deceit.

"I am telling the truth," Lazar told Knapp, in his own defense. "I've tried to prove that. What's going on up there could be the most important event in history. You're talking about physical contact and proof from another system, another planet, another intelligence. That's gotta be the biggest event in history. Period. And it's real and it's there. I'm convinced that what I saw is absolute proof of that. There is no way we could've created those systems. There's no way we could've made the discs, the power supply, or anything to go with them."

At the end of the news story, one of Knapp's coanchors comments that keeping captured flying saucers secret would be quite difficult. Knapp responded with what Lazar said his superiors told him: "They say it's the easiest secret in the world to keep. It's leaked out many times before and no one believes it."

Lazar may have changed that for some. In the decades since he went public, his tale has inspired UFO hunters to visit Area 51, hoping to spot a flying saucer themselves. "Hidden here is the technology to end all wars, to end hunger, to provide an endless supply of energy," said one of them, a psychic and screenwriter named Sean David Morton. He and three friends journeyed to the complex in 1993. "I'm outraged that they're not showing it to the world."

But is there anything to show? Is Lazar history's biggest whistleblower, or is he a next-generation George Adamski? In the past thirty-plus years he's maintained the same story, with the same details and conviction. Naturally, as with any UFO-related story, he has his believers, deniers, and a fair share of I-don't-know-what-to-thinkers.

Nuclear physicist and ufologist Stanton Friedman, who, as we saw in Chapter 1, had faith in Roswell witnesses, struggled to trust Lazar. He didn't believe that his academic records had been erased, but, instead, that they just didn't exist as he claimed they did. In fact, Friedman's research found that Lazar had attended Pierce Junior College outside of Los Angeles. "If one can go to MIT, one doesn't go to Pierce," Friedman wrote in his 2008 book, *Flying Saucers and Science.*

When Russian scientists synthesized the extremely radioactive ununpentium in 2003, it was added to the periodic table as element 115 (now known as moscovium). Lazar's supporters immediately shared the news with Friedman as evidence that his story was genuine. But based on the production time needed to create the element, and its fraction-of-a-second half-life, Lazar's claim that the element made space travel possible didn't hold up for Friedman. "His scheme was science fiction," he commented.

Like Friedman, Christopher Mellon, the former deputy assistant secretary of defense for intelligence, takes issue with Lazar's dishonesty about his education. Mellon, who's been to Area 51, didn't see the "sport model" or anything else Lazar described, though he acknowledges it's a huge, expansive range. "There are some very secret things for sure that our government does, and has, but his particular story isn't really working for me," Mellon told me.

In addition, a trustworthy source who knew Lazar's supervisors claimed that his real job was checking radiation badges of people going in and out of the gate at the border. Though Mellon can't independently confirm this information, it has contributed to his doubt of Lazar's tale.

UFO researcher and TV host Ben Hansen has wavered on the story. He was also concerned by Friedman's research, but then he began analyzing video of Lazar. Hansen, as a former federal agent, is well trained in understanding body language.

"If he is lying, he has to be one of the greatest liars, that has perfected this over the years, and he's told the story a lot," Hansen told me. "But most people are not great liars. And to be able to conceal your body language and things that would give you away, I tend to side with him now that he might be really telling the truth."

Without actual evidence, Lazar's story remains just a story. But as David Marler stressed to me, it doesn't change the bigger picture: "Whether he's telling the truth or not, there is still a whole UFO phenomenon above and beyond Bob Lazar."

Whether you find Lazar credible or not, Marler is right, as evidenced by all the preceding stories and more recent cases discussed in Chapter 5. It's also about who might be engineering UFOs—or at least have the potential to do so. Finding out whether such extraterrestrial life exists has been a search taken on and theorized about by many credible scholars and astronomers for hundreds of years. In many cases with the belief that contact could happen any day now.

CHAPTER 4

THE SEARCH FOR EXTRATERRESTRIAL INTELLIGENCE

Scientific Exploration from Galileo to the Galileo Project

> "There are approximately ten thousand advanced extraterrestrial civilizations in our Milky Way Galaxy alone. I believe that what they have to tell us is of supreme importance. . . . And therefore I maintain it is worth doing everything in our power to ensure that we receive their signal at the earliest possible moment."
>
> —DR. FRANK DRAKE, in his preface to his 1992 book *Is Anyone Out There?*

When Nicolaus Copernicus stared up at the sky in the early sixteenth century and suggested his radical heliocentric theory—that the earth (and other planets) revolves around the sun rather than the other way around—it did not go over well. He challenged something bigger than the astronomical theories of his predecessors; he challenged a foundational, centuries-old belief system and the powerful Catholic Church. How dare this man suggest that the entire cosmos did not revolve around the earth?

Today, we know the universe is far bigger than even Copernicus ever imagined. The Milky Way alone has an estimated 100 billion to 400 billion stars and roughly one exoplanet per star (an exoplanet being any planet that exists outside our solar system). Since the early 1990s, when the first exoplanets were discovered, more than 5,000 have been found—with the amount doubling roughly every twenty-seven months. Based on those numbers, most scientists believe that somewhere out there, life exists. Whether that life is intelligent enough to have traveled here in a flying saucer is another story. But at its core, life elsewhere means that once again we're faced with the reality that this wondrous universe of ours doesn't revolve around us. That notion, not unlike Copernicus's theory about the sun, challenges the beliefs of every major religion.

While the discovery of exoplanets may be relatively new, the scientific notion of intelligent extraterrestrials living on other worlds is anything but. The question, as Nobel Prize–winning physicist Enrico Fermi famously asked in 1950, is: *where is everybody?* Scientists have been trying to answer that question for centuries. Let's explore how their beliefs, methods of exploration, and ability to collect data has changed over the course of time, starting with the early 1600s, when luminaries of astronomy were pretty sure extraterrestrials were more or less everywhere.

The Dawn of the Telescope Finds the Possibility of Life

Ideas about extraterrestrial life began coming into focus in 1610 after Galileo Galilei gazed through one of the first-ever telescopes and spotted the four moons of Jupiter. His scientific peer Johannes Kepler delighted in the discovery and took it as evidence that the solar system had other citizens. "Those four little moons exist for Jupiter, not for us," he stated. "Each planet in turn, together with its occupants, is served by its own satellites. From this line of reasoning we deduce with the highest degree of probability that Jupiter is inhabited."

Kepler didn't stop there. Galileo's telescopic observations of our own moon led him to believe it had an atmosphere of air and clouds and that its surface was similar to earth—complete with water. Therefore, why not life? To Kepler, Galileo's descriptions of the terrain indicated the presence of caves, which he expected must have been dug out by its dwellers. The moon continued to stir Kepler's imagination for decades. In his novel *The Dream*, published posthumously in 1634,

The seventeenth-century German astronomer Johannes Kepler believed life existed elsewhere in the solar system.

he suggested the harsh lunar living conditions would not be suited to human-like beings, but instead might host giant winged, reptilian, and amphibian creatures.

Eighteenth-century astronomer William Herschel, whose biggest claim to fame is the 1781 discovery of Uranus, had similar beliefs. In fact, he suspected all the planets were inhabited—and even the sun. During the late 1700s he frequently observed the giant ball of hot plasma and determined that dark spots were breaks in its "luminous atmosphere," indicating a solid surface "diversified with mountains and vallies" which made it nothing more than "a very eminent, large, and lucid planet." As for the people of the sun, Herschel presumed they had developed organs adapted "to the peculiar circumstances of that vast globe." He applied the same line of thinking to beings on all the planets.

Herschel, like Kepler, also believed the moon was likely inhabited. His logic, at the time, seemed perfectly sound: "While man walks upon the ground, the birds fly in the air, and fishes swim in water; we can certainly not object to the conveniences afforded by the moon, if those that are to inhabit its regions are fitted to their conditions as well as we on this globe are to ours."

IN THE BEGINNING, GOD CREATED MAN, WOMAN, AND FLYING SAUCERS: WAS EZEKIEL'S CHARIOT A UFO?

When Johannes Kepler and William Herschel speculated about beings on other planets, they never imagined that those beings had visited earth. Today, however, many believe aliens have been here as long as we've been here. In 1968, Swiss author Erich von Däniken popularized these ideas with his international best seller *Chariots of the Gods?* The book observes ancient texts and artifacts and, as the title indicates, asks the question: does the Bible speak of UFOs?

Von Däniken's curiosity is backed up with various biblical passages, but the story that comes closest to sounding like an ancient flying saucer is Ezekiel's vision.

In the Book of Ezekiel, the prophet says he beheld God's chariot from the banks of the river Chebar in Babylonia, but ancient astronaut theo-

Ezekiel's vision has led ancient astronaut theorists to believe the prophet described a UFO in the terminology available to him.

rists allege the passage is a description of a UFO. Based on this excerpt, it's not hard to see why:

> I looked, and I saw a windstorm coming out of the north—an immense cloud with flashing lightning and surrounded by brilliant light. The center of the fire looked like glowing metal, and in the fire was what looked like four living creatures. . . . As I looked at the living creatures, I saw a wheel on the ground beside each creature with its four faces. This was the appearance and structure of the wheels: They sparkled like topaz, and all four looked alike. Each appeared to be made like a wheel intersecting a wheel. As they moved, they would go in any one of the four directions the creatures faced; the wheels did not change direction as the creatures went. Their rims were high and awesome, and all four rims were full of eyes all around.

After Ezekiel spoke to God, he heard "the noise of the wings of the living creatures that touched one another, and the noise of the wheels over against them, and a noise of a great rushing. So the spirit lifted me up, and took me away."

In 1961, an aircraft mechanics instructor named Arthur W. Orton proposed that the vision was an account of an extraterrestrial landing. "If you concede that it is possible that we can visit other star systems in a future not too distant, why then could we not have been visited some time in the past?" he reasoned.

The four faces Ezekiel described (a man, a lion, an ox, and an eagle) may have been his interpretation of the ancient astronauts' respiratory apparatus and communications gear, using the only points of reference available to him. Orton made his case in an illustrated comparison of modern flight equipment to the prophet's vision and asked, "How much better could a man living six centuries before Christ" describe such a sight?

He assumed the visitors arrived in a large mother ship, stayed in orbit, and sent a scout ship with helicopter-like blades (the "wheels") to the earth's surface to search for inhabitants and to "determine the level of radioactivity, air components, spore and bacteria count and ra-

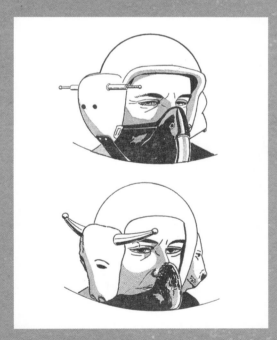

In 1961, Arthur W. Orton suggested Ezekiel's description of a four-faced creature was his interpretation of flight gear. The two illustrations demonstrate how each face might correspond to a piece of equipment.

dio signals incapable of penetrating the atmosphere." Not unlike we might do someday in a similar position.

Von Däniken added to Orton's argument in *Chariots of the Gods?*, stating that whoever spoke to Ezekiel "were certainly not 'gods' in the traditional sense of the word, or they would not have needed a vehicle to move from one place to another. This kind of locomotion seems to me to be quite incompatible with the idea of an almighty God."

Orton and von Däniken had their share of readers who agreed with their ideas and those who entirely dismissed them. Among the former was NASA engineer Josef F. Blumrich, who had helped build the Saturn V rocket that sent Apollo 11 to the moon. "I began to read von Däniken with the condescending attitude of someone who knows beforehand that the conclusions presented can by no means be correct," he said in the introduction to his 1974 book *The Spaceships of Ezekiel*. But after reading von Däniken's theories about the prophet's vision, Blumrich thought differently of the biblical passages. They appeared to be sophisticated details of a spaceship. Rather than refute von Däniken, he acknowledged he was wrong and embraced the fascinating possibilities.

"The prophet could only describe his encounters with space vehicles and their crews in the terms available to him—with words and comparisons familiar to him and his contemporaries," Blumrich reasoned. "So I began taking Ezekiel seriously, in an engineering sense."

His book presents a thorough explanation of the mechanics and mathematics behind the chariot. "The overall result, then, is a space vehicle technically feasible beyond doubt and very well designed to suit function and purpose; its technology is in no way fantastic but, even in its extreme aspects, lies almost within our own capabilities of today," Blumrich wrote.

The engineer's design for the "wheel intersecting a wheel" even received a patent. It is known as the Omni wheel and has been used in autonomous robots. So whether you believe Ezekiel encountered God or got abducted by an alien, his experience at least led humanity to advancements in technology.

ARE THE VON DÄNIKEN THEORIES REALLY TRUE?
WAS EARTH ONCE VISITED FROM OUTER SPACE? DID ALIEN BEINGS WALK OUR PLANET? A MAJOR NASA ENGINEER REVEALS SOME ASTONISHING FACTS!

THE SPACESHIPS OF EZEKIEL
BY JOSEF F. BLUMRICH

In 1974, NASA engineer Josef F. Blumrich authored a book explaining how a space vehicle could be built based on Ezekiel's description.

Hello, Planetary Neighbors: Early Attempts to Make Contact

With so many prominent figures holding strong convictions about a populated solar system, the next logical step for science was to determine ways in which we might make contact with its citizens. In 1820, German mathematician and physicist Carl Friedrich Gauss suggested a plan that would speak to any aliens out there through the universal language of math. He wanted to create a massive right triangle and three squares—symbolizing the Pythagorean theorem—on the Siberian tundra using pine trees and fields of wheat. If any interplanetary people were intelligent enough to develop their own telescopes, they'd surely see that we earthlings knew geometry and would know we were worthy of their attention. Twenty years later, Austrian astronomer Joseph Johann von Littrow proposed the creation of an even bigger spectacle by digging ditches in the shapes of triangles, squares, and circles in the Sahara Desert and filling them with kerosene to burn through the night. The sides and diameters would measure up to twenty miles in length. Such flaming symbols might signal a race of pyromaniacs, but it would assure exploring extraterrestrials that for better or worse, they weren't alone in the universe. Unfortunately, neither idea came to fruition.

Soon after von Littrow's proposal, when electricity was still in its infancy, French scientist Charles Cros built upon his predecessors' grand plans and hoped to erect giant electric lights in geometric forms to signal Martians. If spotted and reproduced, we would have proof of their intelligence and would continue developing shapes—an intergalactic alphabet of sorts—to begin a conversation. Cros also pitched a scheme to the French government that would direct the sun's rays at Mars using a giant mirror to imprint large figures of numbers and shapes right onto the Red Planet's surface, like some form of solar graffiti. The proposal was rejected, perhaps out of concern for the response that burning messages into an inhabited planet might elicit.

The idea, however, of communicating with the Red Planet escalated in fervor and creativity in 1877 when Italian astronomer Giovanni Schiaparelli peered through his telescope and spotted a network of crisscrossing lines across the surface of Mars. He called the lines *canali,* meaning "channels," but it was mistranslated everywhere as "canals." This suggested the lines had been artificially created by a planet full of engineers who could dig like no one on earth. By comparison, the Suez Canal had just been completed after ten years of intense labor. Mars, it appeared, had already covered its entire globe in canals.

An ambitious and wealthy astronomer named Percival Lowell marveled at the Martians' ingenuity and championed the notion that they were irrigating water from the polar caps in an attempt to save their planet from dying out. "Not only do the observations we have scanned lead us to the conclusion that Mars at this moment is inhabited, but they land us at the further one that these denizens are of an order whose acquaintance was worth the making," Lowell wrote in his 1908 book *Mars as the Abode of Life.*

Whether these Martians were desperately digging for their lives or not, the widespread certainty of their existence continued to inspire some of the world's greatest minds with ideas designed to establish communications. In 1909, the opposition of Mars positioned it just 36 million miles away from earth, giving scientists hope that contact would finally be made. Harvard astronomer William Henry Pickering proposed building a $10 million grid of fifty mirrors, each twenty-five feet square, to flash light signals across space. Though he didn't buy into the concept of canals, he wanted to determine once and for all if intelligent life roamed our next-door planet.

Based on his lunar observations in 1904, he already proposed vegetation grew on its surface and therefore there was "no reason why animal life should be impossible upon the moon." So sure, why not Mars? Perhaps instead of digging ditches the Martians were creating the lines across the globe by planting trees on plains in rows. Or maybe the lines were simply natural volcanic cracks. A response, or lack of one, might finally provide the answer. Pickering intended to play the waiting game to see if the Martians saw the lights and had the capability to respond.

"In hoping to get such signals back, we must assume, of course, that the Martians, if there are any, have telescopes, eyes, etc., just as human beings have on the earth," Pickering said. If so, he was prepared to de-

Finding Martians From a Lonely Mountain in Arizona

Percival Lowell's theories about Martians and their extraordinary planet-wide canal systems captured the imagination of the press and people everywhere. This article is from the *Boston Post* on December 8, 1907.

With Mars in opposition in 1920, scientists began planning ways to communicate with intelligent Martians. As seen in this headline from the July 13, 1919, *Kansas City Star*, one of them, Amherst professor David Todd, planned to rise 50,000 feet in the air in a hot-air balloon to better receive incoming messages.

Why Men Flirt With Mars.

A Strange Desire to Communicate With The Earth's Most Neighborly Planet Has Attracted Scientists for Decades

One Astronomer Believed He Saw
A Lake of Beer on Mars::
Another Said The Planet
Was Dying of Thirst.

The Ambition of Prof. David Todd, Who
Has Devoted Years in Trying to Send Signals

The People of Mars Think the People on Our Earth Must Look Like This

—Because They Know That the Force of Gravity Is Very Much Stronger on Mars, and Therefore the People of the Earth Must Be Slow, Heavy Creatures, with Shells Like Turtles to Protect Them from Hailstones.

What the Scientists of Mars Probably Think of Us.

WHILE our astronomers are peering at Mars and trying to determine what sort of life, if any, the planet holds, it is interesting to consider what the Martians think of us. In the first place, if their telescopes are no better than ours it is quite reasonable to suppose that they have proved to their own

The telescope must show that our world is full of clouds, storms and rain. Raindrops on the earth are bigger, heavier and fall with more force than on the ruddy planet. How much bigger and heavier they are must be a matter of speculation by the physicists of Mars. Quite reasonably they may conclude that our

The opposition of Mars in 1909 positioned it just 36 million miles away, giving scientists hope that contact would finally be made. In this clipping from the June 20, 1909, edition of the *San Francisco Examiner*, the journalist imagines how Martian scientists might describe us, based on our heavier gravity. Raindrops, for example, would strike us so hard we'd likely have developed hard shells to protect ourselves.

velop a system of dots and dashes to essentially establish an interplanetary Morse code.

The extravagant project never received funding, and so the mystery remained. That same year, Amherst College professor David Todd had a more affordable, but no less ambitious, plan designed to receive communications from Martians. Rather than flash signals or create massive mathematical symbols, he aspired to ascend 50,000 feet in a hot-air balloon to capture messages far above any terrestrial interference.

"I have no doubt the Martians have been sending us messages for hundreds of years," Todd said. "Doubtless they are wondering at our stupidity in not replying." Our silence, he believed, would have given them good reason to assume earth is not inhabited.

Like Pickering's program, Todd's 1909 plan never materialized. Nor did a second attempt in 1920. French astronomer Camille Flammarion, who frequently wrote about the plurality of worlds, surely appreciated Todd's efforts and would've agreed with his concern that we'd long missed Martian messages. Since Mars is an older planet, Flammarion believed its denizens' evolution had gotten a considerable head start and therefore they would be far more advanced than earthlings.

"Martian humanity is most likely more reasonable and is not mixed up with the littleness of frontiers, dialects, customs, national rivalries, etc.," he wrote in 1923. If they tried to signal us, it may have happened "200,000 or 300,000 years ago, before the appearance of man, at a time of the cave-bear or the mammoth" or during the time of the dinosaurs, or just a few thousand years ago. With no sign of intelligence, they may have just given up.

"Dreamers doubtless these men are who are seeking to communicate with a planet 45 million miles away, of whose inhabitants, if there are any, we know nothing. But wait yet a while to laugh. Who a hundred years ago would have thought that man could communicate with another across three thousand miles of space?"

—Unnamed journalist for the *Kansas City Star* on July 13, 1919

ANCIENT ALIEN ARCHITECTS

For decades, people have asked the question: how could the wonders of the ancient world, including the Egyptian pyramids, Stonehenge, and even the Moai statues at Easter Island, have been created without the help of advanced alien technology? In 1898, astronomer Garrett P. Serviss suggested that Martians visited earth long ago and built the pyramids and the Great Sphinx. An advanced race of giant aliens, Serviss contended, would explain "how those gigantic blocks that constitute the great Pyramid of Cheops had been swung to their lofty elevation." Serviss also happened to be a science fiction writer, and that quote appeared in his serialized tale *Edison's Conquest of Mars*. To author Erich von Däniken and other ancient astronaut theorists, however, the idea isn't science fiction at all.

Von Däniken surmised that fifty million people would've been needed for the construction of the Great Pyramid, which would have far exceeded the estimated world population at that time. Give or take a few million, he also notes the complexity of feeding such a workforce. Scientists, however, disagree with his calculations and suggest a more modest 10,000 workers. As for food, it's believed the pyramid builders mustered the strength to do the job thanks to the daily slaughter of enough cattle, sheep, and goats to serve 4,000 pounds of meat for dinner. All in all, no easy task, but quite possible without the aid of an extraterrestrial helping hand or whatever helping appendage they might have.

In August 2022, a team of international researchers published a paper in *Proceedings of the National Academy of Sciences* suggesting that the transport of stones used to build the pyramids might have been less formidable than imagined. Their findings cite evidence showing that 4,000 years ago the Khufu branch of the Nile River ran close to Giza. In other words, Egyptians had a convenient waterway running alongside the site of several major pyramids to help deliver materials.

Human ingenuity and brute strength might explain how the massive boulders that form Stonehenge were transported from quarries. Everything from the use of sledges, rafts, tree trunk rollers, stone balls, and hardworking oxen have been offered as alternatives to crafty aliens. After the long and surely painfully arduous journey, clever use of weights and leverage might have helped Neolithic workers lift the stones into their mysterious circular configuration. This is opposed to antigravity mechanisms or slings from spaceships that ancient astronauts theorists have suggested.

Modern scholars have proposed that Stonehenge served as a sacred burial ground. Its careful alignment also suggests it may have functioned as an astronomical calendar that corresponded to observations of solstices, eclipses, and moon cycles. But why go to such trouble to build a calendar? As von Däniken

An 1876 illustration of the mysterious Moai statues on Easter Island.

writes, "Was it just because they liked a hard life? I refuse to think that the artists of our great past were as stupid as that." Ancient astronaut theorists note the high levels of quartz in many of the standing stones and question whether the rocks may have emitted energy as part of a vast "power network" designed by superior beings.

Enticing as the idea may be, aliens likely didn't visit Easter Island either. The small chunk of land a couple thousand miles off the coast of Chile is famous for its wondrous and mysterious Moai statues that weigh as much as eighty-six tons each. "Even two thousand men, working day and night would not be nearly enough to carve these colossal figures out of the steel-hard volcanic stone with rudimentary tools," von Däniken wrote. "Who did do the work? And how did they manage it?" Once again, these are all good questions.

In the mid-1950s, explorer Thor Heyerdahl led an expedition of archeologists to Easter Island to look for answers. They didn't expect aliens, but the existence of the giant heads was undeniably curious. During the six-month mission, natives demonstrated a carving process that involved softening the volcanic rock with water. Six men carved the outline of a small statue in three days. Another 180 men then pulled the twelve-ton figure on a wooden sled across a hundred yards, proving that they needed no alien intervention.

Heading north from Easter Island, ancient alien theorists contend extraterrestrials visited the ancient Mayans and gave them vast amounts of information. Not only would this explain how they calculated their calendar with remarkable accuracy and predicted solar eclipses hundreds of years in the future, but it would also explain why an astronaut is seemingly carved into the lid of a twenty-ton stone coffin inside the tomb of Mayan king Pakal (who lived from 603 AD to 683 AD).

The ancient astronaut was unearthed following a 1949 discovery by Mexican archeologist Alberto Ruz Lhullier of a hidden staircase leading deep into the Temple of the Inscriptions, a seventy-foot-tall limestone pyramid at the ancient city of Palenque. After three years of excavating rubble, he found the burial chamber with the elaborately decorated twelve-foot-long sarcophagus. It features a man in a seated position, possibly commandeering some form of sophisticated vehicle. Namely, a rocket, as von Däniken and his disciple, Giorgio Tsoukalos—co-executive producer of TV's *Ancient Aliens* and frequent meme star—believe.

"He is at an angle like modern-day astronauts upon liftoff," Tsoukalos told *Scientific American* in 2013. "He is manipulating some controls. He has some type of breathing apparatus or some type of a telescope in front of his face. His feet are on some type of a pedal. And you have something that looks like an exhaust—with flames."

Archeologists argue that Pakal is in fact seated on what's known as the Quadripartite Sun Monster, shown in a state transitioning between life and death, upon which the king is being delivered to his final resting place. Tsoukalos's propulsion flames might instead be roots of the sacred maize tree. With maize being a Maya symbol of rebirth and food for the dead during their journey to the underworld, it seems a more culturally relevant interpretation. Without context, looking at and defining such ancient artifacts as alien-made is essentially a Rorschach test with an extraterrestrial filter.

Does this sarcophagus lid on the tomb of the Mayan king Pakal show a pilot taking off in a spaceship? Ancient astronaut theorists believe it does.

When Martians Sent Messages to Tesla and Marconi

While scientists philosophized on and debated the merits of their interplanetary communication schemes, two of the most brilliant thinkers of the early twentieth century believed they'd already been contacted by beings from the Red Planet. If Martians existed, it appeared as if they didn't have to ask anyone to "take us to your leader"—they knew exactly who to go to. The first was Nikola Tesla. The genius inventor claimed to have received a message in 1899 at his laboratory situated in the high altitude and pure air near Pikes Peak in Colorado Springs.

"I have observed electrical actions which have appeared inexplicable, faint, and uncertain though they were," he announced nearly two years later. "Brethren we have a message from another world, unknown and remote. It reads: ONE—TWO—THREE."

For Tesla, who believed both Mars and Venus were habitable, it was the breakthrough humankind had sought for ages. "I felt as though I were present at the birth of a new knowledge or the revelation of a great truth," he wrote in *Collier's Weekly* in 1901. The inventor felt confident he could contact the people of Mars and establish communications. The first message would simply be a response to the one he'd received: "Four."

"The Martians, or the inhabitants of whatever planet had signaled to us, would understand at once that we had caught their message across the gulf of space and had sent back a response," Tesla explained. "To convey a knowledge of form by such means is, while very difficult, not impossible, and I have already found a way of doing it."

This bold proclamation proved to be a tease since, despite his conviction, he didn't start a counting conversation with Martians. Though it was not for lack of effort. By 1907 he announced he'd been working with electric power companies with immense generating plants at Niagara Falls to project an 800,000,000-horsepower message across space to the Red Planet. Newspapers hailed his plan for months, but no attempts were ultimately reported. Still, Tesla continued working on interplanetary communication schemes—and continued claiming he had the ability to succeed—into his eighties.

Marconi Asks, Is Mars Signaling Earth? Weird Sounds on the Wireless

Mystifying sounds have been picked up in the air by wireless apparatus attuned to receive long wave lengths. This fact has started speculation among scientists.

Marconi, inventor of the wireless telegraph, raises the question, "Is Mars signaling the Earth?"

Views are given to Universal Service by the following noted men:

BY GUGLIELMO MARCONI,
Inventor of the Wireless.

Marconi's otherworldly signals made for sensational headlines, like this one from the January 29, 1920, edition of the *San Francisco Examiner*.

As for the 1899 message the renowned inventor believed he had received, biographer Marc Seifer suggests it was sent not by a Martian but by a Marconi. That summer, Italian physicist Guglielmo Marconi was transmitting the Morse code signal for S (dot-dot-dot) across Europe and the English Channel, "which precisely corresponds to the three beats Tesla said he intercepted while he was in Colorado," Seifer observed.

Oddly enough, Marconi is the other innovator who claimed to have detected messages from Mars. Though he's best remembered today as the inventor of the wireless telegraph and the father of radio, a chat with aliens would have far surpassed those achievements.

In January 1920, Marconi announced to the press that he'd received a series of mysterious signals on 150,000-meter wavelength while experimenting with his wireless instruments. This was well above any wavelength known to be in use on earth at the time. "Most striking of all is the receipt by me personally of signals which I believe originated in the space beyond our planet," the famed physicist said. "I believe it is entirely possible that these signals may have been sent by the inhabitants of other planets to the inhabitants of earth."

Marconi spent the next two years listening for more otherworldly messages, but no one reached out. It wasn't until 1922 that the source of the signals was discovered. In what must have been a moment of profound disappointment, the answer to Marconi's great mystery turned out to be the far less exotic locale of Schenectady, New York—home of General Electric. Upon a visit to the company's labs, one of the researchers admitted to conducting experiments with a wavelength of 150,000 meters. The experiment had been unannounced, and the current had raced across the planet to Marconi.

Tesla and Marconi never heard from the aliens they'd hoped might be out there, but as higher frequency radio receivers became available in the 1930s, their idea of listening to the cosmos would be expanded on and developed into an entire new branch of astronomy: radio astronomy. The man who started it all? A guy from the phone company.

Radio Astronomy and the Wizard of Project Ozma

Physicist Karl Jansky had no intention of finding extraterrestrial life in the universe. In 1932, his mundane job at the Bell Telephone Laboratories simply required him to find the source of static in phone signals. So, using a motor and Ford Model T tires, he designed an antenna that could rotate 360 degrees as he pointed it at the sky in search of noise.

As Jansky listened for interference, he found that his equipment produced a steady hiss throughout the day but spiked at a certain time. He noted the time, then listened the next day to see if it would repeat. It did, but it came four minutes early. This told him the signal was repeating on a cycle of 23 hours and 56 minutes, which aligned with the earth's rotation relative to the stars, as opposed to the sun. That meant the signal originated from somewhere out in the Milky Way. It was, as science writer Willy Ley said, "the first piece of evidence that radio waves from space reach the ground."

Jansky's accidental discovery was published, and by 1937 an inspired amateur astronomer named Grote Reber cobbled together a sheet metal dish with a thirty-one-foot diameter in his Wheaton, Illinois, backyard. It became the first dedicated radio telescope. Over the next few decades, more advanced dishes were built, and astronomers suddenly weren't restricted to telescopes dependent on light. They now had a "second window" into the universe. While Project Blue Book was studying flying saucers over earth in the late 1950s, radio astronomers were exploring new aspects of the universe, like the fiery cores of distant galaxies called quasars.

Around this time, a young doctoral candidate at Harvard named Frank Drake grew interested in this budding field. The radio telescope, he realized, "was the prime instrument for detecting and even communicating with extraterrestrial beings." It could beam messages into space, and if aliens were equally curious about us, it could receive signals they may be directing at us.

One night while manning the sixty-foot telescope at Harvard's observatory to study the Pleiades star cluster, Drake thought he'd gotten just such a signal. It was too regular to have a natural origin, and unlike anything he'd seen before. Somewhere, four hundred light-years away, Drake believed someone was saying hello.

He was just twenty-six years old at the time. Reflecting on the experience decades later in his book *Is Anybody Out There?*, he wrote, "I'm past sixty now, and I still can't adequately describe my emotions at that moment. I could barely breathe from excitement … what I felt was not a normal emotion. It was probably the sensation people have when they see what to them is a miracle: You know the world is going to be quite a different place—and you are the only one who knows."

Before celebrating, Drake had to be sure the signal was truly originating from the Pleiades. So he turned the telescope away, and much to his dismay, the signal continued. That meant only one thing: the signal was coming from earth. It most likely originated from the military, Drake assumed.

The young radio astronomer would soon find himself with another chance to greet aliens when he joined the staff at the National Radio Astronomy Observatory nestled in the Allegheny Mountains of Green Bank, West Virginia. Shortly after arriving in the spring of 1958, his team began building a new radio telescope with an eighty-five-foot receiving dish. This size, along with new improvements in the technology of receivers, he believed, was sufficient for a serious search.

"I had extraterrestrial designs on the telescope the moment it was finished," Drake wrote.

The telescope's increased sensitivity could detect signals from as far as twelve light-years away—roughly 70 trillion miles. Drake reasoned that if an intelligent alien civilization had a similar radio telescope, he could pick up their signals. Two stars, Tau Ceti and Epsilon Eridani, for example, are about eleven light-years away, putting them well within range.

"The implausible had suddenly become possible," Drake believed.

Now he just needed to sell the idea of using the observatory's new telescope to find aliens, instead of just signals from natural processes in stars and galaxies. Drake took his chance over greasy diner burgers and fries one afternoon with his colleagues. To his delight, the head of the observatory gave him the green light before the waitress brought their check.

In addition to needing extra equipment and a team, the project needed a name. Given the nature of the quest, and his childhood affection for L. Frank Baum's Oz stories, Drake named the program Project Ozma, after the princess from the Land of Oz. "Like Baum, I, too, was dreaming of a land far away, peopled by strange and exotic beings."

At the same time Drake was preparing his ambitious project, two Cornell physics professors published a paper in the September 1959 issue of *Nature* called "Searching for Interstellar Communications." Guiseppe Cocconi and Philip Morrison had come to the same conclusion as Drake, and acknowledged the immense difficulty in finding success. But by April 1960, Ozma was ready to go, meaning those chances got slightly better. For as Cocconi and Morrison wrote at the end of their article, without a search "the chance of success is zero." Their combined efforts and curiosity marked the beginning of what would become known as SETI, the Search for Extraterrestrial Intelligence.

Drake had prepared the Green Bank telescope with a special device to filter out terrestrial radio interference and focus on signals from space to be received at a frequency of 1,420 megacycles. This specific number corresponded to the vibration frequency of interstellar hydrogen atoms, which, due to their abundance throughout the universe, is the radio astronomy frequency Drake believed would most likely to be chosen by intelligent aliens trying to reach another planet. Perhaps this ubiquitous frequency was how other civilizations had been meeting for billions of years and, in today's terms, we'd finally found the Zoom link to join the interstellar meeting.

In the wee hours of a cold, foggy April 8 morning, Drake and two student assistants pointed the giant ear toward Tau Ceti, eager for a historic moment.

"Then there was nothing to do but wait," Drake recalled in *Is Anybody Out There?.* "You will perhaps not be surprised to learn that we waited with breathless anticipation. It was as though we expected the aliens to speak to us at any moment. We were that hopeful, that excited."

A simple output device squiggled lines on a moving strip of paper representing sounds from space. But the squiggles gave no indication of anything unusual. Nothing that could only originate from another civilization's technology.

Later in the day they aimed the telescope to their second target: Epsilon Eridani. Suddenly, things got a lot more exciting.

"Scarcely five minutes passed before the whole system erupted. WHAM!" Drake wrote. "A burst of noise shot out of the loudspeaker, the chart started banging off the scale, and we were all jumping at once, wild with excitement."

Drake was reliving the thrill he'd felt while observing the Pleiades. It was just the kind of signal he was expecting to get from a civilization waving its arms through interstellar space to get noticed. And this time, when he turned the telescope, the signal didn't follow. That indicated it must've been coming from Epsilon Eridani. But when he pointed the telescope back at the star, the signal disappeared. So did his team's adrenaline rush.

To fine-tune their experiment, the astronomers added another device designed to detect terrestrial interference. If the signal came back from Episilon Eridani, it would only come through the telescope, rather than through both devices. After ten days of waiting for a return burst of activity, they finally got it. Unfortunately, the terrestrial device picked it up as well, and Drake determined the signal had merely come from a passing plane.

The project recorded about two hundred hours' worth of observation time between April and July. During that time, the press took interest in the possibility of finally establishing communication with another world. Listening was great, but if we heard something, reporters wondered how we would respond.

"This project is still worrying about its ears," one member of the Ozma team told the press in May. "It has not even thought about a mouth yet." But Drake gave the public hope by suggesting that a one-megawatt transmitter would be powerful enough to send a signal back. Like scientists before him, he suspected any conversation would be in the language of mathematics. At least to start. Any communication offered the prospect of developing into something more robust, as one reporter wishfully anticipated: "Although it would take twenty-two years to get an answer, the far-off Wizards of Ozma might be able to tell us how to cure cancer or how to live in peace."

The months-long experiment came to an end when no more telescope time could be committed to the project. The Land of Oz remained elusive, but Drake's exploration marked a beginning of what became a much broader search.

"We had set out looking for advanced alien civilizations the way a drunk searches for lost keys: by hunting under the light of a streetlamp, where the effort is easy, instead of the dark places out of sight—where searching may yield results," Drake wrote, looking back. "Beyond the perimeter of the lamp glow, out beyond the reach of the eighty-five-foot telescope, lay billions more stars to be explored before the question could be answered."

How Many Aliens Are Out There? Do the Math: The Drake Equation

Not long after Project Ozma came to a close, Drake's efforts to discover extraterrestrial intelligence caught the attention of the Space Science Board of the National Academy of Sciences. A staff officer, J. Peter Pearman, telephoned Drake in hopes of organizing a conference at the National Radio Astronomy Observatory's Green Bank observatory to discuss the potential of his research. The two compiled an invite list right there on the phone, which included a young Dr. Carl Sagan, who at the time had made a name for himself as an "exobiologist"—meaning he studied life beyond earth. Sagan's mentor, Dr. Joshua Lederberg, a genetics professor at Stanford and the chairman of the Academy of Science's Panel on Extraterrestrial Life, made the list as well. Rounding out the group were six other esteemed minds from the fields of astrophysics, astronomy, electronics, chemistry, and neuroscience. The latter was represented by Dr. John C. Lilly, who'd been studying communication with dolphins.[+] Dolphins aren't aliens, but they were the closest thing we had to an intelligent nonhuman life form.

Drake and Pearman planned a three-day conference for this meeting of the minds, beginning November 1, 1961. But with this much scientific firepower gathered in one setting, Drake needed an agenda to get the most out of their time together.

[+] By the end of the conference, the team had dubbed itself the Order of the Dolphin.

The father of SETI, Dr. Frank Drake, stands in front of the eighty-five-foot radio telescope at the National Radio Astronomy Observatory in Green Bank, West Virginia, where he conducted Project Ozma.

"What do we need to know about to discover life in space?" he asked himself. With that basic question in mind, he began listing each of the relevant points, including the number of suns that could be expected to have a system of planets, the number of planets that might support life, and, of those, the chances that that life might be intelligent. The factors were interdependent, which led Drake to write his entire agenda for the conference as a single equation:

$$N = R f_p n_e f_l f_i f_c L$$

At a glance, this galactic calculus may appear as difficult to understand as the physics-defying spaceships people were seeing on a regular basis, but the logic is simple and brilliant. The answer, N, is the number of intelligent civilizations that exist in space and are looking to chat. Finding that answer, however, is based mostly on educated guesses for each variable, which, as Drake described them, are: the rate of star formation (R), times the fraction of stars that form planets (f_p), times the number of planets hospitable to life (n_e), times the fraction of those planets where life actually emerges (f_l), times the fraction of planets where life evolves into intelligent beings (f_i), times the fraction of planets with intelligent beings capable of interstellar communication (f_c), times the length of time that such a civilization remains detectable (L).

Today it's known as the Drake Equation. But during the conference, each term was an individual discussion point. Without going into the nitty-gritty of astrobiology and the specifics behind their astronomical calculations, the group began with R and confidently resolved that the rate of star formation each year in any given galaxy was one. With that, their minds were off and running into the cosmos.

The next variable, f_p, had no set answer, but the team agreed that one-fifth to one-half of the stars might have a system of planets. So how many might support life? For n_e, they looked within our solar system, which clearly has one planet supporting life, though Mars still may prove to host life, or may have once hosted life. At the time, Venus was also believed to possibly support some form of living organism. That's three within the habitable zone. Sagan suggested an atmospheric greenhouse effect could help support life even at distances from a star that might seem too far. So they settled on one to five planets per planet-hosting star.

Over time, the group believed, "it was reasonable to expect life to arise through the sheer force of the laws of physics and chemistry." Basically, if a planet could host life, it eventually would. They determined that the value for f_l was one. And if life could evolve, it was believed intelligence would eventually prosper. This could, as Lilly had been discovering, include creatures like dolphins. Therefore, they also assigned f_i a value of one.

Intelligence is one thing, but to evolve into a being capable of sending interstellar communications, a few other conditions must be met. For example, no matter how brilliant our dolphin friends may be, they're stuck in the oceans. They can glimpse the sky only during the brief moments when they leap out of the water, giving them limited chances of understanding there's an entire universe out there. Even if they could, their flippers would make it tricky to design telescopes and develop rocketry. But assuming other planets had beings that lived on land and possessed an anatomy capable of creating technology, they might give off signals even if they had no intention of doing so. We certainly have. Electromagnetic signals from television have been leaking out into space since the first shows aired. Any intelligent civilization more than sixty light-years away may (or may not) be enjoying wholesome episodes of *I Love Lucy* and *Leave It to Beaver* by now. With this in mind, the conference assigned f_c an estimated value of one-fifth to one-tenth.

The final term, L, proved especially difficult to predict. Just how long might an intelligent civilization survive? We've arrived at the point where we're perfectly capable of wiping ourselves out. Or an asteroid could do the job for us, as it did for the dinosaurs. Then again, perhaps those issues can be avoided for another few thousand years. Could advanced civilizations have found ways to live in peace and ward off threats from space? Drake's team settled on a wide range, netting out at anywhere from one thousand to hundreds of millions of years.

With values assigned to each variable, and most canceling one another out, Drake determined that in the end, N essentially equaled L.

Thus, he announced their collective conclusion: "Our best estimate is that there are somewhere between one thousand and one hundred million advanced extraterrestrial civilizations in the Milky Way."

That's a whole lot of potential aliens. Drake would later refine his estimate to ten thousand, which is significantly less than the higher end of his original statement, but it still predicts a healthy extraterrestrial population out there. This brings us back to Fermi's question: where is everybody?

With such great numbers of aliens estimated, UFO believers could use them as added validation and tell Fermi the aliens have already found us and visited. Drake, however, didn't buy into that belief. If contact were to be made, he was convinced it would be through radio. UFOs were certainly not visiting from Venus, Mars, or elsewhere in the solar system, and the next closest star, Alpha Centauri, is roughly 25 trillion miles away. That meant if an alien civilization did indeed catch episodes of *Leave It to Beaver* and wanted to annihilate us for it, sheer distance would keep us safe.

"The laws of physics guarantee there is no way for an alien civilization to attack us or exploit us," Drake said years later, in 1996. "The distances between the stars create an interstellar quarantine."

Contemporary Scientists Reexamine the Drake Equation

But not all scientists agree with Drake's idea of an "interstellar quarantine." If at least one of the intelligent extraterrestrial civilizations evolved thousands of years before us, isn't it reasonable to think that they've figured out ways to make the seemingly impossible trip? Considering our own progress in just the past hundred years, what might other intelligent beings with a head start of a thousand or even five hundred years be capable of?

Astronomer Marc D'Antonio thinks it's quite possible. Otherworldly beings have been an interest of his since childhood, when he joined MUFON at age eleven. Today he serves as the organization's chief photo and video analyst, combining his scientific skills with photography and computer-generated graphics to frequently debunk UFO images.

"There's life elsewhere without a doubt," he said in a phone interview with me. "I think they've made it here. I think that just because it's not in scientific purview yet, it certainly doesn't mean it's not in some other life-form's purview yet. So why here? Why in all the stars in the universe, why in the heck would they find us? It's not like we're quiet. And what I mean by that is not our radio and not our TV, but what we've been pumping out for over two billion years. And that is the signal that there's oxygen in our atmosphere."

So if there's another civilization out there, perhaps they could've detected some form of life here as early as a couple billion years ago. Perhaps they've been sending probes out into the universe just like NASA has been. "If we're looking for life, why can't some other species somewhere else be looking for life?" D'Antonio asks.

Other scientists agree with this possibility, but it's often left to the realm of imagination, not science. "Given how fast technology has progressed, and how undistinguishable from magic it can become, it's perfectly reasonable to be open to the idea that an alien civilization could be traveling through space and time in such a way that they might appear to us as fleeting unrepeatable UFO events," planetary scientist Dr. Pascal Lee told me. "But having said that, therein lies the problem. Our scientific method is geared toward studying things are repeatable events, are testable."

As Lee points out, it comes back to Carl Sagan's mantra: "Extraordinary claims require extraordinary evidence." A UFO with an extraterrestrial pilot in a space-time craft is indeed an extraordinary claim. "We need extraordinary evidence for that. And short of actually making contact and them spending some space and time with us, you really don't know," Lee said.

Lee also questions the possibility because he believes the N in the Drake Equation is significantly smaller than 10,000. Despite recent data that suggests the number of planets in the universe is about 100,000,000,000,000,000,000,000 (that's 100 sextillion, in case you were wondering) with a trillion of them in the Milky Way alone, Lee suggests it's closer to one. That would be us.

In his lecture, "N~1: Alone in the Milky Way," Lee explores each of the seven terms in the Drake Equation and explains how he arrived at a far different result. At a glance, the discrepancies are largely due to the many statistical challenges involved with arriving at an intelligent civilization that's capable of communicating with us. Looking within our own galaxy, for example, many of the potentially habitable planets that might orbit a star, within 30,000 light-years of the Milky Way's center, face daunting odds of being exposed to intensely powerful gamma ray bursts that would wipe out all life on the surface. To put the danger of these rays in perspective, a burst radiates as much energy in hours or days as the sun radiates over the course of its life. That's extremely bad news for a planet within its range. We earthlings are considerably safer hanging out on the outer edge of the galaxy where gamma ray bursts are less frequent. Lucky us.

We're also fortunate in other ways. Life started forming on earth early on, at least in microbial form. "Life itself might be a relatively straightforward process," Lee said. Based on that, he speculated, "Microbial worlds in our galaxy might be relatively common." Take Europa, one of Jupiter's moons. It has an ocean that's a hundred kilometers deep, capped by a twenty-kilometer-thick ice cap. By comparison, earth's oceans at their deepest are about ten kilometers. "What could possibly be lurking at depth?" Lee wonders. Still, we humans, an intelligent species that learned to use tools and interact with our environment, are about a million years old. It took a long time for us to get here, and if not for the giant asteroid that wiped out the dinosaurs and left a few burrowing mammals alive so they could evolve into us, there'd likely be no us.

That's not the only good luck. We're not like the dolphins Drake's team discussed. We live in an environment that allows us to look up and learn and, as Lee notes, our gravity is conducive to sending telescopes into space to allow us to keep learning. We also haven't been wiped out by a space rock or killed off by a pandemic or war (yet). These are among the many conditions Lee discusses that make us unique.

What if Lee's calculation is right and we truly are alone in the galaxy? Even if we weren't, some civilization would have to be the first. Could that be us? It's possible that we're the starting point for intelli-

"Most people look at our galaxy and think that you're open-minded if you think we're not alone. That somehow you're forward-thinking by claiming there are other civilizations out there. The truth is we might be it. It's a very daunting and unsettling perspective, because if it's true, and it could be true, then wow, nobody's coming here to help us anytime soon. We're on our own, baby. It's a big vast galaxy and we are it. Nobody's going to show us how to warp drive for us, unless we come back and visit ourselves from the future. I find it very intriguing that although we could be the natural evolution of things, we could be such a rare outcome that it's almost giving us some divine responsibility."

—DR. PASCAL LEE, planetary scientist at the SETI Institute and chairman of the Mars Institute, in a September 2021 interview with the author gent communicative folks in the universe and others are centuries or millennia behind.

But what if Lee's calculation is off by one? Let's imagine for a moment that there's one other intelligent civilization in the Milky Way. Based on the scale of the galaxy and the statistics of having two civilizations, we could estimate their distance as being 50,000 light-years away. And let's assume our civilization and our far-away neighbors both last a generous 10,000 years. Our signal would take 50,000 years to get there, and theirs would take the same. That means if we picked up their signal, they would be tens of thousands of years more advanced than us and would likely be gone by the time we heard them.

"Not only do distances between civilizations affect their ability to communicate, but if civilizations are short-lived, then that's also a barrier to our ability to overlap in time and communicate effectively," Lee explained.

It's a bleak outlook. But there's a whole universe outside our potentially very lonely galaxy, filled with a hundred billion other galaxies, as Lee noted, "many of whom will be far more advanced than we are, from the statistics they could be more advanced by billions of years."

Distance, of course, still makes things especially tricky. The nearest large galaxy is Andromeda, and that, as we've learned from the alleged extraterrestrial immigrant in the 1969 Condon Report (see page 73), is more than two million light-years away.

"If you were to detect a signal from an alien civilization from a nearby galaxy, it would be a very scary prospect because that would mean they'd have a two-million-year head start on us," Lee said. "But that's the kind of time scale that might allow them to travel through wormholes or travel through space-time that we have no inkling of now."

Until we figure out wormholes or warp speed, or aliens show up and make their presence undeniably known, scientists will keep listening. As Coccino and Morrison said in 1959, there's still a chance of finding someone else out there as long as we look. And regardless of the different possible solutions to the Drake Equation, those searches continue to keep hope alive.

PASCAL LEE'S 14 POSSIBLE EXPLANATIONS TO THE FERMI PARADOX

In his lecture titled "N~1: Alone in the Milky Way," planetary scientist Dr. Pascal Lee details his conclusion to the Drake Equation. But first he explores a world in which Drake's *N* variable is high, indicating that many intelligent civilizations exist somewhere in the galaxy. If such a scenario were correct, then as Fermi asks, "Where is everybody?" Lee offers the following explanations (and interpretations) for the lack of evidence of extraterrestrial life.

EXPLANATION	INTERPRETATION
Interstellar communications and travel are too difficult.	Not worth pursuing.
Intelligent civilizations (ICs) are too alien.	Lost in translation.
ICs are too advanced or too busy.	We mean nothing to them. They've got other fish to fry.
ICs are not radio-loud for long.	They've all switched to cable.
ICs are avoiding us.	Best proof they're intelligent.
ICs are breeding us.	We're someone's ant colony.
ICs are protecting us.	They follow the Prime Directive.
ICs are studying us.	We're someone's science project.
ICs are training us.	We're not worthy yet (not potty-trained yet).
ICs can't agree on what to do.	They have a Congress too.
ICs are here, but unseen.	We're in a LOT more trouble than we think.
Search for Extraterrestrial Intelligence (SETI) is young.	We've only just started.
SETI is misguided.	We're not doing the search right.
SETI is suppressing evidence.	(This space intentionally left blank.)

A Glass of Water Out of the Ocean: Dr. Jill Tarter and the Founding of the SETI Institute

To date, scientific efforts have yet to receive a signal from a remarkably advanced civilization that's either thriving light-years away or long gone. But what happens if it does? Carl Sagan explored the idea in his 1985 novel, *Contact*, which was adapted into the 1997 film starring Jodie Foster. The Academy Award–winning actress plays scientist Ellie Arroway, who discovers a signal repeating a sequence of prime numbers emanating from the Vega star system about twenty-six light-years away. But the real math gets complex as the world contends with the social and political ramifications of extraterrestrial life.

Sagan naturally had the scientific background to make the story as true to life as science fiction might get. That includes the character of Arroway, who was inspired by the real-life astronomer and cofounder of the SETI Institute, and the current Chair Emeritus for SETI Research, Dr. Jill Tarter.[†]

Tarter hadn't planned to further Frank Drake's SETI work and make a career out of listening for aliens. But while finishing her graduate studies at Berkeley, an astronomy professor named Stuart Bowyer was looking to pursue research into extraterrestrial intelligent life and needed someone who could program a computer to help analyze data from the Hat Creek Radio Observatory, located about 300 miles north of San Francisco. In the mid-seventies, programming was a rare skill, and Tarter happened to have spent her first year at Berkeley working with one of the world's first minicomputers, the PDP-8/S.

"Someone gave him this computer," Tarter recalled in a phone interview. "He said, 'What the hell do I do with this?' They said, 'Well, Jill's still here, why don't you go ask her?'"

So Bowyer did. And to help explain his plan for it, he brought along a copy of NASA's 1971 plan to search for radio signals from extraterrestrial civilizations, code-named Project Cyclops. The 243-page report

---

[†] Jill Tarter loves the movie *Contact*. But when a clip was played at Carl Sagan's memorial just months before the film's release, there was an error in Arroway's simplified version of the Drake Equation. "She's taken 10^{11}, multiplied it by 10^{-18}, and come up with 10^6. And it's just so many orders of magnitude wrong," Tarter shared with me. "At the end you just heard scientists and engineers do a collective groan because *we* could see how wrong it was. . . . I like the movie but didn't like the innumeracy."

called for a thousand dishes, each a hundred meters in diameter, covering more than sixty square miles of land. With the ability to discover radio signals from up to a thousand light-years away, scientists hoped they'd finally detect another civilization. Success, they believed, might unlock a "galactic heritage"—a vast pool of knowledge created by advanced races around the galaxy. Access to such information could reveal solutions to the planet's environmental issues, energy shortages, war, and other problems. Unfortunately, one of those other problems—a budget—prevented the roughly $10 billion project from ever taking off. The idea behind it, however, never lost steam.

"I read the Cyclops report from cover to cover," Tarter explained. "I just really got excited about the fact that I was in the right place at right time, with the right skills to maybe be able to do something about answering this whole question. So I just got hooked and I've stayed hooked ever since."

As radio astronomy searches for extraterrestrial intelligence continued over the years, NASA got involved, and by 1985 the SETI Institute had begun its operations as a nonprofit corporation headed by Tarter and San Francisco State's director of research, Tom Pierson. But just as its survey of the sky was beginning, Congress cancelled the project—despite its cost of less than 1 percent of NASA's annual budget, and far less than Cyclops's price tag.

"Not a single Martian has said 'Take me to your leader,' and not a single flying saucer has applied for FAA approval," said Senator Richard Bryan of Nevada in a 1993 press release after leading the charge to kill SETI's funding. His words and actions were not only a blow to the search for extraterrestrial intelligence but a testament to the lack of intelligence on our own planet.

At the time, Tarter called it a "loss of the most visionary opportunity scientists have ever put together." But fortunately, intelligence is much easier to find outside of Congress, and the SETI Institute has stayed afloat through private contributions. The Allen Telescope Array at Hat Creek Observatory in northern California was donated by Microsoft cofounder Paul Allen and allows scientists to conduct daily searches.

Tarter, for one, remains hopeful about discovering extraterrestrial intelligence one day. That's in part because there's still a lot of places

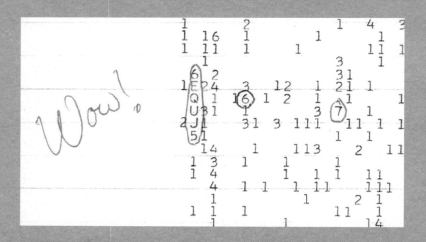

Dr. Jerry Ehman's written excitement gave the "Wow! signal" its name. The unusual signal was captured in 1977 at the Big Ear Radio Observatory at Ohio State University.

to look. In 2010, at the fiftieth anniversary of Project Ozma, she did a series of calculations to compare the volume of the nine dimensions of the universe with the volume of all the earth's oceans to illustrate how much exploration had been done to date.[†] "The answer was essentially that it's explored one glass of water out of the ocean," she said.

A Blip of Hope: The Wow! Signal

Despite the lack of verified contact from galactic neighbors, SETI researchers have had blips of excitement. On the night of August 15, 1977, for example, one of those blips lasted for seventy-two seconds in a signal recorded at the Big Ear radio telescope at Ohio State University.

Built in the sixties, the Big Ear was about the size of three football fields with two receiver horns. Its initial purpose was to map the radio sky, but when that mission ended in 1972, volunteers began using it to listen for extraterrestrial civilizations. That August night, at 10:16 p.m. when the extraterrestrial phone rang, no one was home to answer the call. But the unsupervised computer took a message, which was bundled into the reams of printouts from days of data and then delivered to astronomy professor Dr. Jerry Ehman's house. To his surprise, a single page showed a brief spike from one of the receivers—thirty times higher than the levels of random radio noise.

"It was a narrowband signal, just what we were looking for [with SETI]," Ehman told *Astronomy* in 2016.

He responded to this potential first-ever signal from another intelligent civilization by scribbling "Wow!" in the margin. With that single word, a SETI legend was born. The "Wow! signal," as it became known, showed a readout of "6EQUJ5," which was far from the usual 1s and 2s that typically filled the pages. The lower digits are the usual signals that come from natural noises. Anything greater than 5 is significant. Signals registering higher than 9 switched to letters. Ehman's find showed a sequence way beyond anything they'd seen that seemed to originate from the Sagittarius constellation in the center of the Milky

---

† Nine dimensions? Yes, while we go about our day in three of them, there are others we don't think about: time, two polarization dimensions, central frequency, modulation, and sensitivity.

Way. Could "6EQUJ5" be a friendly extraterrestrial greeting?

Ehman shared the potentially existence-changing printout with his colleagues Dr. Robert Dixon, head of the university's SETI program, and Dr. John Kraus, director of the observatory. The Wow! signal's frequency at 1420 megahertz and anomalous intensity pattern ruled out planets, asteroids, and stars as sources. Since 1420 megahertz is an internationally protected wavelength reserved for scientific research, they also ruled out terrestrial technology, including satellites, spacecraft, and aircraft. Lastly, they determined there had been no equipment malfunction. None of it added up. Decades later, it still doesn't.

As the years passed, Dixon remained supportive of the Wow! signal, saying it was "unmistakably of intelligent origin and had all the hallmarks of coming from an intelligent civilization." In 1992, Dr. Frank Drake called it "one of our all-time best candidate signals—a candidate for true evidence of extraterrestrial intelligence." But because the signal never repeated, he added it was "either a very-hard-to-explain fluke, or the real thing."

Ehman and the Wow! signal even penetrated pop culture, getting a mention in a 1994 *The X-Files* episode titled "Little Green Men." When Dana Scully gets help from a scientist to understand the meaning of a printout from the giant Arecibo telescope in Puerto Rico, he looks in awe at the signal and tells her, "In August 1977, my buddy, Jerry Ehman, found a transmission on the print-out like this. The Wow! signal is the best evidence of extraterrestrial intelligence."

On the signal's twentieth anniversary, Ehman revisited the data and his original sentiment held true. "Since all of the possibilities of a terrestrial origin have been either ruled out or seem improbable, and since the possibility of an extraterrestrial origin has not been able to be ruled out, I must conclude that an ETI (ExtraTerrestrial Intelligence) might have sent the signal that we received as the Wow! Source," he wrote on the Big Ear Radio Observatory website.

That said, as a scientist, he acknowledged that he'd need to wait for additional signals that could be further analyzed. "There is simply too little data to draw many conclusions. In other words, as I stated above, I choose not to draw vast conclusions from half-vast data," he said.

Today, the mystery of the Wow! signal remains. However, in recent years astronomers have discovered a new phenomenon from the far reaches of the Milky Way and other distant galaxies called a fast radio burst (FRB) that could offer a new possible explanation. If nothing else, these very brief but incredibly bright radio pulses serve as a reminder that new discoveries continue to be made, and perhaps a clear answer will eventually be found—if not by astronomers, maybe through more advanced equipment able to capture an undeniable extraterrestrial message.

> "Since all of the possibilities of a terrestrial origin have been either ruled out or seem improbable, and since the possibility of an extraterrestrial origin has not been able to be ruled out, I must conclude that an ETI (ExtraTerrestrial Intelligence) might have sent the signal that we received as the Wow! Source."
>
> —DR. JERRY EHMAN in his 1998 article "The Big Ear Wow! Signal: What We Know and Don't Know About It After 20 Years"

RELIGION, NEAR-DEATH EXPERIENCES, AND EXTRATERRESTRIAL GUIDANCE

"And worlds without number have I created; and I also created them for mine own purpose; and by the Son I created them, which is mine Only Begotten.

"And the first man of all men have I called Adam, which is many.

"But only an account of this earth, and the inhabitants thereof, give I unto you. For behold, there are many worlds that have passed away by the word of my power. And there are many that now stand, and innumerable are they unto man; but all things are numbered unto me, for they are mine and I know them."

While scientists search for extraterrestrial intelligence, the notion of other worlds and aliens living on them is quite clear according to the Church of Jesus Christ of Latter-day Saints. The quotes above come directly from the nineteenth-century prophet Joseph Smith's book of Moses (chapter 1, verses 33–35), published in the mid-1800s.

Mormons' acceptance of alien life is what attracted NASA scientist, engineer, and astrophysicist Chrishma Singh-Derewa to the religion. I didn't know about his acceptance of Mormonism when we first met during my research for my book on Mars. But as we discussed other worlds during the start of this project, he explained that after personally experiencing an extraterrestrial or extradimensional presence, it was the only faith that would align with the truth he had found as a young child. It was a discovery that came to him right after he died.

When he was just three years old, Singh-Derewa was running to a friend's house on a cold February day in Connecticut and got stuck while climbing over a picket fence. "My coat tip was the only thing holding me to the inside of the fence, and was covered with snow," he said. "No one could see or find me."

Hanging there in the cold for hours, his heart stopped. He remembers leaving his body and seeing it externally, then having a vision involving "a multitude of individuals, like light." The powerful and unforgettable near-death experience set him on a career path and settled any questions of life beyond life—and earth.

"They said that I needed to go back," Singh-Derewa recalled. "And I said, 'Why?' They were clear—to expand humankind into the stars. I questioned what a three-year-old could be helpful with. Even at forty-seven I still ask myself this, how can I possibly be of help? I thought, there's six billion other people on the planet that are still there. Perhaps one of them can do it? I am happy here."

Eventually his father and the police found and rescued him. When he woke up, back in his body, he found himself instilled with a purpose in life. "I felt from that moment on a duty to these beings that sent me to return—they felt like family, enlightened somehow, I remember feeling my unborn daughter was among them. And I pursued that duty painfully. Because, you know, seven degrees in aerospace and astrophysics is a painful thing."

In adulthood, Singh-Derewa has worked as an engineer and scientist at NASA Jet Propulsion Laboratory and other NASA contractors to help lead humans to space, including the Artemis mission to bring us back to the Moon and onward to Mars. Perhaps his "duty" has been part of a larger plan to help more people understand the nature of the universe and life that exists within it. So we can all be as certain of that fact as he.

Dr. Lynne Kitei, a physician based in Phoenix, Arizona (whom we met in Chapter 3), had a similar experience to Singh-Derewa during a near-death experience in 1956 when she was eight. It happened while she was undergoing what she described as "major dental work." The kind that required sedation. The mask over her face apparently administered slightly more anesthesia than it should have, as it sent her into a deep, almost-permanent sleep.

"I began to experience myself being slowly pushed through what seemed to be a revolving door," she described in her book, *The Phoenix Lights: A Skeptics Discovery That We Are Not Alone*. "There was a strange harp sound, like a haunting musical tune repeating over and over again; I felt myself slowly turning around and around." Kitei then reached a barrier—one that, if passed, she believed would offer no return. She began playing back her short life, then found herself "shooting above the earth" and floating among the clouds.

"I actually met three giant beings above the earth, with giant hoods, like glowing white robes with giant hoods over their head," Kitei told me in a phone interview. "And I couldn't see their faces, but I felt their unconditional love for me, and I have felt they have been with me ever since."

During that state between life and death, Kitei recalled looking down on earth and wondering if our lives are all predetermined. And if we don't have control over the future, she realized we still have control over how we handle situations, treat others, and interpret events.

"If this were true, would it mean that our own actions and reactions, the results of the multitude of lessons we learn throughout our lifetime, will lead us to who we will become in our future?" she asks in her book. "What we will become as the human race on Earth? Is that what they are watching?"

Call them extraterrestrials, God, or angels, but the *they* Kitei referred to and the questions she raised are essentially the roots of most every religion and belief system. It's the same story, just with different names for the main characters.

Advances in SETI and the Search for Bio- and Technosignatures

The more scientists can listen, of course, the better the chances are of hearing something. It's without question a matter of finding a needle in a haystack that's literally the size of the universe. As Dr. Seth Shostak, senior astronomer at the SETI Institute, explained to me, "We never got an email or a text message from E. T. saying, 'Hey, I'll be at 1453 megahertz on the dial.' You don't know where to tune. You can sort of have an idea from physics the best frequencies to look at, but, in fact, you don't know exactly."

Ten years ago, he noted, the receivers SETI was using had about twenty million channels. "We thought it was a lot—it's like having twenty million radios, and you tune each one slightly differently so you're listening to twenty million spots on the radio dial. But today, that number is more like two hundred million. In fact, it's more than that in the best cases."

Beyond two hundred million radios, SETI is also looking for flashes of light, in a recent effort known as LaserSETI. It's based on the idea that advanced civilizations could be sending messages through light waves, like interstellar fiber optics. Light has a distinct advantage over radio in that it can convey about a half million times as many bits of information per second.

As technology continues to advance, there will be other ways to expand the search. I spoke with Dr. Ravi Kopparapu, a planetary scientist at the NASA Goddard Space Flight Center, about ways to detect different types of technosignatures. But before understanding his ideas, it's best to understand what a technosignature is. The term was first coined in a 2007 article by Jill Tarter, in which she described it as "evidence of some technology that modifies its environment in ways that are detectable." Finding such evidence implies that an intelligent technologist created it.

Kopparapu's been working on a technosignature project with a small team of scientists from Berkeley, Penn State, and other institutions. One method of detection to explore, for example, is to study the pollution in the atmospheres of exoplanets. Finding that pollution, and concluding with any confidence that intelligent beings are responsible for it, however, is quite complex. As a starting point, we can look to our own industrialized civilization. Because we use a lot of fossil fuels, we emit high levels of nitrogen dioxide globally. During the COVID-19 pandemic lockdown in 2020, those levels significantly decreased, offering scientists a more defined representation of humanity's emissions when we're operating as our normal industrial selves—and distinguishing those levels from what the planet might create naturally. Lightning, for example, produces nitrogen dioxide. So what if a planet just happens to be one gigantic Tampa, Florida? As Kopparapu explained, scientists first have to understand the atmosphere and environment of a given exoplanet, which will allow them to run climate models and learn if the gases detected together could have been created by lightning or other natural processes, or not. If the models say no, things start to get interesting. Especially if the scientists can detect other gases, such as chlorofluorocarbons (CFC), which cannot be produced naturally.

"If you detect nitrogen dioxide and CFCs, together, that's a really, really good sign that that planet [hosts] a technologically advanced species," Kopparapu said.

Okay, so how do we do that? The equipment needed to discover this type of alien technology won't be available until around 2045, when the successor of NASA's James Webb Space Telescope and the Roman Space Telescope, LUVOIR Surveyor, is expected to launch. LUVOIR, which stands for "large ultraviolet optical infrared," is designed to analyze the atmospheres of exoplanets and detect biosignatures (oxygen, methane, carbon dioxide, etc.) from any life that may exist on them. This is possible because when light from a star goes through an exoplanet's atmosphere and reaches the surface, it then gets reflected back through the atmosphere and absorbs gases in certain wavelengths (or "colors"). Once these wavelengths reach LUVOIR, it will analyze the gases collected along the way.

If we look ahead to when we can find the answers Kopparapu is seeking, there might still be questions about the origin of the technology detected. As he points out, "a planet doesn't need to have biology for technology to exist." Strange as that sounds, it's true right here in

The Allen Telescope Array, located at the Hat Creek Observatory about 300 miles north of San Francisco, is the first radio telescope purposely built for SETI efforts.

The James Webb Space Telescope is peering into the history of the universe and may detect signs of life in the atmospheres of exoplanets. Artist conception seen here.

our solar system, with rovers on Mars and orbiters around Jupiter and Saturn. This means if we find evidence of technology on another planet, but detect no biosignatures, it's possible that we will have found a world that another intelligent civilization already reached. That would lead to the next questions: *Who* and *where* are they?

Detecting optical technosignatures and listening to larger and larger swaths of star systems may eventually yield results. Then again, they may not. But what about looking closer to home? As we've seen, there've been numerous unexplained cases in ufology. They just lack the data for scientists to study and gain results to stand behind. Fortunately, that's finally beginning to change, thanks to a Harvard University astrophysicist, Dr. Avi Loeb.

The Thing from Interstellar Space: 'Oumuamua Scouts the Solar System

Avi Loeb is a rare breed in his field. He's a scientist who's not afraid of the UFO stigma, or to suggest that scientists should study unidentified objects in earth's vicinity, like the one that was discovered passing through our solar system in October 2017. This first interstellar object to float our way was detected by a telescope at the Haleakalā Observatory in Hawaii, and was thus given the Hawaiian name 'Oumuamua, meaning "a messenger from afar, arriving first" or "scout."

Its anomalous size and shape, which appeared to be formed like an oblong cigar or flattened disk the size of a football field, along with its unusual tumbling speed and lack of cometary tail, didn't fit the profile of any known rocks that typically gallivant through space. That has led some scientists to regard it as a type of rock we've never encountered before, like an iceberg made of molecular hydrogen or pure nitrogen. Some scientists have done modeling to show how such an object could reproduce the shape and size of 'Oumuamua during its lengthy journey, with solar radiation removing some of its gases along the way.

Loeb, however, finds the hydrogen and nitrogen rock theories to be problematic considering 'Oumuamua's mass and interstellar excursion. So given that it lacks the characteristics of a comet or asteroid, why limit theories to new types of rocks and not explore the idea that it could be something else? That something else, as Loeb argued in his 2021 best-selling book, *Extraterrestrial: The First Sign of Intelligent Life Beyond Earth*, could be equipment from an extraterrestrial technological civilization. Among the science community it's a radical point of view. But Loeb stands by it.

When I spoke to him via Zoom, he likened the situation to a caveman finding a cell phone and determining that the device is just a type of rock he's never seen before. "Of course if you get enough data, if you're curious, you will figure out by pressing a button that it records the voice, and if you press another button it records the image, and that will tell you it's not a rock," he said. "But for that you need to be open-minded."

Sometimes being open-minded isn't easy. In fact, in a summary PDF Loeb shared with me in advance of a 2022 talk at Oxford University, he noted that some scientists would prefer the interstellar object hadn't entered the solar system—or their minds—at all: "When a colleague of mine, specializing in solar system rocks, heard about 'Oumuamua, he said: 'this interstellar object is so weird . . . I wish it never existed.' His statement explains why innovation is often suppressed in the face of anomalies."

Dismissing sightings of anomalous objects teaches us nothing, but dismissing the taboo could teach us what humanity has wondered forever. It all starts with data.

"If we want to identify any floating objects that might be alien technology we have to also understand what's the background rate of just random interstellar rocks floating through the solar system," Dr. Jacob Haqq Misra, an astrobiologist and senior research investigator at the Blue Marble Space Institute of Science, told me in a phone interview. "We should look for more things like 'Oumuamua. Not necessarily because that one was to me convincing as alien technology, but because there is stuff floating through space and some of it could be alien technology—garbage or functional technology, so we should study any of those things just to understand what to expect and when is there an anomaly."

An artist illustration of 'Oumuamua, the interstellar object detected in October 2017 as it passed through our solar system. Harvard's Dr. Avi Loeb suggests that it's extraterrestrial in nature.

> "Ridiculing the notion that 'Oumuamua may have been artificial in origin will not get rid of our neighbors. As Galileo Galilei instructed us four centuries ago, the nature of celestial objects must be found through our telescopes rather than philosophical prejudice."
>
> —DR. AVI LOEB, Frank B. Baird Jr. Professor of Science at Harvard University and founder of the Galileo Project, in 2021

If the Government Won't Release Data, We'll Get Our Own: The Galileo Project and Alien Archaeology

Avi Loeb's conviction is starting to create a change in attitudes. The success of *Extraterrestrial* has led to enough substantial private donations for him to found the Galileo Project, an organization entirely dedicated to researching other 'Oumuamua-like objects and unidentified aerial phenomena. Since launching the project a month after the Pentagon's UAP report to Congress on June 25, 2021, Loeb's had more than a hundred scientists join his quest for answers, including Jacob Haqq Misra and Seth Shostak.

Together, they're collecting and discussing their own data rather than waiting for or hoping the government releases any of its own—even though Loeb has heard from politicians that there is "high quality data that indicates there is something weird in our sky." Without the constraints of classified information, they'll openly share their findings and offer transparent analysis. And why not? As Loeb stresses, the sky is not classified. Ideally, the Galileo Project will find more data on UAPs to study and understand, unlike what Project Blue Book was limited to, and look in places where the brilliant minds exploring the stars through radio astronomy haven't.

"It's doing it in the wrong way," Loeb told me, speaking passionately of SETI's methods and the change in thinking he believes is needed. "That includes the Drake Equation, which is completely irrelevant for searching for equipment, and moreover, it includes the Fermi paradox, which is completely the wrong question. It asks, 'Where is everybody?' Because we are searching for something exactly at the same technological phase that we are, which we have possessed for 126 years. That's out of the 4.5 billion years of the earth. For the last hundred years we've been transmitting radio waves and then we are looking for things we've been doing for just the last hundred years. What's the chance that someone else is exactly synchronized with us, using the same communication?"

Instead, Loeb compared his approach to that of archeology. "If you look for a civilization that predated you, you are not trying to have a phone conversation," he explained. "You're not asking, 'I want to speak with the ancient Greeks on the phone to learn about what they actually knew.' That will not be possible because they're not alive anymore. Most of the stars formed billions of years before the sun, why would they be within a hundred years of our technological development right now and still alive? Like, what's the chance of that? Tiny! A hundred years out of billions of years? So a much more sober approach is to search for equipment."

Within two to three years, he hopes to have collected valuable data that could tell us more about possible alien archeology, and that may finally provide the extraordinary evidence that Carl Sagan famously said is required for extraordinary claims; the kind of evidence ufologists and UFO observers so far haven't been able to share with scientists.

SETH SHOSTAK'S EMAIL IS FILLED WITH LOADS OF ALIENS AND ONE BILLIONAIRE: THE BEGINNING OF BREAKTHROUGH LISTEN

When your full-time job is to search for signs of intelligent extraterrestrials, people are eager to help. The senior astronomer at the SETI Institute, Dr. Seth Shostak, knows this firsthand, as he explained to me from his home in California during a Zoom call.

"I get a lot of bonkers emails," he said. "Every day I get people who have problems with aliens in their personal lives or whatever it is. These emails usually begin with, 'I've got some really important news for you.' Okay. And the important news is that the aliens have been spotted in, you know, Trenton, New Jersey, or something. Could be. But some of them are much more interesting. They claimed an alien has moved into their house, or their daughter's dating an alien or whatever."

Usually he'll ask if they have some form of proof to support these claims—photos, videos, something besides their own story that he can investigate and offer an educated opinion on. About half of them say they do, but most of them don't want to share it. When someone does offer a photo, Shostak is happy to offer what he can.

"Almost all of them are very, very simple artifacts of cameras," he said. "And photography happens to be one of my hobbies, my number one hobby I would say. So I recognize these diffraction patterns in the optics. And I write them back and I say, 'Well, I looked at this, and this is what I think it is.' Their response to that is usually anger. They never say thanks."

A little more than a decade ago, one of Shostak's emails turned out to be considerably less bonkers. Though he almost didn't realize it. The message essentially said, "Yuri Milner would like to speak with you," and was signed by a Russian assistant.

"The name didn't mean anything to me and I was about to delete it," Shostak recalled. "But then I decided to take the time to google-search this guy. It turns out he was this Russian billionaire, who lives not terribly far from where I'm sitting. So I decided to answer the email."

Soon after, the two met and Shostak learned that Milner wanted to establish a multi-million-dollar prize for anyone who could find a true alien. Like a Nobel Prize for alien hunting.

If Milner was going to offer a prize for discovering extraterrestrials, he wanted help establishing rules and criteria. Shostak spent a few years working out details regarding what would constitute good evidence and discussing potential issues.

"If you just put out a prize like that to the

first person to find E. T., you're going to get a lot of responses, mostly from the UFO crowd," he explained. "You're gonna say, 'Yeah, I saw them last night in my neighbor's yard or whatever.' So the question was, how do you decide whether you're going to take this entry seriously, or toss it as more bananas thinking?"

Ultimately, Milner opted against the prize and instead decided to donate $100 million over ten years toward what would be the most ambitious and comprehensive search for extraterrestrial intelligence yet: a large-scale, open-source program called Breakthrough Listen, based at the SETI Research Center at the University of California, Berkeley.

In addition to Shostak's backing, the project also received support from many other luminaries, including Stephen Hawking, Frank Drake, Jill Tarter, Avi Loeb, and, from a totally different corner of the universe, *Family Guy*'s Seth MacFarlane.

"We would typically get 24–36 hours on a telescope per year, but now we'll have thousands of hours per year on the best instruments," project leader Andrew Siemion told *Nature* at Breakthrough Listen's 2015 launch. "It's difficult to overstate how big this is. It's a revolution."

In comparison, SETI's previous efforts had been funded by an estimated $2.5 million a year from various research grants and private foundations.

"They have what in this field is considered real money, millions of dollars a year, it's nothing compared to what the Department of Energy spends on fusion or whatever, but for this kind of project, that's a lot of money," Shostak emphasized. "So that's Breakthrough Listen. Now, they haven't had the breakthrough yet. But they are listening."

What Happens If First Contact Happens?

Should the Galileo Project detect another interstellar object in our solar system before it's on its way out, a space mission to intercept its path could be designed to capture imagery and help scientists understand whether the object is natural but anomalous, or artificial in origin. If it turns out to be some form of extraterrestrial engineering, that raises a whole new set of questions—starting with, *what now?* What is the protocol for dealing with such a discovery? Suddenly the answers would no longer be the stuff of science fiction.

For SETI, the plan isn't far off from what was depicted in *Contact*. First, the findings would be confirmed at the discovery site, and then the discoverers would seek out an independent verification.

"You try to do it quietly," Tarter explained. "And then if you get an independent verification, you tell the world."

SETI would build out teams of local experts at observatories around the planet, ready to answer questions and collaborate with their local press. Experts from various fields, including the media, communications, religion, and social science would also collaborate to help the public at large deal with the fact that the debate is over, and that we're not alone.

"How would your life change if you found [extraterrestrial intelligence]?" Seth Shostak asks about such a scenario. "How is that going to influence your job? Well, I don't know. 'I work as an investment advisor in a Price Waterhouse,' or whatever, 'and it's not gonna affect my job at all.' Which is sort of true. There's no doubt society would change. But, you know, in very subtle ways, I think. Unless, of course, once having found them, you could somehow figure out what they're saying, assuming they're saying anything, or you could get in touch. That would change things a bit. But I'm not sure any of that is very likely."

What might change things drastically is if the message received is far more than a friendly greeting. Frank White, author of *The SETI Factor*, believes that finding an intelligent civilization could be less about having a ridiculously long-distance relationship and—like NASA's Project Cyclops had hoped—more about the potential information. "If they send us the Encyclopedia Galactica, they could really have a huge impact on earth, because what if they have a way of doing computing

"We often forget how much unites all the members of humanity. Perhaps we need some outside, universal threat to make us recognize this common bond. I occasionally think how quickly our differences worldwide would vanish if we were facing an alien threat from outside this world."

—President RONALD REAGAN, addressing the United Nations General Assembly in 1987 that's way beyond anything IBM or Apple know about?" he proposed during a phone interview with me. "They could have an enormous impact on us."

That type of knowledge could help human advancement leap forward in unimaginable ways. In the process, all that helpful knowledge would also have a ripple effect across society. "All of our institutions would collapse," White suggested. "They could send us medical information that could make every medical school obsolete. And on and on."

Finding a piece of equipment in our solar system, however, could be an entirely different sci-fi story brought to life. "If you engage with it inappropriately, it could have immediate consequences for humanity," Loeb cautioned.

That equipment might not be alien space junk. It might be perfectly functional. And just like our own machines sent out into space, it might be equipped with artificial intelligence. "So then the question is, what is the intent of the equipment?" Loeb asked. Is it monitoring us? If so, what do we do about it? Those decisions, Loeb suggested, shouldn't be left to "the scientific whims of the group that discovers this thing" but instead might best be determined by a committee at the United Nations.

If such equipment were found, whether through a discovery by the Galileo Project, SETI, or even another organization, maybe the presence of an alien civilization could truly unite the nations. As Ronald Reagan said at the UN in 1987, "We often forget how much unites all the members of humanity. Perhaps we need some outside, universal threat to make us recognize this common bond. I occasionally think how quickly our differences worldwide would vanish if we were facing an alien threat from outside this world."

With the government beginning to release information about UAPs and science taking a more serious look, might we soon prove Reagan right?

NASA released this James Webb Space Telescope image, called "Pillars of Creation," on October 19, 2022. It shows interstellar gas and dust in a region where young stars are forming, roughly 6,500 to 7,000 light-years from earth. It's a beautiful reminder of just how vast the universe is—and of the potential to find life somewhere out there. Or of that life finding us first.

CHAPTER 5

THE TRUTH IS OUT THERE, OFFICIALLY

The Government Acknowledges UFOs

Deep Throat: Mr. Mulder, why are those like yourself who believe in the existence of extraterrestrial life on this earth not dissuaded by all the evidence to the contrary? Mulder: Because . . . all the evidence to the contrary is not entirely dissuasive.

—*THE X-FILES*, Season 1, Episode 2, "Deep Throat," 1993

W hen Project Blue Book closed in 1969, it left about 6 percent of its cases marked as unidentified. Say what you will about its sources and the availability of data, but its ability to offer explanations was far greater than that which the Office of the Director of National Intelligence (ODNI) offered Congress on June 25, 2021.

In its "Preliminary Assessment: Unidentified Aerial Phenomena" report covering 144 UAP incidents originating from U.S. government sources from November 2004 to March 2021, it identified one object as a large, deflating balloon. The other 143 cases "remain unexplained." That's 99 percent unexplained. Granted, it claimed to have limited data, but the government still conceded to the public that there are a whole lot of things flying around in the sky that it doesn't understand. The report's executive summary states: "Most of the UAP reported probably do represent physical objects given that a majority of UAP were registered across multiple sensors, to include radar, infrared,

50 U.S.C. § 3024(i)   1.4(a)
Observed UAP usually traveled between ███ and ███████ Altitudes varied
for these objects, but frequently registered between 1.4(a) and 1.4(a) ███ mean sea
level (MSL). We have ███ cases, however, in which the observer perceived that the
1.4(a)   UAP demonstrated 1.4(a) ███████ and another in which the UAP was
detected 1.4(a) ███ feet MSL.

(U) And a Handful of UAP Appear to Demonstrate Advanced Technology

50 U.S.C. § 3024(i)
In **18** incidents, described in **21** reports, observers reported unusual UAP movement
patterns or flight characteristics, and/or 1.4(a)(g) ███████ A few of these reports
describe UAP behavior 1.4(a)(g) ██████
████████

50 U.S.C. § 3024(i) Some UAP appeared to remain stationary in winds aloft, move against the wind,
maneuver abruptly, or move at considerable speed, without discernable means of propulsion. In
a small number of cases, military aircraft systems processed radio frequency (RF) energy
associated with UAP sightings as 1.4(a)(g)
Although there are 1.4(a)(g) ████████████████ we would 1.4(a)(g)
████████████████████ Recordings of radar displays suggest these UAP 1.4(a)(g)
████████████████████

50 U.S.C. § 3024(i)
In 1.4(a)(g) ███ a Navy pilot in an 1.4(a)(g) ████████████ in
altitude. He noted the winds aloft were greater than 1.4(a)(g) ███ and he was "fighting
to keep his aircraft in the airspace." 1.4(a)(g) was 1.4(a)(g) ████ and its
position was unaffected by the 1.4(a)(g) The pilot 1.4(a)(g)
████████████████ object was 1.4(a)(g)
████████████

50 U.S.C. § 3024(i)
In 1.4(a) ███ a Navy report documented a 1.4(a)
████████████ but then appeared to change course and speed,
1.4(a) ██████ from 1.4(a)
50 U.S.C. § 3024(i)
In ███████ a UAP exhibited 1.4(a)
████████ according to 1.4(a) ████████████ The
1.4(a)   UAPTF has ███ additional reports of aircraft indicating 1.4(a)
██████ that appear to 1.4(a)

50 U.S.C. § 3024(i)
The UAPTF holds a small amount of data that appear to show UAP demonstrating
acceleration or a degree of signature management 1.4(a)(g)(e)
However, this 1.4(a)(g)(e)
Additional rigorous analyses is necessary by multiple teams or groups of technical experts to
determine the nature and validity of these data. We are conducting further analysis to determine
if breakthrough technologies were demonstrated.
50 U.S.C. § 3024(i)
According to 1.4(a)(g) ████████ during a 1.4(a)(g) incident the UAP
1.4(a)(g) ████████████

A redacted version of the Office of the Director of National Intelligence's June 25, 2021, report to Congress was released on TheBlackVault.com in March 2022. The site's founder, John Greenewald Jr., has published hundreds of thousands of pages of declassified government documents obtained through Freedom of Information Act requests.

electro-optical, weapon seekers, and visual observation."

As Frank White, author of *The SETI Factor*, opined online shortly after the report's release, "This is a really important statement, because detractors of UFO stories have often implied or stated outright that the witnesses are probably hallucinating or imagining what they think they are seeing." He acknowledges that people are capable of imagining that experiences are physically real when they're not, but "this report does not default to that explanation, or even consider it as one of the possibilities for explanation."

In a nutshell, the United States now officially recognizes the existence of unidentified flying objects. The report added that "if and when individual UAP incidents are resolved" they'll fall into one of five categories: airborne clutter; natural atmospheric phenomena; U.S. government or U.S. industry developmental programs; foreign adversary systems; and "a catchall 'other' bin."

It's that "other bin" that leaves the door open for something extraterrestrial. And who knows what's lurking behind all the redactions in the for-their-eyes-only classified version.

For this reason, many still believe a secret program exists deep within the government dating to the 1940s and '50s that's hiding evidence of contact with aliens. And that decades of disinformation are slowly leading to disclosure, presumably about intergalactic friends, foes, or maybe a little bit of both, here among us.

I quoted Lee Speigel at the end of Chapter 2 describing the problem of a government admitting there's something out there it can't protect us from. So what led the ODNI to release a report in the first place? Turns out all it took was a newspaper article.

The Day the Earth Stood at Attention: The *New York Times* Breaks a UFO Story

Seventy years after the air force released a statement claiming that a flying saucer crashed in Roswell, the government once again reported a UFO. Well, an ex-government employee, that is. It was October 4, 2017, and Luis Elizondo had just resigned that morning. He shared video evidence and his role in running a shadowy government program called the Advanced Aerospace Threat Identification Program (AATIP) with the *New York Times* for an article that would run two months later, on December 16, and forever change the course of the UFO conversation.

Previous to investigating UAPs, Elizondo had spent two decades working in counterintelligence, counterterrorism, and counterespionage for the Department of Defense. It was a position that fielded intense terrestrial threats from the Taliban, ISIS, and Al-Qaeda. He had no interest in UFOs or UAPs. But in 2008, his skill set was deemed ideal for looking into whatever advanced technology seemed to be traversing American airspace. Elizondo approached the job the same way he approached hunting terrorists or spies, and soon enough he found himself studying a far different menace than ever before. Yet, no one cared.

"I took an oath to defend this country from all enemies, foreign and domestic," he told me on a Zoom call from his heavily guarded home in a part of the country I won't disclose. "And it turns out that the biggest enemy on this topic was bureaucracy. And so in a very weird sort of way, I actually left the department out of loyalty, not disloyalty. I simply had to leave the department to finish the very mission that they gave me in the first place."

In Elizondo's resignation letter to the secretary of defense, General James Mattis, he expressed his alarm at the "bureaucratic challenges and inflexible mindsets" within the department. "This is particularly true regarding the controversial topic of anomalous aerospace threats," he stated. "Despite overwhelming evidence at both the unclassified and classified levels, certain individuals in the Department remain staunchly opposed to further research on what could be a tactical threat to our pilots, sailors, and soldiers, and perhaps even an existential threat to our national security." Mattis's underlings kept the letter from him until the day before the *Times* article was set to run.

"No one wanted to tell the emperor he had no clothes on," Elizondo added. "And that's a problem."

Before Elizondo's resignation, Christopher Mellon, the deputy assistant secretary of defense for intelligence, had attempted to shake up the system. He happened to know two people who were direct reports to General Mattis and asked them to take a briefing on the situation—crazy as it sounded—and then push it through to the top. But the system continued to reject the evidence. The taboo of UFOs, it seemed, proved mightier than the military. Mattis's staff was not going to let their boss take a briefing on a subject that, despite the evidence, still suffered from the stigma of flying saucers.

"They were concerned about damaging his press prestige," Mellon explained to me during a phone interview. The staffers feared that Mattis's political adversaries would use it as ammo to discredit him or tarnish his character. "They love the guy. They revered him. All the people around him had just incredible loyalty and the highest regard for him. And it was largely out of protective concern for his reputation and interests that they didn't want him to touch the issue at all."

But Mellon viewed the UFO issue as a pressing matter of national security. "Nobody knows where they're from or why they're there," he said. "And nobody in the community was doing a goddamn thing. Nobody was investigating. Nobody was even reporting. They weren't sending any alerts or notifications. This was just going on and being completely ignored. It's mind-boggling. . . . I was, frankly, kind of embarrassed as an intelligence person. What is wrong with all these other intelligence people? How can they not be inquisitive and curious? And how can they not be sounding the alarm and trying to take some action here?"

Whatever pilots had been seeing with their own eyes had been detected by radar and captured on video. Despite the billions of dollars being spent on the defense of America, these objects were evading the highest trained pilots in the most advanced aircraft on the planet. Whatever they were, they were doing it all without wings or any visible signs of propulsion. In general, they were defying physics as we know it.

If the technology belongs to a foreign adversary, it means the American military is far behind someone else's. That may be a larger cause for concern than if the technology is extraterrestrial, since aliens—assuming it's them—don't seem interested in harming us. At least, not yet. But as Mellon pointed out, what if China has developed aircraft and weaponry that greatly surpasses America's and, in a naval encounter, a flotilla gets wiped out in the South China Sea?

"Everybody's going to look back, and what possible excuse is anybody going to have at this point for not following up on all this data, these warnings? I mean, it's just going to be ludicrous," Mellon said. "I tell people that it reminds me both of December 7, '41, and 9/11. In the Pearl Harbor bombing, we saw stuff—there was a radar battery that detected the Japanese planes approaching Hawaii. And the lieutenant operating that battery didn't think to report it up the chain. He thought it was probably some U.S. aircraft or had some innocent explanation. So he didn't bother to report it, and the alarm was not sounded. [With] 9/11 we had a problem with the CIA and FBI not sharing information that might have prevented that tragedy. And we have that in spades in a much larger degree with this UAP issue. So are we learning the lessons of history? What are we doing? How many times do we have to make these mistakes?"

Mellon and Elizondo met while working together for To the Stars Academy of Arts and Science, a UFO investigative group cofounded by former Blink-182 guitarist and vocalist Tom DeLonge in 2017. Their colleagues included parapsychologist and physicist Hal Puthoff and former senior CIA intelligence officer Jim Semivan. With the bureaucracy being the problem rather than a solution, Mellon and Elizondo knew the only way to make things happen was to go to the press. In a move reminiscent of Deep Throat's Watergate rendezvous with Bob Woodward, an unnamed source met Mellon in a parking lot and handed over three videos featuring U.S. Navy fighter pilots tracking UAPs, entitled "FLIR" ("Forward Looking Infrared"), captured in 2004 near the Nimitz aircraft carrier about two hundred miles off the coast of San Diego; "Go Fast," recorded off the East Coast by an F/A-18 Super Hornet pilot in 2015; and "Gimbal," also obtained in 2015 near the Florida coastline. Sharing the videos, secretive as they were, was totally legal. All had been declassified and accompanied by official paperwork labeled APPROVED FOR PUBLIC RELEASE AUGUST 2017.

Together, Mellon, Elizondo, Puthoff, and Semivan met with investigative journalist Leslie Kean at a Pentagon City hotel bar to offer her the story of her career. Kean had a respected track record of writing

The 2015 "Gimbal" video captured off the coast of Florida shows an object that remains unidentified.

about aerial anomalies over the previous seventeen years. She spent years lobbying for the government to pay more attention to the phenomenon, and in 2010 penned the *New York Times* best seller *UFOs: Generals, Pilots, and Government Officials Go on the Record.* Along the way, she'd made strong connections with people in high places, including the men who arranged the meeting—who now needed her help.

The clandestine gathering was an attempt to turn heads and change minds by going public with compelling videos and stories directly from experienced navy fighter pilots. Strange objects flying in restricted airspace around aircraft carrier strike group workups and naval aviation training missions off both coasts had been happening almost daily for years. As deputy director of naval intelligence Scott Bray told politicians at the May 17, 2022, congressional hearing on UAPs, there have been "at least eleven near misses." But for far too long, there were not nearly as many questions about what the objects are.

There at the hotel with Kean, Elizondo was crossing a line he never expected to. Until that day, he had avoided the press at all costs. "It was terrifying. . . . Once you're out of that proverbial airlock, that's it," he said. "You don't go back and you can't get back in the airlock. And so I knew I was giving up a lot." Sitting with Mellon, Puthoff, and Semivan, he told Kean about the government's secretive efforts to study UAPs, beginning in 2007 with a $22 million allocation by the Department of Defense—all at the request of Senate majority leader Harry Reid—and showed her the three declassified videos (but gave her only "FLIR" and "Gimbal"—"Go Fast" was held back in order to generate further press at a later date). Not only did Kean have impeccable witnesses, she had actual evidence. Proof that something is happening, right now.

"I was absolutely stunned, just bowled over by it," Kean told me as we discussed the events over the phone. "I mean, this was probably the most important moment of my whole career covering UFOs. The pinnacle moment that I never would have dreamed would have happened. So I was just shocked and amazed and thrilled. I knew that the power of what they were showing to me was so incredible."

But the story still lacked the acknowledgment and backing of the highest levels of government, so Kean and her coauthors of the *New York Times* article, Ralph Blumenthal and Helene Cooper, reached out to the recently retired Reid, who'd had a lifelong interest in UFOs. He had initiated the Advanced Aerospace Weapon System Application Program (AAWSAP) in 2007, which sought to find out who or what had technology that was leaps and bounds ahead of America's.

From 2007 to 2012, the AAWSAP team became the first group to explore the *Nimitz* case and interview the pilot witnesses. It also built a database of global UAP sightings, reported on historical cases of UAPs around nuclear sites, and dedicated a good portion of time to investigating paranormal activity at Utah's Skinwalker Ranch.

So it was no surprise when Reid decided to answer the *Times'* call in 2017 and go on the record for its article. It was a move he initially hesitated making. "I had recently retired from the senate, and there was still a stigma attached to the issue—'little green men' and all that," Reid wrote in his foreword to the 2021 book *Skinwalkers at the Pentagon*. "But it became clear to me that the reporter was interested in this as a substantive issue and focused on the science. So, I decided to tell her what I knew."

> **"As I became increasingly interested in UAPs, my staff warned me not to engage. 'Stay the hell away from this,' they said. But I couldn't help it—I was curious."**
>
> —Former U.S. senator **HARRY REID**, in his foreword to the 2021 book *Skinwalkers at the Pentagon*

As far as Kean was concerned, Reid's willingness to participate was crucial to the story. They had the video evidence, the news about the allocated funds, and the Senate majority leader at the time confirming all of it. With that, the article ran online first, and followed on the front page of the next day's print edition emblazoned with the headline:

REAL U.F.O.'S? PENTAGON UNIT TRIED TO KNOW.

"Within an hour of it going up on the internet, it was just everywhere," Kean recalled. "It was pretty remarkable."

She wasn't exaggerating. The story was picked up globally and suddenly a more serious collective conversation about UFOs began. To help add more fuel to the UAP fire, Mellon finally released the third video, "Go Fast," to the *Washington Post* in March 2018 as part of an op-ed titled THE MILITARY KEEPS ENCOUNTERING UFOS. WHY DOESN'T THE PENTAGON CARE? Each of the videos immediately went viral upon its release. As the months passed, there was no fourth film to feed to the media, but Mellon needed to keep the momentum going with the public and to continue pushing the Pentagon to care. He'd gained some ground with the Senate Armed Services and Intelligence committees, but the appropriations committees were still skeptical. According to Mellon, they had not taken the time to meet with any of the navy aviators and hear their firsthand accounts.

"I knew we couldn't really get any funding for anything," Mellon said. "And one of the old tricks I've used in the past on the Hill is to ask for a simple report that does not require an appropriation [of funds]. So my suggestion to the oversight committees was just ask for a report from the executive branch on the topic. Tell them what you want. Specify the parameters. And you don't need an appropriation. All you have to do is put in a report requirement. And that will help validate what we're suggesting is actually going on and the extent of it, and you'll have the benefit of that information—and then that will help keep the issue alive and maintain people's attention."

Mellon continued writing op-eds and meeting with staffers to push the idea for two years. He finally found success after meeting with Florida senator Marco Rubio's staff director, who understood that presenting important information at no cost to taxpayers was a good idea. With Rubio's backing, the Pentagon had no choice but to pay attention and deliver its report. This became the June 25, 2021, "Preliminary Assessment" presented to Congress, which made history as the first public admission of the reality of UFOs by the United States government.

A BRIEF TOUR OF SKINWALKER RANCH

If you were a billionaire with a fascination with the paranormal like Robert Bigelow, how could you not snap up Utah's ultra-spooky Skinwalker Ranch for a mere $200,000? Bigelow made the purchase in 1996, freeing owners Terry and Gwen Sherman from the many frights they reported on the 480-acre property within the Uinta Basin. The Shermans spoke of numerous anomalies, including UFOs of varying shapes and sizes, airborne lights, crop circles, cattle mutilation, and a shape-shifting werewolf-like creature that Native American folklore calls "The Skinwalker." As if all that wasn't strange enough, Terry even heard voices in unfamiliar languages that seemed to hover about twenty-five feet above him, though he could see nothing there.

"For a long time we wondered what we were seeing, if it was something to do with a top-secret project," Terry Sherman told the Associated Press in 1996. "I don't know really what to think about it."

A local retired junior high school teacher, Joseph Junior Hicks, believed any top-secret projects came not from the government but from somewhere unknown. Hicks had investigated hundreds of UFO sightings in the region since the 1950s. Over the years he had spoken to truckers who'd claimed to have been followed by UFOs and met with several people who said they witnessed humanoid beings looking out through the portholes of flying saucers.

"I think what's happening is we are being visited from beings from another world or some other place," he explained in the same article. "I think primarily it's research and exploration."

Under Bigelow's ownership, the investigation changed hands from the schoolteacher to a team of scientists from his own organization, the National Institute for Discovery Science. Among their bizarre experiences on the spooky property, according to the 2005 book *Hunt for the Skinwalker*, was witnessing a roughly six-foot-tall, four-hundred-pound creature emerge from a three-dimensional tunnel seen through night vision goggles. By the time Bigelow's team was operating under the government-funded AAWSAP program in 2008, there were reports of an "infectious entity" from the ranch attaching itself to visiting intelligence agency personnel and following them home. Their wives and children "were subjected to nightmarish 'dogmen' appearing in their backyard" and "black shadow people standing over their beds when they awoke." Not to mention colorful orbs parading through their homes and yards.

These are all disturbing claims. To Dr. Mark Rodeghier of CUFOS, so is the fact Bigelow's exploration of Skinwalker used AAWSAP funding. "I've been crossing my fingers since I've heard about all this that the powers that be in Washington don't bring this up," he told me. "Because if I was skeptical about current government activities and the program that they've funded, I would get up and I would say, 'Well, this whole thing started with complete foolishness at the Skinwalker Ranch, and that thing had nothing to do with UFOs directly, and that's behind all of this and I don't think we should fund it.' And I think that's a wrong argument, because of course, the UFOs were part of it. But if I was a skeptic, that's the argument I would take. In other words, they left themselves open to that criticism."

AAWSAP's funding ended after two years. No reasons have been given. "It's possible it wasn't funded, you know, for what you might think of as legitimate reasons," Rodeghier con-tinued. "Because you guys are spending half your money at the ranch."

Bigelow hasn't disclosed any findings, though he has hinted at them. "The main mysteries at Skinwalker were never solved," Bigelow told the *New York Times* in 2021. "Lots of things have never been made public that we have, things that I personally initiated that we have photographs of."

The curious billionaire sold the ranch to Utah real-estate mogul Brandon Fugal in 2016. Investigations across the Uinta Basin continue, many of which are now funded by the History Channel show *The Secret of Skinwalker Ranch*.

"My first story was in the year 2000, in the *Boston Globe*, and then right up until 2017, my main point was, 'Hey, guys, UFOs are real.' That was the bottom-line point of everything I was doing in three words, 'UFOs are real.' And here we are now where it's absolutely, officially acknowledged that they're real. So it's been very satisfying to me to be able to see this happen after pushing for it for so long."

—LESLIE KEAN, investigative journalist and author of the *New York Times* best-selling book, *UFOs: Generals, Pilots, and Government Officials Go on the Record*, in a March 2022 interview with the author

The Declassified Navy Videos: "FLIR," "Gimbal," and "Go Fast"

What was so special about the three UFO videos that forced the U.S. government to finally admit the existence of UFOs? Let's examine them more closely.

For about two weeks prior to the 2004 "FLIR" recording, captured on November 14, USS *Princeton* radar operator Kevin Day had been detecting unusual clusters of five to ten objects flying at about 28,000 feet and 138 miles per hour. Day, whose job description essentially boils down to identifying things that fly, found himself stymied.

"I had never seen anything fly like that before," he told Ben Hansen on *UFO Witness*. Their elevation was too high for them to be birds and the relatively slow speed was too slow to be aircraft. Day and his team tested their equipment and concluded that everything was working properly, yet these things kept showing up. The team was convinced they were real objects, not artifacts left in the system. As Hansen told me, "If we can't determine what's a solid object or not on a radar, we're in trouble, because this is the best in the world."

Given that confidence, it was time to dispatch a pilot to intercept the entity in hopes of identifying it. So when navy fighter pilots were conducting training operations off the nearby USS *Nimitz* carrier, Commander David Fravor of the Black Aces fighter squadron and Lieutenant Commander Alex Dietrich—each accompanied by a weapons systems officer in the back seat—were sent to get a closer look. And as they raced through the sky in the F/A-18F Super Hornets, they did. The encounter lasted about five minutes, with the object mirroring their moves, as if it was fully aware of their presence.

Fravor described the UAP as looking like a smooth, white, forty-foot-long Tic Tac breath mint. Round on both ends, without wings or windows, and no sign of a propulsion system. It moved in all directions, abruptly, unlike what a helicopter would be capable of.

"You know, I think that over beers, we've sort of said, 'Hey man, if I saw this solo, I don't know that I would have come back and said anything,' because it sounds so crazy when I say it," Dietrich told Bill Whitaker in a May 2021 interview on *60 Minutes*.

"I don't know who's building it, who's got the technology, who's got the brains—but there's something out there that was better than our airplane," Fravor added.

After they returned, pilot Chad Underwood took off to get another look—this time armed with more advanced sensory technology, namely the $6 million FLIR camera. Sure enough, Underwood got a blip on his radar and spotted the same object hovering at around 20,000 feet with no exhaust fumes.

"The thing that stood out to me the most was how erratic it was behaving," he told *New York* magazine in 2019. "And what I mean by 'erratic' is that its changes in altitude, air speed, and aspect were just unlike things that I've ever encountered before flying against other air targets."

As Underwood went on to explain, the object didn't do what any aircraft, piloted or not, is required to do: obey the laws of physics. "The Tic Tac was not doing that. It was going from like 50,000 feet to, you know, 100 feet in like seconds, which is not possible."

Underwood's FLIR pod managed to capture one minute and sixteen seconds of the mystifying object, which appears as a blurry dot that eventually zips out of frame, as if to say it had entertained the pilots enough. Show's over. But for everyone involved, it was an unforgettable performance.

"Fifty-five hundred people that were on the *Nimitz* in 2004 when this happened, and I guarantee every single one of them knows that this event happened," Fravor said in the 2020 documentary *The Phenomenon*.

Despite their experience, the officers just got back to work. With the taboo still firmly in place, they didn't make any noise about UFOs. As Underwood explained to *New York* magazine, he wasn't interested in conversations about extraterrestrials.

"At no point did I want to speculate as to what I thought this thing was—or be associated with, you know, 'alien beings' and 'alien aircraft' and all that stuff," he said. "I'm like, 'No. I do not want to be part of that community.' It is just what we call a UFO. I couldn't identify it. It was flying. And it was an object. It's as simple as that."

The objects seen off the East Coast were just as astonishing and puzzling. Former navy pilot Lieutenant Ryan Graves told *60 Minutes*

"What we were shown at least is that there are some very credible pilots who in flight are seeing stuff that cannot be explained by them. And it's also caught on video, but we basically can't make out what it is. It leaves us with a question mark. People hate question marks. They feel compelled to give an answer. I think that's how religions are so attractive, because they provide answers to a lot of things, when you have an urge to get an answer. Science takes time. It doesn't come up with an immediate answer for you."

—DR. PASCAL LEE, planetary scientist, on reserving judgment
about the nature of the objects seen in the declassified Pentagon videos,
in a September 2021 interview with the author

that his squadron began seeing UAPs in restricted airspace near Virginia Beach in 2014 just after they updated their jets' radar to focus on objects with infrared targeting cameras. This continued nearly every day for two years during training sessions. In "Gimbal," the pilot can be heard commenting excitedly as he gave chase: "Look at that thing, it's rotating! My gosh! They're all going against the wind, the wind's 120 knots to the west. Look at that thing, dude!"

Skeptics and Skepticism About Skeptics

As with every UFO case, debunkers and skeptics weighed in on the declassified videos, oftentimes claiming the objects seen in the footage were technological artifacts. Mick West, a science writer who runs the debunking site Metabunk.org and experiments with camera systems, light, and motion, has been among the most vocal skeptic. He believes the "Gimbal" video, for example, is showing a deceptive infrared glare from the engines of a distant jet.

"I looked up the camera's patents; these revealed a de-rotation mechanism used to correct for 'gimbal roll,' which would inevitably mean glares would rotate in the manner seen in the video," West told the *Guardian* in June 2021. "This is also probably why the Navy gave it the code name 'Gimbal,' rather than, say, 'Flying Saucer.'"

As for the other two navy videos, he suggests the speed exhibited in "Go Fast" is more of an illusion caused by the parallax effect. Rather than a UFO, West believes the object zipping across the ocean is "consistent with a balloon drifting in the wind." The "FLIR" video, featuring the flying Tic Tac, "did not show a craft moving like a ping-pong ball, but instead looked more like a distant plane with the apparent movement caused by the camera switching modes and performing gimbal rolls."

West's theories are based solely on the videos, not on what pilots witnessed with their own eyes, which in the case of "Gimbal" includes more objects seen outside the camera's frame. "There's a whole fleet of them," one of the pilots is heard saying. These theories don't sit well with those who were directly involved.

"It's funny how people can extrapolate stuff who've never operated the system know for sure," Fravor said dismissively on the *Lex Fridman Podcast* in 2020.

Mellon finds the debunkers' explanations utterly disrespectful, particularly because of "the degree of incompetence that they're implying" by suggesting Fravor and the other pilots don't know what they're seeing on their radar scopes, with infrared, or with their own eyes. The theories rely on the short videos and disregard the other facts.

"I think that's intellectually dishonest, and I think it takes a lot of nerve for guys who've never been in an F-18, to have never operated any of the systems, to assume that these guys don't know how to operate them or don't know what they're looking at," he said.

According to Elizondo, the sightings are continuing to happen every week by navy pilots, special operators, and others on the ground. "It's not secret anymore," he told me. "I think if this was a jury, with the evidence we have, you know, we're well beyond reasonable doubt. The jury would have in this case no option but to convict because the evidence is overwhelming."

So, what are these advanced things flying circles around our most brilliant technology? Extraterrestrials or something else equally mind-boggling? Through all of his experiences and with the knowledge gained at AATIP and in the years since, Elizondo's approach has been to keep an open mind. As he points out, there was once a time when life on earth was viewed as either plants or animals. Then fungi were added to the list. Not long after, microorganisms were discovered.

"A hidden kingdom right in front of our nose," as Elizondo said. "It's been here the whole time. Is it possible that these UAPs, these UFOs are like that? Had they always been here? Are they just as natural to this planet as we are and we're just now at the point where technologically we can interact? Are they from under the oceans? Are they from outer space? We don't know. Are they interdimensional? The possibilities are limitless and that's why we have to be very careful not to think in a binary way—it's either from here or from outer space—because chances are there's a lot of other options in between."

CONGRESS GETS THE WILSON-DAVIS MEMO

During the May 17, 2022, congressional hearing, Wisconsin representative Mike Gallagher asked Scott Bray and Ronald Moultrie of the UAP Task Force if they were aware of something known as the Wilson-Davis memo. This 2002 document includes notes from a private conversation between Dr. Eric Davis, an astrophysicist and senior science advisor to EarthTech International, and Admiral Thomas Ray Wilson, former director of the Defense Intelligence Agency.

The memo was leaked in 2019 after being retrieved from the estate of the late Apollo 14 astronaut Edgar Mitchell. Mitchell and Davis had worked together at Robert Bigelow's National Institute for Discovery Science in the early 2000s. Among the memo's numerous revelations that got ufologists buzzing are remarks from Wilson about the existence of a UFO cabal, crashed and recovered spacecraft, and that technology *"not of this Earth—not made by man—not by human hands"* is being reverse engineered. Just as Bob Lazar has claimed. Discussions of Roswell, Socorro, Rendlesham Forest, and MJ-12 are also briefly noted. But is the memo real?

Wilson has fully denied the authenticity of the document, and various researchers have called it a hoax. Davis has kept quiet on the subject, but in July 2020 he told the *New York Times* that he gave a classified briefing to a Defense Department agency just a few months earlier about retrievals of materials from "off-world vehicles not made on this earth." He gave similar briefings to staff members of the Senate Armed Services Committee in October 2019.

So who's telling the truth? Christopher Mellon, who knows both Wilson and Davis, believes the conversation occurred. "I can't really comment about it, but the memo is real."

Bray and Moultrie claimed they were unaware of the document. Whether they decide to read it and evaluate its veracity remains to be seen. Regardless, the controversial memo has gone from UFO lore directly into the public record.

WHEN UFOS REACHED THE UNITED NATIONS

etween the closing of Project Blue Book in 1969 and the launch of the Pentagon's secret AAWSAP program in 2007, world leaders didn't entirely ignore flying saucers. On November 27, 1978, a United Nations session explored the evidence. And why not? The UN promotes international peace and security, social progress, and advancing human rights, so if UFOs threaten to disrupt those goals, the General Assembly should attempt to do something about it.

UFOs began their journey to the UN three years earlier, after the prime minister of Grenada, Sir Eric Gairy, spotted a strange object in the small island nation's sky. Curious and confused, he began a personal crusade to understand the phenomenon. Grenada and other small countries could learn more if they had help from other nations, he thought. So Gairy went to the UN and attempted to establish an international committee that would aid the sharing and studying of UFO-related data. He hoped members would heed the aliens' "positive, friendly, godly message."

"The intent of the extraterrestrial beings is to try to instill in mankind and earth a better way of life," he once told reporters. No one took him seriously.

But when reporter and historian Lee Speigel caught wind of Gairy's struggles, he offered to help. He'd been on his own mission to learn more about these visitors and recently produced a documentary record album called *UFOs: The Credibility Factor*. Speigel had the connections to organize a group of credible scientists and witnesses, and the materials to develop a video presentation. He just needed Grenada to sponsor the proposal, which Gairy was happy to do.

"J. Allen Hynek was the first person I contacted," Speigel says. "I said, if I could do something at the United Nations, would you like to do it with me? He was like, 'Are you kidding?'"

Hynek had more than a hundred countries represented in his CUFOS database and was eager to promote a global approach to understanding what or who the world was seeing in the skies. "I have always strongly urged that the United Nations provide mechanisms for facilitating the exchange of UFO information between interested scientists in various countries," he wrote in response to Speigel's proposal.

Hynek brought fellow UFO investigator, scientist, and author Jacques Vallée to the team. Astronomer Claude Poher, nuclear physicist Stanton Friedman, astronaut Gordon Cooper, and U.S. Army Reserve captain Lawrence Coyne rounded out the group.

While the scientists swapped data and theories, both Cooper and Coyne had personal unexplainable experiences to share. From the seat of his jet fighter, Cooper witnessed several UFOs flying well above him over Europe in 1951. More than a decade later he saw another while orbiting the earth. The object Coyne saw from his helicopter, as noted in Chapter 1, was much closer and nearly made impact.

When the day of the meeting arrived, the delegation testified before a hearing of the Special Political Committee, along with representatives from the Committee on the Peaceful Uses of Outer Space. Gairy and his minister of education, Wellington Friday, gave their opening remarks, then Hynek took the stage. He first complemented Grenada for having the courage to "trod where mightier nations feared to tread" and then stressed the number of global reports made by credible persons, such as commercial pilots, radar experts, and members of the military. He concluded by emphasizing the fact that scientists and specialists around the world had no means to share their results and collaborate with other countries. The UN could create such a framework to further scientific study and, as Speigel saw it, "to work together to figure out this UFO thing." It would be a win for Grenada and the rest of planet earth.

Following the presentation, Decision 33/426 was adopted. Among its several points, it stated: "The General Assembly invites interested member states to take appropriate steps to coordinate on a national level scientific research and investigation into extraterrestrial life, including unidentified flying objects, and to inform the secretary-general of the observations, research and evaluation of such activities."

The committees intended to gauge the response and work with Grenada at the General Assembly's next session. Unfortunately, it never had a chance to. On March 13, 1979, an armed revolution overthrew Gairy's government and ousted him from power. That put an end to his quest for answers with the UN. As for Grenada, well, it suddenly had more immediate issues to deal with.

"Back then, there was no other country that I could've originally gone to for support of my proposal," Speigel says. "Only Grenada, because of Gairy. So with him out of the picture, the U.S. and Russia probably loved this, because now they didn't have to deal with another UFO presentation any time soon. And that's kind of where it ended."

As various countries are beginning to seriously look into unidentified aerial phenomena, the subject may make a return to the United Nations. In January 2023, the parliament of San Marino, a European microstate situated at the northern edge of Italy, voted to submit a proposal to the secretary general to create an office like Gairy sought: one that would share data internationally and scientifically study UAPs. Speigel has been invited to join a team to once again raise the discussion at the UN and seek its cooperation.

"If we can get this new resolution passed, history will be made," he told me. "And I will be very honored if I'm still part of that."

His Excellency Sir Eric Matthew Gairy
Prime Minister of Grenada
addresses the
Thirty-Third Session
of the
General Assembly
of the United Nations
on October 12, 1978

More than a month before the November 27, 1978, UFO presentation at the United Nations, Sir Eric Gairy, prime minister of Grenada, urged member nations to attend. "Sighting of UFOs are not restricted to just one or two parts of our planet," he told the General Assembly. "Reports come from all over the world today, and scientific analysis of these reports strongly suggest not only that a growing number of people believe that a more in-depth investigation into this phenomenon might make a significant contribution towards the well-being of the earth planet as well as towards man's better understanding of himself and of his purpose on earth."

"I have waited most of my life for the truth. Serious researchers, such as myself, have known this for years. Yet, we have faced ridicule, ad hominem attacks, and have been marginalized in the mainstream media and by certain so-called skeptics. I feel heartened that the truth is being revealed, fragment by fragment, as so not to incite public hysteria."

—KATHLEEN MARDEN, author, researcher, and niece of Betty and Barney Hill, in a February 2022 email to the author

Even Presidents of the United States See UFOs

The political scene has come a long way since ignoring and mocking the UFO issue following the closing of Project Blue Book. Former Democratic presidential candidate Dennis Kucinich would surely agree. During a 2007 debate, moderator Tim Russert asked him if it was true that he'd spotted a triangular UFO silently hovering over actress Shirley MacLaine's home in Washington State. Kucinich answered, "Uh, I did. It was an unidentified flying object, okay? It's like, it's unidentified. I saw something." As the audience erupted in laughter, Kucinich attempted to roll with it yet still defend himself by reminding viewers that his experience was hardly an isolated case.

"I'm also going to move my campaign office to Roswell, New Mexico, and another one in Exeter, New Hampshire, okay?" he said.[†] "And also, you have to keep in mind that Jimmy Carter saw a UFO and also that more people in this country have seen UFOs than I think approve of George Bush's presidency."

Carter's UFO sighting occurred in 1969 on his way to giving a speech in north Georgia. He described it as a bright object in the sky that came toward him and changed colors from green to blue to red to white and then took off. During his 1976 presidential campaign, he vowed to support the study of UFOs: "If I become president, I'll make every piece of information this country has about UFO sightings available to the public and scientists." However, when he won the election and pursued the topic, the director of the CIA, George H. W. Bush, wouldn't answer any questions. Carter let it go and claimed there were no government cover-ups.

Ronald Reagan claimed to have seen something unusual while flying in a Cessna Citation aircraft while he was governor of California in 1974. He discussed the sighting with Norman C. Miller, then Washington bureau chief for the *Wall Street Journal*. "We followed it for several minutes. It was a bright white light," Reagan told Miller. "We followed it to Bakersfield, and all of a sudden to our utter amazement it went straight up into the heavens." There were no follow-up reports on what it might have been.

---

† Kucinich was referencing a 1965 case in which a luminous egg-shaped UFO was spotted by civilians and police officers in Exeter.

In May 2021, just a month before ODNI's report to Congress, the collective shift in attitude was evident when Barack Obama spoke about the possibility of UFOs on late-night television. "Well, when it when it comes to aliens, there's some things I just can't tell you on air," he told James Corden, presumably joking. But then in a more serious tone, he referenced the *Nimitz* sighting and other recent phenomena: "There's footage and records of objects in the skies, that we don't know exactly what they are, we can't explain how they moved, their trajectory. They did not have an easily explainable pattern. And so, you know I think that people still take seriously trying to investigate and figure out what that is."

The Interstellar Road Ahead

Christopher Mellon's mission to keep the UAP conversation moving forward is working. As discussed in Chapter 4, a month after the ODNI presented its report to Congress, Avi Loeb launched the Galileo Project to collect and analyze scientific data. In addition, aviator Ryan Graves is working with engineers and scientists, including Dr. Ravi Kopparapu, at the American Institute of Aeronautics and Astronautics (AIAA) to investigate the topic further. NASA established the UAP Independent Study to explore the space a little closer to home. And in Washington, DC, the government continues to take notice. More importantly, it's continuing to take action.

In December 2021, New York senator Kirsten Gillibrand announced the inclusion of her unidentified aerial phenomena amendment in the 2022 National Defense Authorization Act. Senator Marco Rubio and Arizona Democratic congressman Ruben Gallego worked alongside her in a bipartisan effort to establish an office with access to Department of Defense and Intelligence Community data related to UAPs.

"Our national security efforts rely on aerial supremacy and these phenomena present a challenge to our dominance over the air. Staying ahead of UAP sightings is critical to keeping our strategic edge and keeping our nation safe," Gillibrand said in a press release.

It's the type of coordination that should be a no-brainer for all government programs, and one that may actually lead to understanding, as Gillibrand stated, "whether these aerial phenomena belong to a foreign government or something else altogether."

In addition to centralizing data and testing scientific theories, the UAP office must provide unclassified annual reports to Congress and classified semiannual briefings on intelligence analysis, reported incidents, health-related effects, the role of foreign governments, and nuclear security.

The legitimacy of "aerial supremacy" and understanding what's in our airspace has made it okay to talk about the subject. As Leslie Kean told me, "The stigma against having anything to do with UFOs is diminishing, because they do have that national security component. And I mean, how can you ridicule that?"

As we enter a new era of UFO investigation, perhaps what's most surprising about recent efforts is that they didn't happen sooner. Maybe someday we'll discover that a small covert group does in fact hold all the secrets, but for now, as is often the case, the government might simply be plagued with ignorance. "I think some [members of Congress] felt well, how come I wasn't briefed about this earlier?" Kean said. "It just wasn't happening. The different agencies were sitting on their data, nobody was communicating, nobody wanted to deal with this. The 2017 article forced the issue, and congressmen and representatives on the Hill became curious about this and they wanted to know more."

The Gillibrand amendment assures they, and all their constituents, will. "There's a lot more to come," Kean added. "I really believe that and I'm excited."

Staring over the Next Horizon

Luis Elizondo agrees with Kean's assessment that the process of UFO investigation and disclosure has just begun. "This is just the tip of the iceberg," he promises. "I think when the full breadth and scope of this topic finally comes out, people are going to be shocked." Aside from shock, he also believes it will be a necessary moment of growth "in order to evolve as a species." Much like when humankind first harnessed fire and illuminated the darkness, and when explorers braved the seas by journeying over the horizon. "Maybe in very much the same sense, we are, yet again, as a species standing on a stuning beach, and just staring over the next horizon we're about to sail over," he says.

The question is, what will we find? Will we uncover a new wrinkle of physics that redefines how things work? Or a new species that redefines our place in the universe—one that proves there's another pale blue or green or red dot in the vast universe with the intelligence to guide it here and discover the same thing? Fascinating as this would be, it creates another mystery.

As CUFOS's president and scientific director, Mark Rodeghier, puts it: "Imagine instead that a year from now an alien spaceship does show up openly and contacts us and we start talking to them and everything's fine. They're not killing us, they're talking, and here we are. And finally, of course sooner rather than later somebody says to them, 'Well, glad you're open to contact now, after all these years of not.' And the alien says, 'What do you mean? We just got here! We haven't been here since '47. I don't know what you're talking about.' Meaning, of course, we still wouldn't know what the UFO phenomenon was."

However, if we ever make contact with one advanced alien civilization, surely there could be more, just as the Drake Equation has suggested. Perhaps another civilization could explain the sightings since the 1940s, or as some believe, since the beginning of humanity. Could they be millions of years ahead and find us as interesting as we find a colony of ants? Or could they be our creators? Are religion and the idea of God rooted in an extraterrestrial beginning? In some ways, the idea is nothing more than semantics. Followers of the world's religions have little trouble believing in a supreme being and angels—both of which reside in a realm outside of this physical earth and provide answers to unexplainable problems. The same could be said of aliens. Both reflect our desire for something more. But we humans like to think we're special, and if another race of beings out there is exponentially smarter than us, we're not so special.

Perhaps, as Jacques Vallée suggested, those beings exist right alongside us in another dimension, occasionally poking their heads out for a select few to see. They could be living in a world hidden to us all this time, just like the kingdom of microorganisms, or even lurking in the depths of the ocean, as Elizondo has considered. Or is that invisible world even closer? Buried inside each and every one of us, within our own minds? It's a suggestion professor emeritus of religious studies at the University of North Carolina at Chapel Hill David Halperin shared with me. He wonders if scientists and ufologists are looking in the wrong direction. Rather than reaching out to the stars, he suspects that understanding the UFO phenomenon might require that we look deeper within. We just might find what he calls "visitors from *inner* space."

"There are things we just do not understand about ourselves, about our minds, how our minds interact with our bodies," Halperin said. "Because I think that the phenomenon of physiological effects of a UFO sighting is fairly well established." If he's right, if the mind can create the UFO phenomenon on such a mass scale, we might one day discover that we're even more special than we thought.

Whether it's inner space or outer space or an entirely different space, it's clear that something is happening. It's not visitors from Venus or other planets in our solar system as contactees proudly proclaimed in the fifties. But more than seventy-five years after the term *flying saucer* first entered our culture, the government has publicly acknowledged the phenomenon exists and has adopted an open-minded approach. Curious scientists have shed the stigma, allowing them to focus on gathering and following data without following a narrative. Just as critically, more people are willing to listen to what's being seen and learned. The question is no longer whether UFOs exist, but rather: what are they? Until we uncover the truth of what's out there, and it changes our entire concept of the reality that surrounds us, the search for answers will keep us wondering. And, alone or not, keep us human.

Declassified Sources

In addition to the many ufologists, experiencers, investigators, scientists, and other people I interviewed, the following articles, books, documents, films, shows, online videos, and podcasts were helpful in creating this book. They are all fully accessible; no security clearances needed.

INTRODUCTION
GREETINGS, EARTHLING READERS

Associated Press. "Man Says Object Buzzes Vehicle." *Burlington Daily Times*, July 3, 1964.

"Boy Burned in Mystery Mishap Leaves Hospital." *Lubbock Avalanche-Journal*, June 12, 1964.

"Many See Mysterious Object." *Morgantown Post*, May 26, 1964.

"Set Afire by Black Blob." *National Enquirer*, August 22, 1964.

United Press International. "Flying Object with Bad Smell Reported in Toccoa." *Macon News*, July 16, 1964.

CHAPTER 1
ATTACK OF THE FLYING SAUCERS

Arnold, Kenneth, and Raymond Palmer. *The Coming of the Saucers: A Documentary Report on Sky Objects That Have Mystified the World*. Amherst, WI: self-published, 1952.

Associated Press. "12 'Saucers' Escape Jets over Capital." *San Francisco Examiner*, July 28, 1952.

———. "Balls of Fire Stalk U.S. Fighters in Night Assaults over Germany." *New York Times*, January 2, 1945.

———. "Army Declares Flying Disc Found." *Spokane Daily Chronicle*, July 8, 1947.

———. "'Disc' Found near Roswell Is Weather Balloon, Kite." *Abilene Reporter*, July 9, 1947.

———. "'Flying Disc' Is Caught but Army Identifies It as Weather Kite." *Daily Oklahoman*, July 9, 1947.

———. "Flying Discs Still a Mystery." *Missoulian*, July 10, 1947.

———. "'Flying Saucer' Controversy Rages with Reports of 'Tumbling' Objects." *Opelika Daily News*, June 30, 1947.

———. "Flying Saucer Puzzle Grows." *Monroe News Star*, July 7, 1947.

———. "Illinois Engineer Confirms Report of Flying Disks." *Green Bay Press-Gazette*, June 27, 1947.

———. "Newspaper Announces Ban on 'Saucer' Stories." *Battle Creek Enquirer*, August 7, 1952.

———. "'Saucers' Over Washington." *News and Observer*, July 22, 1952.

———. "UFOs Only Swamp Gas, Expert Says." *Capital Times*, March 25, 1966.

Bragalia, Anthony. "The Socorro UFO Hoax Exposed!" The UFO Iconoclast(s) blog, September 28, 2009. https://magonia.com/wp-content/uploads/2017/07/socorro-hoax-exposed.pdf (accessed November 15, 2022).

Broad, William. "Wreckage in the Desert Was Odd but Not Alien." *New York Times*, September 18, 1994.

Brosnan, John. "Heads Up, Folks! The Discs Are Flying Again." *Times News* (Twin Falls), August 15, 1947.

Clark, Ed. "Men Who See 'Em Say Foo-Fighters Can't Be Poohed." *Stars and Stripes*, February 19, 1945.

Considine, Bob. "Did Flyer Die Chasing Real Saucer?" *St. Louis Post-Dispatch*, November 20, 1950.

Corso, Philip J., and William J. Birnes. *The Day After Roswell*. New York: Gallery Books, 2017.

Daugherty, Greg. "George Adamski Got Famous Sharing His UFO Photos and Alien 'Encounters.'" History Channel, January 9, 2020. https://www.history.com/news /george-adamski-ufo-alien-photos (accessed November 3, 2021).

David, Jay, ed. *The Flying Saucer Reader*. New York: The New American Library, Inc., 1967.

Davis, Isabel, and Ted Bloecher. "Close Encounter at Kelly and Others of 1955." Center for UFO Studies, 1978.

"Do UFOs Exist?" *Larry King Live*. CNN, aired July 1, 2003. https://cnn.com /TRANSCRIPTS/0307/01/lkl.00.html (accessed November 5, 2021).

Dunning, Brian. "Lonnie Zamora and the Socorro UFO." *Skeptoid* podcast, August 1, 2017. https://skeptoid.com/episodes/4582 (accessed May 5, 2022).

Edwards, Frank. *Flying Saucers—Serious Business*. New York: Bantam, 1966.

Feola, Eloise. "Fighter Pilot Killed Chasing UFO; 'Lubbock Lights' Remain Mystery." *Pittsburgh Press*, March 8, 1967.

"Fiery Object Sighted near Levelland Still Deep Mystery to All Officials." *Lubbock Evening Journal*, November 4, 1957.

Friedman, Stanton T. *Flying Saucers and Science: A Scientist Investigates the Mysteries of UFOs*. Pompton Plains, NJ: New Page Books, 2008.

Garwood, Darrell. "Camera Battery May Soon Tell." *Miami Daily News*, July 30, 1952.

Gillette, Halbert P. "Fireball?" *Los Angeles Times*, February 28, 1942.

Hastings, Robert. "Recent Russian Newspaper Article Discusses UFO Incidents at Soviet and American Nuclear Weapons Sites." UFOs & Nukes, June 21, 2010. https://www.ufohastings.com/articles /recent-russian-newspaper-article-discusses -ufo-incidents-at-soviet-and-american-nuclear -weapons-sites (accessed May 2, 2022).

Houran, James, and Stephen Porter. "Statement Validity Analysis of 'The Jim Ragsdale Story': Implications for the Roswell Incident." *Journal of Scientific Exploration* 12, no. 1, 1998. https://www.scientificexploration.org /docs/12/jse_12_1_houran.pdf (accessed November 30, 2021).

Hynek, J. Allen. *The Hynek UFO Report*. London: Sphere Books Ltd., 1978.

———. *The UFO Experience: A Scientific Inquiry*. New York: Ballantine Books, 1972.

Jacobs, David Michael. *The UFO Controversy in America*. Bloomington: Indiana University Press, 1975.

Keyhoe, Donald. *Flying Saucers from Outer Space*. New York: Henry Holt and Company, 1953.

———. *The Flying Saucers Are Real*. New York: Fawcett Publications, 1950.

"Knox Indicates Raid Just 'Jittery Nerves.'" *Los Angeles Times*, February 26, 1942.

Lhote, Henri. *Search for the Tassili Frescoes: Story of the Prehistoric Rock-Paintings of the Sahara*.

Translated by Alan Houghton Brodrick. London: Hutchinson & Co., 1959.

Meyer, Philip. "The Great Flying Saucer Boom." *Detroit Free Press*, April 3, 1966.

Oliphant, John. "Calling Occupants of Inter-planetary Craft—Still." *Vancouver Sun*, July 5, 1997.

"Paul & Joel Hynek." *Edge of Reality Radio with Lee Speigel*. KGRA Digital Broadcasting, February 27, 2020.

"Reports of Flying Saucers Aren't New." *Minneapolis Star*, August 11, 1965.

Ruppelt, Edward J. *The Report on Unidentified Flying Objects*. New York: Doubleday & Company, 1956.

Sagan, Carl. *The Demon-Haunted World*. New York: Ballantine Books, 1996.

Sagan, Carl, and Thornton Page, eds. *UFO's: A Scientific Debate*. Ithaca, NY: Cornell University Press, 1972.

Saulsbury, Jim. "Space Enthusiasts Meet." *San Bernardino County Sun*, March 14, 1955.

"Says That Life on Venus Is Probable." *Rutland Daily Herald*, December 5, 1922.

Thomas, David E. "A Different Angle on the Socorro UFO of 1964." *Skeptical Inquirer* 25, no. 4 (Jul/Aug 2001).

Treloar, Jim, and Bill Serrin. "'This Thing Like a Ball of Fire' . . . Just Gas?" *Detroit Free Press*, April 3, 1966.

United Press. "'Flying Saucer' Eye-Witness Wishes He'd Never Mentioned It." *Daily News Journal* (Murfreesboro, TN), June 27, 1947.

———. "Jittery Hillbillies See Duck-Walking Whattizit." *Windsor Star*, September 15, 1952.

———. "Los Angeles 'Raid' Mystery Deepens." *Scranton Tribune*, February 27, 1942.

———. "Mystery Aircraft Caused Los Angeles Raid Alarm." *News and Observer* (Raleigh, NC), February 27, 1942.

———. "Pilot Fussed; FBI Won't Check Into Flying Saucers." *Des Moines Register*, June 29, 1947.

———. "Shiny Disks Hurtling High in Sky May Have Been Jets." *Spokane Chronicle*, June 28, 1947.

United Press International. "Michigan UFOs Debunked: They're Swamp Gas, Scientist Says." *Star Tribune* (Minneapolis, MN), March 26, 1966.

Vallee, Jacques. *Anatomy of a Phenomenon*. New York: Ace Books, 1965.

"Weather Is Blamed for Flying Saucer Mystery but Radar Men Insist Object Is 'Something.'" *Palladium-Item and Sun-Telegram* (Richmond, IN), July 31, 1952.

Zochert, Donald. "Room for Doubt in Report on UFOs." *Philadelphia Inquirer*, February 9, 1969.

CHAPTER 2

CLOSE ENCOUNTERS

Abrahams, Brad, dir. *Love and Saucers*. Curator Pictures, Perceive Think Act Films, The Orchard, 2017.

Adamski, George. *Inside the Flying Saucers*. New York: Paperback Library, Inc., 1967.

Adamski, George, and Desmond Leslie. *Flying Saucers Have Landed*. New York: The British Book Centre, 1953.

Associated Press. "Did UFOs Cause the Northeast Blackout?" *Troy Record*, July 30, 1968.

———. "NASA Scientists Will Check Men's 'Visit to UFO.'" *Alamogordo Daily News*, October 15, 1973.

———. "Space-Age Aspirant Quits, Is for Kennedy." *Chattanooga Daily Times*, October 24, 1960.

Barker, Gray. *They Knew Too Much About Flying Saucers.* New York: University Books, Inc., 1956.

"Believers, Skeptics Attend Space Show." *Courier News* (Plainfield, NJ), September 17, 1958.

"The Bellero Shield." *The Outer Limits.* Season 1, episode 20, aired February 10, 1964.

Briggs, Katherine M. *British Folk Tales and Legends: A Sampler.* London: Granada Publishing, 1977.

Carlson, Peter. "Ike and the Alien Ambassadors." *Washington Post*, February 19, 2004. https://www.washingtonpost.com/archive /lifestyle/2004/02/19/ike-and-the-alien -ambassadors/4698e544-1dc8-4573-8b8d -2b48d2a6305e (accessed September 4, 2022).

Davis, Russ. "Lehigh Valley Flight to Venus? Easy via Saucer, the Man Says." *Sunday Call-Chronicle* (Allentown, PA), June 9, 1957.

Dellquest, Wilfrid. "Gabriel's Trumpet." *Eagle Rock Sentinel*, August 11, 1960.

Dickinson, Terence. "Zeta Reticuli Update." 1980. Clippings folder, International UFO Museum & Research Center.

Feeney, Mark. "Pulitzer Winner Is Killed in Accident." *Boston Globe*, September 29, 2004.

Fox, Margalit. "Budd Hopkins, Abstract Expressionist and U.F.O. Author, Dies at 80." *New York Times*, August 24, 2011.

Friedman, Stanton T., and Kathleen Marden. *Captured! The Betty and Barney Hill UFO Experience.* Franklin Lakes, NJ: New Page Books, 2021.

Fry, Daniel W. "My Experience with the Lie Detector." *Saucers* 2, no. 3 (September 1954). https://danielfry.com/controversies /polygraph-test (accessed September 2, 2021).

———. *The White Sands Incident.* Louisville: Best Books Inc., 1966.

Fuller, John G. *The Interrupted Journey: Two Lost Hours "Aboard a Flying Saucer."* New York: Dial Press, 1966.

Golfen, Bob. "UFO Believers Share Their Experiences at Conference." *Arizona Republic*, October 6, 1994.

Hartzman, Marc. "Promises of Utopia: A Look Back at Kennedy vs Nixon vs the UFO Spacemen's Candidate." Weird Historian. https://www.weirdhistorian.com/promises -of-utopia-a-look-back-at-kennedy-vs-nixon -vs-the-ufo-spacemens-candidate (accessed September 1, 2021).

Hickson, Charles, and William Mendez. *UFO Contact at Pascagoula.* Gautier, MS: Charles Hickson, 1987.

Hillinger, Charles. "Twilight of Flying Saucers." *San Francisco Examiner*, April 19, 1970.

Hopkins, Budd. *Missing Time: A Documented Study of UFO Abductions.* New York: Richard Marek Publishers, 1981.

———. *Witnessed: The True Story of the Brooklyn Bridge UFO Abductions.* New York: Pocket Books, 1996.

Jefferson, David J. "A Harvard Doctor Offers Trauma Relief for UFO 'Abductees'." *Wall Street Journal*, May 14, 1992.

Klass, Philip. *UFOs Explained.* New York: Random House, 1974.

Knight News Wire. "Scientists Supporting UFO Claim." *Hartford Courant*, November 28, 1975.

Kolberg, Rebecca. "Fantasy-Prone Psyche May Lie Behind Strange Visitations." United Press International (*Newhall Signal & Saugus Enterprise*), June 19, 1988.

Kottmeyer, Martin. "The Eyes That Spoke." *Skeptical Briefs* 4.3 (September 1, 1994). https://skepticalinquirer.org/newsletter /eyes-that-spoke (accessed February 15, 2022).

Kummer, Frank. "Bordentown UFO Con-ference Offers Bizarre Tales." *Courier-Post* (Camden, NJ), November 6, 1998.

"L.A. Flying Saucer Meet Ends with Blast at Unbelieving Earthlings." *Pasadena Indepen-dent*, July 13, 1959.

"Loving the Alien." *Independent*, October 26, 1996.

Mack, John E. *Abduction: Human Encounters with Aliens.* New York: Charles Scribner's Sons, 1994.

———. *Passport to the Cosmos: Human Trans-formation and Alien Encounters.* New York: Crown Publishers, 1999.

"Marjorie Eleanor Fish." *News Herald* (Port Clinton, OH), April 10, 2013.

Morgan, Joseph. *Phoenix Britannicus: Being a Miscellaneous Collection of Scarce and Curious Tracts [. . .], Vol. 1.* London, 1732.

Moseley, James W. "Some New Facts About 'Flying Saucers Have Landed.'" *Saucer News*. Special issue 1, October 1957.

Musgrove, Paul. "Planetarium Probes UFOs." *Vancouver Sun*, October 26, 1983.

Norris, Fred. "Fact or Fiction? A Novelist's Close Encounter." *Birmingham Evening Mail*, May 23, 1987.

Palmer, Barry. "Portsmouth Couple Awes 600 Persons Here; Describes Near-Contact with Alien Spacecraft." *Nashua Telegraph*, December 1, 1965.

Raduga, Michael, Andrey Shashkov, and Zhanna Zhunusova. "Emulating Alien and UFO Encounters in REM Sleep." *International Journal of Dream Research* 14, no. 2 (October 2021). https://journals.ub.uni-heidelberg.de /index.php/IJoDR/article/view/78599/78539 (accessed September 22, 2022).

Redfern, Nick. "UFO Events Fabricated by Government Agencies: Manipulating Minds and Using Helicopters." Mysterious Universe, May 28, 2021. https://mysterious universe.org/2021/05/ufo-events-fabricated -by-government-agencies-manipulating -minds-and-using-helicopters (accessed online March 20, 2022).

Richard Dolan Intelligent Disclosure. "Astonishing 1961 Abduction Case (Helen Wheels) | The Richard Dolan Show w/Peter Robbins." YouTube, uploaded February 9, 2021. https://www.youtube.com/watch?v =RsHSnh_f5As (accessed November 2, 2021).

Salla, Michael E. "Eisenhower's 1954 Meeting with Extraterrestrials: The Fiftieth Anniver-sary of First Contact?" Exopolitics, research study 8, January 28, 2004. https://exopolitics .net/Study-Paper-8.htm (accessed Decem-ber 9, 2021).

"Saucer Expert Seeks Presidency." *Whittier News*, August 10, 1960.

Steiger, Brad. *Strangers from the Skies.* New York: Award Books, 1966.

Stranges, Frank E. *Stranger at the Pentagon.* 4th revised ed. New Brunswick, NJ: Inner Light Publications, 1991.

Strieber, Whitley. *Communion: A True Story.* New York: Beech Tree Books, 1987.

Stringfellow, Kim. "Giant Rock, Space People and the Integratron." The Mojave Project,

May 2018. https://mojaveproject.org/dispatches-item/giant-rock-space-people-and-the-integratron (accessed September 8, 2021).

Szymanski, Mike. "Eisenhower Great-Granddaughter Discusses Time Travel, Mars and ETs." Patch, May 16, 2012. https://patch.com/california/studiocity/eisenhower-great-granddaughter-discusses-time-travel-5503567164 (accessed April 30, 2022).

"Tibetan Monastery, First in America, to Shelter Cult Disciples at Laguna Beach." *Los Angeles Times*, April 8, 1934.

Twitchell, Cleve. "A Conversation with Daniel W. Fry, Scientist Living in Merlin." *Medford Mail Tribune*, January 6, 1963.

United Press International. "Fishermen Claim UFO Abducted Them." *Galesberg Register-Mail*, October 13, 1973.

———. "UFO? He Doesn't Believe What He Saw." *Miami Herald*, November 4, 1973.

Webb, Walter N. "A Dramatic UFO Encounter in the White Mountains, New Hampshire, Sept. 19-20, 1961." NICAP Report, August 30, 1965. Clippings folder, International UFO Museum & Research Center.

Williamson, George Hunt. *The Saucers Speak: A Documentary Report of Interstellar Communication by Radiotelegraphy.* London: Neville Spearman, 1963.

"Woodcutters Fooled the World, Say Aviation and Lie Detector Experts." *San Antonio Express*, August 1, 1976.

CHAPTER 3

THE PHENOMENON CONTINUES

Aldridge, Dorothy. "UFO Pilots Not Cause of Cattle Mutilations." *Colorado Springs Gazette Telegraph*, August 3, 1975.

"Ariel School Encounter Witness, Salma Siddick & Filmmaker Randall Nickerson, 10-18-17." *Martin Willis Live Shows, Podcast UFO*, streamed live October 18, 2017. https://www.youtube.com/watch?v=1rtJpw_WWDg (accessed April 22, 2022).

Becker, Bob. "Mutilators Are Considered Dangerous by Law Officers." *Colorado Springs Gazette Telegraph*, August 3, 1975.

"Bob Lazar describes Alien Technology Housed at Secret S-4 Base in Nevada — Part 5." Originally aired May 15, 1989, on KLAS-TV Las Vegas. https://www.youtube.com/watch?v=4UjqFaQq_7I (accessed February 10, 2022).

Cardoso, Rodrigo. "The official history of the ET of Varginha" (A história oficial do ET de Varginha). Translated by browser. Istoé, May 12, 2021. istoe.com.br/105958_A+HISTORIA+OFICIAL+DO+ET+DE+VARGINHA (accessed April 22, 2022).

Christie, Sean. "Remembering Zimbabwe's Great Alien Invasion." *Mail & Guardian*, September 4, 2014. https://mg.co.za/article/2014-09-04-remembering-zimbabwes-great-alien-invasion (accessed April 13, 2022).

Daugherty, Greg, and Missy Sullivan. "Huge, Hovering and Silent: The Mystery of 'Black Triangle' UFOs." History Channel, July 22, 2020. history.com/news/black-triangle-ufos-facts (accessed January 15, 2022).

Dunning, Brian. "The 1994 Ruwa Zimbabwe Alien Encounter." *Skeptoid* podcast, December 29, 2020. https://skeptoid.com/episodes/4760 (accessed April 3, 2022).

Duran, Marlys. "Engineer Probes UFO Mystery." Scripps Howard News Service, July 21, 1999.

Epstein, Jack. "The Extraterrestrial Invasion of Brazil." *San Francisco Examiner*, August 11, 1996.

"ETs Captured in Brasil." Edited by Cynthia Hind. *UFO AfriNews* 15 (January 1997).

Fiscus, Chris, and Richard Ruelas. "Phoenix Sighting in U.S. Spotlight." *Arizona Republic*, June 20, 1997.

Goodyear, Toni. "UFO Researcher Declares Sightings Are 'Valid'." *Robesonian*, April 13, 1975.

Green, Jessica. "Has the Mystery of 'Britain's Roswell' Finally Been Solved? Rendlesham Forest UFO 'Landing' Was a Prank SAS Tricksters Played on US Airmen, Insiders Claim." *Daily Mail*, December 30, 2018. https://www.dailymail.co.uk/news/article -6539849/Has-mystery-Britains-Roswell -finally-solved.html (accessed March 12, 2022).

Hazlewood, Lynn. "Strangeness in the Night." *Hudson Valley*, October 1997.

Hind, Cynthia. "Report on Space Activity in Zimbabwe." *Mufon UFO Journal*, December 1994.

Iasimone, Ashley. "Kesha Recalls UFO Sighting That Influenced New Album 'Rainbow.'" Billboard, July 8, 2017. https://www.billboard .com/music/pop/kesha-ufo-sighting-joshua -tree-spaceship-rainbow-album-7858028 (accessed May 1, 2022).

Jacobsen, Annie. *Area 51: An Uncensored History of America's Top Secret Military Base.* New York: Little, Brown and Company, 2011.

"Kesha Talks Praying, Rainbow and Space- ships." *Zach Sang Show*, YouTube, uploaded July 7, 2017. https://www.youtube.com /watch?v=R7LoDjHoahI&t=27s (accessed May 2, 2022).

Kitei, Lynne. *The Phoenix Lights: A Skeptic's Dis- covery That We Are Not Alone.* 20th anniversary ed. Waterfront Press, 2019.

Lazar, Bob. *Dreamland.* Cardiff by the Sea, CA: Interstellar, 2019.

Lennon, John. "Interview/Interview with by/ on John Lennon and/or Dr. Winston O'Boogie." *Andy Warhol's Interview* IV, no. 11, 1974.

Letter to unknown from Inspector - Opera- tions (Planning), July 28, 1999. Suffolk Police Files. https://www.suffolk.police.uk/sites /suffolk/files/unusual_lights.pdf.

Marler, David. *Triangular UFOs: An Estimate of the Situation.* Self-published, 2013.

Masciola, Carol. "Tourists Are Haunting the Deserts of Nevada, Hoping for a Close En- counter of the Alien Kind." *Salt Lake Tribune*, June 1, 1993.

Moffett, Matt. "Tale of Stinky Extraterrestrials Stirs Up UFO Crowd in Brazil." *Wall Street Journal*, June 28, 1996.

Naughty But Nice Rob. "Fran Drescher Believes She Was Abducted by Aliens." HuffPost, January 26, 2012. https://www .huffpost.com/entry/fran-drescher-aliens -interview_n_1232688 (accessed May 1, 2022).

Nickerson, Randall, dir. *Ariel Phenomenon.* String Theory Films, 2022.

"Phoenix Has Flair for Paranormal." *Arizona Republic*, October 30, 1997.

Pope, Nick, John Burroughs, and Jim Penniston. *Encounter in Rendlesham Forest: The Inside Story of the World's Best-Documented UFO Incident.* New York: Thomas Dunne Books, 2014.

Ridpath, Ian. "Jim Penniston's notebook." Author's website, October 2021. http://www .ianridpath.com/ufo/pennistonnotebook .html (accessed March 12, 2022).

Ruelas, Richard. "Air Guard: Valley's UFOs Were Our Flares." *Arizona Republic*, July 25, 1997.

———. "Phoenix Lights, Plus a Year." *Arizona Republic*, March 13, 1998.

"Shaq on Kobe's Hall of Fame Induction, Seeing a UFO & Most Expensive Thing He Ever Bought a Stranger." *Jimmy Kimmel Live*, YouTube, uploaded May 18, 2021. https://www.youtube.com/watch?v=u-YMnJyJL2I (accessed May 2, 2022).

Sheaffer, Robert. "The Rendle-Sham Case: Phony and Phonier." *Skeptical Inquirer* 39, no. 6 (November/December 2015). https://skepticalinquirer.org/wp-content/uploads/sites/29/2015/11/p23.pdf (accessed March 12, 2022).

Silva, Samantha, and Régis Melo. "Varginha ET: case completes 20 years with mysteries and uncertainties" (ET de Varginha: caso completa 20 anos com mistérios e incertezas). Translated by browser. Globo.com, South of Minas (Sul de minas), January 20, 2016. https://g1.globo.com/mg/sul-de-minas/noticia/2016/01/et-de-varginha-caso-completa-20-anos-com-misterios-e-incertezas.html (accessed April 23, 2022).

Sims, Paul. "Britain's Most Famous UFO Sighting 'Was a Top Secret Military Experiment.'" *Sun*, May 11, 2020. https://www.thesun.co.uk/news/11600899/ufo-sighting-military-experiment-claim (accessed March 12, 2022).

Simon, Stephanie. "Ill. Folks Know Truth Is Out There, but Flying Object Is Still Unidentified." *Los Angeles Times*, January 18, 2000.

Speigel, Lee. "Lumberton, North Carolina, April 3–April 9, 1975." Report submitted to J. Allen Hynek on May 8, 1975.

Tingley, Brett. "We Talk Giant V-Shaped Airships, Space, and Phoenix Lights with JP Aerospace's Founder." The Drive, February 5, 2020. https://www.thedrive.com/the-war-zone/32082/we-talk-giant-boomerang-shaped-airships-space-and-phoenix-lights-with-jp-aerospaces-founder (accessed January 20, 2022).

"Transcript of Bergstrom AFB Interview of Betty Cash, Vickie & Colby Landrum – August 1981." Transcript of taped interview from Bergstom Air Force Base Law Library. https://www.cufon.org/cufon/cashlani.htm (accessed October 24, 2022).

"Two Women Pursue UFO for Distance of 10 Miles." *Berkshire Eagle*, March 10, 1967.

"UFO Report Launches Demands for Inquiry." *Honolulu Advertiser*, June 21, 1997.

United Press. "Seattle Men in Plane Photograph California 'Flying Triangles'." *Siskiyou Daily News*, July 21, 1950.

Unsolved Mysteries. Season 4, episode 10, NBC, November 10, 1991.

Walzer, E. B. "More Than a Flight of Fancy." *Daily Times* (Mamaroneck, NY), September 11, 1983.

CHAPTER 4

THE SEARCH FOR EXTRATERRESTRIAL INTELLIGENCE

Ball, Gloria. "Earth Scientists Checking Sounds For Other-Star Intelligent Being." The Science Service (*Austin Statesman*), May 5, 1960.

Betz, Eric. "The Wow! Signal: An Alien Missed Connection?" Astronomy, September 30, 2020. https://m.astronomy.com/news/2020/09/the-wow-signal-an-alien-missed-connection (accessed December 28, 2021).

Boyd, Robert. "A Galaxy-Wide Search for Intelligent Life." *Miami Herald*, May 12, 1996.

Cocconi, Guiseppe, and Philip Morrison. "Searching for Interstellar Communications." *Nature,* September 19, 1959.

Cohen, Jennie. "Solving the Riddle of Stonehenge's Construction." History Channel, February 19, 2020. history.com/news /solving-the-riddle-of-stonehenges -construction (accessed April 26, 2022).

Collyns, Robin. *Did Spacemen Colonize the Earth?* Chicago: Henry Regnery Company, 1976.

Dixon, Robert S. "A Statement Regarding the Claim That the "WOW!" Signal Was Caused by Hydrogen Emission [. . .]." Naapo.org. June 6, 2017. http://naapo.org/WOW CometRebuttal.html (accessed December 28, 2021).

Drake, Frank, and Dava Sobel. *Is Anyone Out There?: The Scientific Search for Extraterrestrial Intelligence.* New York: Dell Publishing, 1994.

Ehman, Jerry R. "The Big Ear Wow! Signal: What We Know and Don't Know About It After 20 Years." Big Ear Radio Observatory, September 1, 1997, revised February 3, 1998. http://www.bigear.org/wow20th.htm (accessed December 25, 2021).

Elias, Thomas D. "Congress Abandons Search for Intelligent Life." Scripps Howard News Service (*The News Journal*), November 7, 1993.

Flammarion, Camille. *Dreams of an Astronomer.* Translated by E. E. Fournier d'Albe. New York: D. Appleton and Company, 1923.

Greenewald, John. "Ronald Reagan's Own Handwriting Emphasizes Importance of "Alien Threat" Reference in UN Speech, 1987." The Black Vault. theblackvault.com /documentarchive/ronald-reagans-own -handwriting-emphasizes-importance-of -alien-threat-reference-in-un-speech-1987 (accessed March 13, 2022).

Halperin, David J. *Intimate Alien: The Hidden Story of the UFO.* Stanford University Press, 2020.

"Hello, Earth! Hello! Marconi Believes He Is Receiving Signals from the Planets." *Baxter Springs Herald*, March 25, 1920.

Herschel, William. "On the Nature and Construction of the Sun and Fixed Stars." December 18, 1794. The Royal Society. https:// royalsocietypublishing.org/doi/pdf/10.1098 /rstl.1795.0005 (accessed December 27, 2021).

Hoverstein, Paul. "They Missed the 'Wow Signal.'" *News-Press* (Fort Myers, FL), October 9, 1992.

Jarus, Owen. "How Were the Egyptian Pyramids Built?" Live Science, June 14, 2016. https://www.livescience.com/32616-how -were-the-egyptian-pyramids-built-.html (accessed March 3, 2022).

Kennedy, Courtney, and Arnold Lau. "Most Americans Believe in Intelligent Life Beyond Earth; Few See UFOs as a Major National Security Threat." Pew Research Center, June 30, 2021. https://www.pewresearch. org/fact-tank/2021/06/30/most-americans -believe-in-intelligent-life-beyond-earth-few -see-ufos-as-a-major-national-security- threat (accessed March 12, 2022).

Kitei, Lynne. *The Phoenix Lights: A Skeptic's Discovery That We Are Not Alone.* Waterfront Press, 2019.

Kopparapu, Ravi, and Jacob Haqq-Misra. "'Unidentified Aerial Phenomena,' Better Known as UFOs, Deserve Scientific Investigation." Scientific American, July 27, 2020. https:// www.scientificamerican.com/article /unidentified-aerial-phenomena-better -known-as-ufos-deserve-scientific -investigation (accessed December 2, 2021).

Lee, Pascal. "N~1: Alone in the Milky Way with Dr. Pascal Lee." Mt Tam Astronomy, YouTube, https://www.youtube.com /watch?v=cuJDkIUuDBg&t=1398s (September 20, 2021).

Loeb, Avi. *Extraterrestrial: The First Sign of Intelligent Life Beyond Earth*. New York: Houghton Mifflin Harcourt, 2021.

———. "Looking Through the Window with New Telescopes." Unpublished manuscript, PDF emailed to author, December 31, 2021.

Marconi, Guglielmo. "Marconi Asks, Is Mars Signaling Earth? Weird Sounds on the Wireless." *San Francisco Examiner*, January 29, 1920.

Merali, Zeeya. "Search for Extraterrestrial Intelligence Gets a $100-Million Boost." *Nature*, July 20, 2105. https://www.nature.com /articles/nature.2015.18016 (accessed February 18, 2022).

Morelli, Keith. "MOSI Scientist Sets Out to Explain 'Wow Signal.'" *Tampa Tribune*, April 25, 2016.

"Pickering's Idea for Signaling Mars." *New York Times*, April 25, 1909.

Seifer, Marc. *Wizard: The Life and Times of Nikola Tesla: Biography of a Genius*. New York: Citadel Press, 1998.

Serviss, Garrett P. *Edison's Conquest of Mars*. Los Angeles: Carcosa House, 1947.

Shermer, Michael. "How Beliefs in Extraterrestrials and Intelligent Design Are Similar." Scientific American, July 1, 2013. https:// www.scientificamerican.com/article/how -beliefs-extraterrestrials-and-intelligent -design-are-similar (accessed May 13, 2022).

Story, Ronald D. "Von Däniken's Golden Gods." *Zetetic*, Fall/Winter 1977.

Tesla, Nikola. "Talking with the Planets." *Collier's Weekly,* February 9, 1901.

"There Is Life on the Moon, Science Now Declares: Then What Do the Moon People Look Like?" *San Francisco Examiner*, October 9, 1904.

"Venus, Not Mars, He Says, Wires Us." *Kingsport Times*, February 3, 1920.

Von Däniken, Erich. *Chariots of the Gods? Unsolved Mysteries of the Past*. New York: Bantam Books, 1973.

———. *Gods From Outer Space: Return to the Stars, or Evidence for the Impossible*. New York: Bantam Books, 1973.

White, Frank. *The SETI Factor: How the Search for Extraterrestrial Intelligence Is Revolutionizing Our View of the Universe and Ourselves*. New York: Walker and Company, 1990.

"Why Men Flirt with Mars." *Kansas City Star*, July 13, 1919.

Yirka, Bob. "Khufu Branch of Nile River Once Flowed Close Enough to Giza to Carry the Stones Needed to Build the Pyramids." Phys.org, August 30, 2022. https://phys.org /news/2022-08-khufu-nile-river-giza-stones .html (accessed October 18, 2022).

CHAPTER 5

THE TRUTH IS OUT THERE, OFFICIALLY

Associated Press. "Utah Family Says UFOs Regularly Visit Their Ranch." *Casper Star-Tribune*, July 5, 1996.

Bender, Bryan. "'A Glowing Red Orb': Wild UFO Theories Move from the Shadows to Congress." Politico, May 18, 2022. https:// www.politico.com/news/2022/05/18/ufo -theories-congress-pentagon-00033497 (accessed July 7, 2022).

Blumenthal, Ralph. "Can Robert Bigelow (and the Rest of Us) Survive Death?" *New York Times*, January 21, 2021. https://www.nytimes.com/2021/01/21/style/robert-bigelow-UFOs-life-after-death.html (accessed August 23, 2022).

Blumenthal, Ralph, and Leslie Kean. "No Longer in Shadows, Pentagon's U.F.O. Unit Will Make Some Findings Public." *New York Times*, July 23, 2020, updated June 3, 2021. https://www.nytimes.com/2020/07/23/us/politics/pentagon-ufo-harry-reid-navy.html (accessed July 7, 2022).

Crowder, Paul, dir. *UFO*. Season 1, episode 3, Bad Robot Productions, Showtime, 2021.

Fox, James, dir. *The Phenomenon*. CE3, 2020.

"Grenada Asks U.N. for Study of UFOs." *Miami Herald*, November 29, 1978.

Kean, Leslie. *UFOs: Generals, Pilots, and Government Officials Go on the Record*. New York: Three Rivers Press, 2010.

Kelleher, Colm A., and George Knapp. *Hunt for the Skinwalker: Science Confronts the Unexplained at a Remote Ranch in Utah*. New York: Paraview Pocket Books, 2005.

Lacatski, James T., Colm A. Kelleher, and George Knapp. *Skinwalkers at the Pentagon: An Insiders' Account of the Secret Government UFO Program*. Henderson, NV: RTMA, LLC, 2021.

Phelan, Matthew. "Navy Pilot Who Filmed the 'Tic Tac' UFO Speaks: 'It Wasn't Behaving by the Normal Laws of Physics.'" *New York* magazine, December 19, 2019. https://nymag.com/intelligencer/2019/12/tic-tac-ufo-video-q-and-a-with-navy-pilot-chad-underwood.html (accessed March 26, 2022).

"Secrets of the State." *UFO Witness*. Season 1, episode 1, Discovery+, 2021.

Speigel, Lee. "WikiLeaks Documents Reveal United Nations Interest in UFOs." HuffPost, October 28, 2016. https://www.huffpost.com/entry/wikileaks-ufos-united-nations_n_5813aa17e4b0390e69d0322e (accessed December 14, 2021).

West, Mick. "I Study UFOs – and I Don't Believe the Alien Hype. Here's Why." *Guardian*, June 11, 2021. https://www.theguardian.com/commentisfree/2021/jun/11/i-study-ufos-and-i-dont-believe-the-alien-hype-heres-why (accessed April 8, 2022).

Photo Credits

169 Collection of Peter Robbins

171 © Arizona Republic, USA TODAY Network

181 Photo by author

188 **TOP** Robeson County Sightings by Dale Hendrickson
BOTTOM National UFO Historical Records Center, www.nufohrc.org

191 Photos by Tim O'Brien

202 Anonymous, unknown author. Public domain, via Wikimedia Commons

204 Matthaeus (Matthäus) Merian (1593-1650). Circa pre-1650. Wikimedia Commons

205 *Analog Science Fact & Fiction*, March 1961

206 Collection of Peter Robbins

209 **TOP** Lowell Observatory Archives
MIDDLE *Kansas City Star*, July 13, 1919
BOTTOM *San Francisco Examiner*, June 20, 1909

213 British Library

214 Madman2001, CC BY-SA 1.0, via Wikimedia Commons

216 *San Francisco Examiner*, January 29, 1920

223 NRAO/AUI/NSF

234 Big Ear Radio Observatory and North American AstroPhysical Observatory (NAAPO)

242 **TOP** Seth Shostak/SETI Institute
BOTTOM NASA-GSFC, Adriana M. Gutierrez (CI Lab)

245 ESO/M. Kornmesser

253 SCIENCE: NASA, ESA, CSA, STScI; IMAGE PROCESSING: Joseph DePasquale (STScI), Anton M. Koekemoer (STScI), Alyssa Pagan (STScI)

257 John Greenewald, Jr., theblackvault.com

262 navair.navy.mil/foia/documents

277 Collection of Peter Robbins

Index

Page numbers in *italics* refer to images.

Acknowledgments

Writing this book was only possible with the help of many fascinating, brilliant, and curious people. I want to first thank my friend Lee Speigel, who has been studying and writing about the UFO phenomenon since the 1970s. You graciously offered information, opinions, and anecdotes and introduced me to many of the people within the UFO community who follow in this list, all of which helped tremendously. That list starts with David Marler.

Thank you, Dave, for welcoming me to your home for two full days, generously sharing your knowledge, offering advice as needed, and giving me access to your remarkably vast collection of historic files, clippings, books, videos, and ephemera.

Thank you, Peter Robbins, for also allowing me to make a visit. I greatly appreciate the hospitality, the discussions about your remarkable life experiences, and the opportunity to explore your amazing UFO collection.

Thank you to the many other researchers, scholars, writers, scientists, experiencers, and friends who took time to speak on the phone, log on to Zoom calls, return emails, make connections, chat as an avatar, and, when possible, talk in person like human beings: Loyd Auerbach, Will Bueche, Kim Carlsberg, Cate Chassé, Larry Christesson, Marc D'Antonio, Pierre d'Entremont, Charles Davis, Chrishma Singh-Derewa, Lue Elizondo, Rani Gran, John Greenewald, Chris Gsell, Lance Hallowell, David Halperin, Lieutenant Colonel Charles Halt, Ben Hansen, Dale Hendrickson, Paul Hynek, Karen Jaramillo, Cheryll Jones, Leslie Kean, Lynne D. Kitei, Ravi Kopparapu, Barbara Lamb, Pascal Lee, Avi Loeb, Kathleen Marden, Cat Martinez, Daniel Matt, Christopher Mellon, Holly Holmes-Meredith, Jacob Haqq Misra, Nick Phillips, Nick Pope, Thom Reed, Mark Rodeghier, Capt. Robert Salas, Daniel Sheehan, Seth Shostak, John Spencer, Mike St. Lawrence, Ray Stanford, J. I. Singh, John Spencer, Jill Tarter, Rachel Tillman, Joseph Villari, Eric Wasser, and Frank White.

Thank you to my agent, Katie Boyle, for sharing a fascination of UFOs and offering guidance throughout this otherworldly journey. As always, I truly appreciate your enthusiasm, time, support, and friendship.

At Quirk, thank you to my editor, Rebecca Gyllenhaal, for your genuine passion, collaboration, and suggestions that helped shape this book. To Jhanteigh Kupihea, for pursuing further explorations into space with me. To Jane Morley for your wonderfully thorough copyediting. To Andie Reid for making these pages beautiful. And to Nicole De Jackmo, Jennifer Murphy, Christina Tatulli, John J. McGurk, Mandy Sampson, Kate Brown, and Kate McGuire for helping put this book into the universe.

To my parents, Bev and Paul Hartzman, thank you for buying me Time-Life's Mysteries of the Unknown books and *Communion* when I was a kid, and getting me to the MUFON conference all these years later.

And lastly, thank you to my wife, Liz, and my daughters, Lela and Scarlett, who may not believe in UFOs, but always believe in me.